W9-AQO-240

$13.95

The Sexual Arena & Women's Liberation

Edward J. Bardon M.D.

rs mold their
which may or may

(especially in the
as heard in his
m to explore in
ple are facing
it. These responses
hich concretely
his book.
es of the men and
he pages of this
ents of Dr. Bardon,
ith names
itification and to
issues remain

In our humor, our literature, our art, and in our everyday speech, there is evidence of anger and confusion between the sexes. What is the women's liberation movement doing to reduce the tension of sexual role stereotypes? Have new problems emerged from this controversial political and social movement?

Many individuals have experienced raw emotions as women struggle to achieve equality in a man's world, but few have acknowledged that their own sexual patterns have been disturbed. Even fewer are able to analyze the positive and negative effects on their performance in the sexual arena.

In this book a thoughtful and concerned psychiatrist presents the necessary information and insights to help us handle our new freedom to explore and choose what suits us best sexually.

Dr. Edward J. Bardon has worked for many years with college students. At close range he has seen and heard the impact of social customs on young adults. His experience reveals that with changing expectations regarding sexual behavior, some cling

g The Sexual
to better equip all
te decisions about
vior. The power of
iany, but its force
and even
r. Bardon. This
vidual tap the
ovement and to
hat might be

will meet new
u to develop the
rage to exercise
care.

iatrist associated
where he treats
s and teaches

psychotherapy and psychiatry.

The Sexual Arena & Women's Liberation

Edward J. Bardon, M.D.

Nelson-Hall nh Chicago

CARNEGIE LIBRARY
LIVINGSTONE COLLEGE
SALISBURY, N. C. 28144

Library of Congress Cataloging in Publication Data

Bardon, Edward J
 The sexual arena and women's liberation.

 Includes index.
  1. Feminism—United States. 2. Sex role.
I. Title.
HQ1426.B28   301.41′2   77-23937
ISBN 0-88229-219-6 (cloth)
ISBN 0-88229-558-6 (paperback)

Copyright © 1978 by Edward J. Bardon

All rights reserved. No part of this book may be reproduced in any form without permission in writing from the publisher, except by a reviewer who wishes to quote brief passages in connection with a review written for broadcast or for inclusion in a magazine or newspaper. For information address Nelson-Hall Inc., 325 West Jackson Blvd., Chicago, Illinois 60606.

Manufactured in the United States of America.

301.412
B427

Contents

106634

During the past ten years, millions of women have been influenced in one way or another by the thinking of the women's movement. These ideas have solved problems for some women and created problems for others. It is from this perspective that Dr. Bardon has written *Women's Liberation and the Sexual Arena.*

Amy was in every way a normal and attractive woman who, like many other women her age, chose to stay at home to raise her young son. Her husband, a well-meaning fellow, decided that it would be best for the child if they did not hire baby-sitters, even in the evenings, so that their child would have the benefit of their uninterrupted attention. Sounds ideal? Perhaps, but a steady diet of home, hearth, husband and baby soon made Amy doubt her sanity and drove her to a psychiatrist's office. It was Dr. Bardon who helped her to recognize and later accept her frustration and anger and to see that she was no less a woman and mother because she wanted a life away from home.

Not all problems are resolved as easily as Amy's.

Lucille was an "old-fashioned" woman who wanted a conventional marriage. Her husband, Peter, failing to understand her wishes, thought he was doing the best for her by trying to coerce her into the role of the "modern woman." As Dr. Bardon points out, Peter and Lucille's communication gap was too deep to be bridged. He says, "When last seen, they were continuing to express their anger in subtle ways, and their sexual relationship was remarkable for its lack of mutual enjoyment."

Dr. Bardon's book is refreshing in its ability to capture slices of life in this sexual revolutionary period.

ISBN 0-88229-219-

Preface

This book is an outgrowth of thirteen years experience as a psychiatrist listening to and working with college students. Being on a university campus, I am in a position to witness the impact of changing social customs on the young adult. Women's liberation has been chief among these forces during the past several years.

Listening to diverse people talk leads to an awareness of the wide variety of responses to the feminist movement. These individual reactions, especially in the sexual area, will be of primary concern in this book. While scores of books have been written on women's liberation, none seem to explore in depth how different individuals are actually reacting.

Many people are facing important choices because of the feminist movement. There is a sense of urgency as they try to come to terms with changing expectations regarding sexual role behavior. Some cling in a desperate way to the old and the timeworn when they are clearly disadvantageous. Others try to mold their behavior into radical new forms which at times do not fit their personalities. Still others manage to make wise decisions which will serve them well now and in future years.

My hope is that people can make better personal decisions regarding their sexuality and role behavior in relation to the messages of women's liberation. A more intimate acquaintance with the feminist movement and the variety of individual responses to it should be helpful in this regard. Women's liberation has the power to benefit many and also the force to bring about conflict, confusion, and in some cases rather disastrous consequences. It is important that we tap the inherent benefit that resides in the women's movement and limit the more pernicious effects that are occurring in some people.

This work touches a personal vein as I have long been aware of the narrowness of traditional masculine-feminine behavior. I am especially indebted to my wife for her patience and her understanding of the underlying issues. As my children grow, they confront me with the limitations of stereotyped roles. The future belongs to them, and I can only hope they have more freedom to explore and choose what suits them best than has been traditionally available in the past.

Above all, I wish to thank my many patients for the help they have given me in understanding these issues. I have learned much listening to people explore their confusion and then develop rewarding life patterns based on self-knowledge. Confidentiality demands these individuals remain nameless. I have taken extreme care to modify case histories where necessary and change all identifying data so that no personal identification is possible.

I also wish to thank the colleagues who helped me develop this material. Their initial warm reception to my ideas encouraged me to pursue this topic.

Chapter 1

Wives, submit yourselves unto your own husbands, as unto the Lord.
For the husband is the head of the wife, even as Christ is the head of the church: and he is the saviour of the body.
Therefore as the church is subject unto Christ, so let the wives be to their own husbands in everthing. **Ephesians V, 22-24.**

The Arrival

The human species is renowned for its unpredictability, complexity, and irrationality. Our absurdities reach their most towering heights as women and men gather in the sexual arena to thrash out their relationships with one another.

Listen!

Esther: Six months ago something happened and I can't seem to get it off my mind. I met this fellow at a bar. I wasn't looking for a pickup, but this guy came up and wanted to buy me a drink.

What could I say? I didn't want to hurt his feelings. Well, we hit it off together and talked until the bar closed. He told me about his jazz collection and asked me up to his apartment to hear his records. I thought maybe I shouldn't go, but what the hell. Why shouldn't I be free to go wherever I want? I'm liberated. Shouldn't I be able to take care of myself? I resent conventions that hem me in. Well, you can guess the rest. He wanted sex. I went along up to a point, but then he forced me. I didn't mind his taking my clothes off and feeling me, but when he tried to go all the way—that's when I really got mad. But it was no fight. He was much stronger and wouldn't take no for an answer. God, he was like some wild animal. He didn't physically hurt me, but I felt so used. Women are exploited. He wanted sex and he didn't care what I felt. Why do men act like that? I really don't understand.

Roy: Ya, it's too bad it happened. I don't know that there's a real reason. I was mugged last year—just walking home minding my own business, and this character slugged me and stole my money. What can you say?

Esther: Men really piss me off. I'm all for women's liberation. It's time we stopped letting men take advantage of us and using us to satisfy their own needs.

Nadine: I know what you mean, Esther. I'm so afraid of men. They try to get you off in a corner and then into bed. A girl has to be so cautious. Sex is wrong before marriage. I would never let a man touch me.

Roy: Boy, that makes me angry. You women think you're so damn put-upon, sitting on your pedestals, waiting to pounce on some innocent guy. Women's lib is for the birds. You already have all the advantages. It's men that need liberating. I fear women. You've taken advantage of me too many times.

Sandra: Roy, that's what women's liberation is all about. Don't you realize it means liberation for men as well?

Roy: What kind of shit is that? Liberation for men? You've already got all the power and control. Now you want more. You just use sex to trap a guy.

Greta: Why are you so bitter, Roy?

Roy: All the pressure to earn money is on me, and it's damn hard. I sweat all day to support some helpless woman. Men are trapped in this society. I really liked this one girl. I spent hundreds of dollars on her, and one day she tells me we're through, that things have gotten too serious. And men are the only ones that get drafted.

Greta: Not if the Equal Rights Amendment is ratified. Then women here will be drafted, just like in Israel. Women don't have that type of temperament—we're more gentle and kind. I don't like all this women's lib business. They want to take away the things I hold so dear. I want a man to take care of me and support me. I don't want to be strong and independent. I like the feeling of being with a guy who is capable and takes control of the situation.

Henry: That's what I feel. I want to take care of a woman. It's second nature to me, right in line with the way I was brought up. I was raised to feel that women are dependent and passive, that a man must be strong and protect them. They can't face the world alone the way a man can. This is my God-given role in life. I want to honor women and help them.

Sandra: I'd like to throw this ashtray at you, Henry. You're just one bundle of stereotyped roles. Women aren't weak and helpless. We don't want to be treated as inferior creatures who need to be taken care of and protected. And, Greta, you're just as bad. It's women like you who keep this thing going. I can feel more sympathy for you, however. You believe what men teach us—that we need them to control our lives. I was raised on that garbage. You just haven't been liberated, Greta. When you are, you will realize how men benefit from keeping us in a subservient position. I hate a man like you, Henry, who treats us this way.

Esther: You said what I feel, Sandra. That's why I joined that women's liberation group. I'm even learning karate to protect myself the next time a man tries to use me sexually. Men have structured marriage and society so that we are kept around just to screw when it fits their needs.

Greta: You feminists can't tell me how to live my life. You think all women have to agree with you. Well, they don't. Many women still want a life with marriage, children, and a home, and we'll fight you tooth and nail.

Sandra: Roy, there is no reason you have to marry if you don't want to. No one is forcing you to support a woman.

Roy: I feel trapped. Society expects me to marry, and I do want a family. Do you realize that 90 percent of all men marry at some time. I can't fight that kind of odds. It's all part of our culture.

Henry: A good Christian accepts these God-given roles. It's all ordained in the Bible, and it works for the benefit of women as well as for men. Women need the protection which men have been called upon to provide.

Sandra: Oh, shut up, Henry! Roles, structuring, society. Hell, I want equality. I want to do away with stereotyped roles for both women and men. I want the freedom to be myself and not have artificial limitations imposed on me. I'm strong and I can take care of myself. I'm not some weak, inadequate woman who needs to be protected by you men who

think you're so damn superior. I want a man to treat me as
an equal partner in everything.
Roy: But women exploit men so much.

Thus the human drama of men and women and their
relationships unfolds. Our propensities for conflict and unpredictability have long taken us in this direction.

Gather a group of women and men who have hitherto been
strangers into an intimate, protected place and they will begin
to discuss associations and interconnections between the sexes.
Then sit back and listen as confusion, misunderstanding,
unrealistic expectations, and anger flow forth.

Amid such seeming chaos, patterns slowly take form. We
hear men who program themselves into a role of dominance and
strength and women into a role of submission and weakness.
We discern women who gladly accept such an inferior position
with its supposed advantages. Then there are the voices of
anger: women who are furious at men for the role they feel
they have been forced to play in our society and the individual
hurts and insults they have sustained at the hands of men—and
men who are enraged at women for similar reasons.

Arising from the turmoil is the increasingly urgent cry for
equality between the sexes, and it has been christened women's
liberation.

In the opening dialogue, Sandra calls for equality. She feels
strong and capable and wants an end to conditioned role
behavior which results in inequality between women and men.
She resents men who would treat her as a submissive, dependent being instead of as an equal partner. Above all she wants
the freedom to develop her potential in any direction with no
artificial restraints imposed by stereotyped roles. She is a
feminist.

What is the reception of a feminist such as Sandra? How do
people greet her messages? As we shall discover, she is different
things to different people. Some women welcome her with open
arms for she seems to promise better things ahead for those
who want more equality and the responsibility which this will
entail. Other women, such as Esther, are equally receptive but
for different reasons. They see women's liberation as a way of

protecting them from men and heterosexuality. They interpret the women's movement in a fashion which provides ready justification for their underlying anger at men. Then there are the women like Greta—legions of more conventional women who are furious at the feminists because they sense a threat to the traditional female role which they have come to rely on and trust.

Men, likewise, display widely diverse reactions when they are confronted head-on by a feminist such as Sandra or the messages of women's liberation. Men such as Henry who are bound up in tradition and God's gift of supremacy to the male look with perplexity and at times humor on women who would want to change their God-given role. Why, they ask with amazement in their voices, would a woman wish to forego her role as wife and mother and her exalted position within the family?

Other men, such as Roy, find more rage and rebellion in their beings as they listen to women demand more equality. These men assume that women already have the best of everything. They have been hurt by the control and power which they feel women possess. How, they ask with bitter incredulity, can women dare ask for more when they already have all the advantages over men who must slave to support and protect them?

Another type of man was not present in the opening group discussion. This is the man who senses a feeling of identity with feminists for he recognizes the legitimacy of their complaints and frequently feels that he, likewise, has been hurt by prescribed role behavior. These men recognize women's liberation as a potentially beneficial force for both women and men. Often they are angry at the traditional masculine role in our society and the manner in which they have been pressured to conform.

All of these are different reactions to women's liberation. Yes, these and many more. Each individual must come to terms with the feminist movement in her or his unique way. This strident cry for equality between the sexes has grown until all of us are being affected in one way or another, some to a great extent, others perhaps to only a minor degree. Women's liberation cannot just be ignored in hopes that it will soon wither away. It is too strong and influential for that. The feminist movement is forcing many to make new choices concerning their own role behavior in relationship to the opposite sex: perhaps important adjustments in a marriage or close relationship are forced upon us, or sexual change itself is called for, or maybe our careers are affected either through expanding opportunities or increasing competition from previously excluded groups.

Chapter 2

Nature intended women to be our slaves . . . they are our
property; we are not theirs. They belong to us, just as
a tree that bears fruit belongs to a gardener. What a mad
idea to demand equality for women!   **Napoleon Bonaparte**

What Is Women's Liberation?

Women's liberation has moved across the land leaving
encouragement and trembling in its path. The rapidity of its
movement and the dynamism with which it flows have left us
surveying a scene which was nonexistent a few years back.
Many have rushed forward to embrace its ghostlike images in
sweeping pronouncements about the public good. Politicians
have hurried to encompass its rhetoric as a vote-getting mechanism. Yet seldom have those in power understood the profound
implications of the movement.

What is women's liberation? What is this movement, this
force, which has created such hope, turmoil, and confusion? In
actuality, there is no possibility of conceptualizing it in a simple,
uniformly agreed upon manner. The feminist movement is too
complex and too full of internal conflicts and inconsistencies to
allow a simple definition.

Feminists seem to argue incessantly as to what the movement
is. One contingent pushes hard for abolition of the traditional
family, a breakup of marriage and sexual patterns and possibly
women banding together in small amazonlike groups. Another
verbal group of feminists identify the movement with female
homosexuality and a refusal to have sexual relationships with
males. Then there is the more radical segment of women's
liberation which is working for no less than the total destruction or breakup of American society with its capitalistic
structure.

Some think women's liberation is the so-called respectable contingent that is working for equal pay and job opportunities for women along with an increase in political power and representation at all levels of government. Others feel it is the group who protests society structuring men and women into basically unequal roles, with women ending up in the inferior position.

Many feminists are vividly aware of this disagreement and write quite logically that women cannot seem to agree on even the barest minimum as to what the movement is or ought to be. Cellestine Ware in her book *Woman Power* states that "The Woman's Liberation Movement is a catch-all phrase that is currently used by a diversity of groups."[1]

Never to be daunted, however, many feminists continue to define what women's liberation means to them. They come up with a colorful variety of impressions. One that is particularly impressive is by Gerri Perreault. She states that "It [women's liberation] is, quite simply, a movement to free women and men from being programmed from infancy into stereotyped roles solely on the basis of sex."[2]

The conciseness and wide implications of this definition appeal to me. Freedom from stereotyped roles would include complete equality between the sexes with no artificial limitations on one's abilities or position in life. If carried out, it would lead to many of the goals advanced by different proponents of women's liberation. It would certainly touch on all the problems associated with programmed role behavior including possible realignment of sexual relationships and of the traditional family and marriage, and it points out that men as well as women are potentially deeply involved.

Although good, this definition is also limited. Many will feel it does not include some pet issues of women's liberation which are crucial to them, such as abortion or the breakup of corporate America. Some will undoubtedly feel it is not a radical enough statement while others will feel it is all too radical.

A movement or cause is perhaps best understood by the ways in which it becomes manifest. They may include quite contradictory or confusing aspects with comfort. For what stormy movement has ever carried logical consistency as its banner? An emotional movement is better known for its results and effects on people than it is for any dictionary definition. By providing a more detailed look at some of the important areas women's liberation has entered, I hope to provide a better answer to the question, "What is women's liberation?"

The area of female-male relationships is one that women's liberation has especially moved into. People of all ages and backgrounds are affected by the changing atmosphere in heterosexual relationships. A twenty-nine-year-old woman informs her husband that she is tired of staying home and caring for their two children. She has decided to develop a career of her own and demands that her husband share equally the household chores. A thirty-five-year-old successful lawyer quits his profession and moves with his family to the north woods. He and his wife want to start from scratch and build a more equal, sharing relationship where role structuring is avoided. A forty-one-year-old woman comes into my office and announces that she is a victim of women's liberation because of increasing pressure on her to obtain outside employment, yet she is optimistic that this will eventually lead to a more rewarding life for both her and her husband. A fifty-year-old mother of three goes into a marked depression when her nineteen-year-old daughter announces that she intends to move in with her boyfriend.

Our youth in particular are in a position to be influenced by women's liberation in their heterosexual relationships. The reasons for this are not mysterious but reside within normal personality development. The young are continually searching for successful ways to relate to the opposite sex. They do not have the fixed personality patterns which characterize those who are older. Their personalities are in a state of flux as they try to meet new impulses arising from within and new pressures from their environment.

No longer can youth rely on traditional methods to guide them. They do not live in a static world but in one that is dynamic. The feminist movement is questioning the basic foundations of traditional masculinity and femininity, marriage, family, and heterosexuality.

Tradition in these areas, although probably containing much inequity and limitation of freedom, has often given a sense of purpose and security. Less and less often is this now available, and youth are being forced into a real and direct confrontation with their unique selves. They must look deep within, discover what is truly important to them, and develop consistent methods for bringing about these desired goals.

Youth are now daring to be free and experiment with new patterns for relating to the opposite sex. The influence of women's liberation is often seen in this. One detects a striving for real equality as young women and men listen sincerely and try to react honestly to complaints of the opposite sex. There is an attempt toward a new openness in communication with many new sensitivity and discussion groups springing into existence.

Patterns of living intimately together are changing. Many find a recent freedom to live together without the benefit of (or without the handicaps of) marriage, often in an experimental fashion. Before lifelong commitment, one can have a trial period to determine personality and sexual compatibility. Marriage itself is frequently frowned upon, by both women and men, as being too restricting, confining, or promoting of inequality. Marriage vows, when marriage does occur, are increasingly being rewritten to reflect the personal views and desires of the participants. Especially subject to change are any phrases which suggest inequality, servitude, or structuring of roles.

Some couples are structuring a mutually agreed upon sexual freedom into their marriage. In these cases, marriage is not seen as restricting; rather each partner is free to have close friendships or sexual relationships with other individuals.

Under feminist influence, the traditional dating situation often seems to disappear. No longer is the male expected to pay the entire cost of time spent together; women feel increasingly free to be more aggressive in asking for dates or sexual contact. With developing regularity, sexual behavior itself is turning into new channels, a subject important enough to be explored in depth.

Traditional role differentiation is breaking down for many couples as women's liberation enters the marital scene. Gone is the old stereotype of the man going out into the big, cruel world to earn a living while the little woman stays home to clean house, knit, tend the babies, and perhaps manage some time for volunteer work. Both sexes (although up until now women have tended to be the most vociferous) often see this role structuring as too degrading to the human potential. Many married women are looking forward to a more active, responsible position in society including a greater degree of economic independence. Home care and husband and child tending are oftentimes not seen as desired end products.

Men are increasingly anticipating economic sharing by their wives as society opens up to more job equality for women. I meet many men who resent not being able to stay home more and help care for the children. Men are beginning to realize they have been missing one of life's great rewards, the intimate contact with and maturing of their children. Housework, although seldom seen as rewarding or desirable by either man or woman, is frequently planned on more of a sharing basis.

Some of these experimental means of relating work out well, bringing great satisfaction to individual couples. Others break down in confusion or anger leaving a disastrous situation with mutual feelings of having been misled or cheated.

Feminism has extended into a wide variety of fringe areas whose connection with women's liberation is difficult, if not impossible, to perceive except by those espousing them. They are often controversial political or social issues which deserve support on their own merit. It is important to look at some of these because they are a part of the general scene of women's liberation. They are supported most vehemently, and at times quite elegantly, by certain feminists while being denounced by the next.

The first of these areas is homosexuality. Articles in support of homosexuality occur with some degree of regularity in the feminist literature.[3] Lesbianism is proclaimed as the prime mover behind women's liberation, the vanguard of the movement. Women are cajoled to take a female lover and do their part for the cause. Heterosexuality is denounced as slavery and exploitation for the woman.

Some writers aggressively assert that by turning to homosexuality one is adopting a more normal, healthy approach to life. Elaborate rationalizations for this are advanced, and in spite of all efforts, it is often difficult for the reader to logically follow their reasoning. Emotions are crystal clear, however, and they contain an abundance of rage toward the male of the species.

Seething passions denounce men as being incapable of love and affection. Bitterness is expressed in ugly epithets, and one gradually senses the hurt that these women must have experienced in their relationships with men.

The subject of homosexuality and its relationship with women's liberation seems important enough to warrant further treatment, including a case history, in a later section.

Support of minority racial groups becomes intertwined with women's liberation in the minds of some. In their literature, one runs across many articles dealing with Black, Indian, and Chicano problems. Women writing these articles tend to feel an identification with racial minority groups even though they are likely to be white middle-class members of the majority sex. Again, the reasoning involved does not seem to follow Aristotelian logic but rather flows along emotional channels into the path of least resistance, a form of thinking characteristic of many radical causes.

White males are conceptualized as the archenemy: dominant, controlling, and power hungry. Men have formed a powerful male hierarchy which voraciously ravishes all other humans. Women and minority groups are the servants, the word "slave" being used repeatedly to describe the status of women. Women are innocent creatures who live in wretched conditions because of their subjugation and bondage. At this point we can sense the identification with the suffering and oppression of the black people.

Men are seen as supporting this system because of the supposed advantages this holds for them. "Men uphold it [the male power hierarchy] because it makes them important and relieves them of all unpleasant work, including emotional work."[4] The feelings are intense and sincere even if the world they describe may be rather open to question.

Corporate, capitalistic America comes under frequent verbal attack from ardent feminists. Many see women's liberation as a political movement, and some trace its evolution from radical and leftist opinions which have been common in our recent past. According to these philosophies, corporate America must be overthrown if women are to ever have equal rights. Women are exhorted to not just work out the best life for themselves, but rather direct their energies into furthering the political movement.

Radical feminist groups at times come with colorful and exotic titles which tell us something of their character and purpose. WITCH is the Women's International Terrorist Conspiracy from Hell, a group which sees marriage as a capitalistic enterprise for the systematic and deliberate oppression of women. SCUM is the Society to Cut Up Men, a rather provocative name which suggests that this group has no rapprochement with men in mind.   The New York Radical Feminists is a group founded in 1969. They have put together a fairly elaborate statement of their philosophy under the title NYRF Manifesto. Their manifesto states:

> The oppression of women is manifested in particular institutions, constructed and maintained to keep women in their place. Among these are the institutions of marriage, motherhood, love, and sexual intercourse.[5]

The Vietnam War was frequently attacked by feminist groups. Marches against the war were organized and supported with the rousing cry, "Vietnam for the Vietnamese! March against the war!" Petitions denouncing President Nixon's latest bombing escapades were circulated and signed as were letters to federal representatives. A photograph is circulated in "A Journal of Female Liberation" showing a dejected captured U.S. airman being guarded by a diminutive North Vietnamese militia women. The implication is quite clear—the Vietnamese woman is the hero, the U.S. airman the villain.[6]

This, however, is definitely not the place to analyze America's longest war. While many of us would agree with the positions taken, it is the connection between women's liberation and the antiwar movement which is germane to our purpose. An impossible connection you say—the antiwar movement and equal rights for women. Maybe yes, maybe no. It depends entirely on whom you talk with.

What this does illustrate is the extent to which women's liberation has extended into a wide variety of social and political causes, some popular—others not so popular. Usually they are well along the continuum toward the leftist or radical end.

Women's liberation is truly a heterogenous movement which defies any simplistic, all-inclusive definition. Many diverse areas are now feeling its presence and influence—areas which are not particularly connected in any logical fashion. Yet it is important to keep in mind the wide scope of the feminist movement and the different ways in which it is interpreted as we examine the multifarious effects it is having on individual people.

Chapter 3

Man for the field and women for the hearth:
Man for the sword and for the needle she:
Man with the head and woman with the heart:
Man to command and woman to obey;
All else confusion.   **Alfred, Lord Tennyson**

Conflict and Confusion

Conflict between the sexes seems to be an inherent part of the American scene. It forms the background and framework within which women's liberation operates—always present and strong in influence. An historic part of our culture, it antedates by eons the commencement of women's fight for equality. Evidence for the widespread presence of this conflict is ubiquitous, showing itself in our humor, our literature, our art, our institutions, and in the everyday speech of our people. Although most measurable in our divorce rate, this is only the tip of the iceberg. The solid, stable appearing marriage can hide intense conflict, couples existing in a nightmarish battle and uniting only for brief periods to maintain their respectable image with the neighbors.

Julia and Max are such a couple. They have been married for twenty-four years, twenty-four years of struggle, bickering, hostility, and intense hurt. Open warfare in full battle array would wax and wane like the moon, but when not present to any extent, it would be replaced by a more insidious type of anger which was even more destructive.

Julia was the initial one to present herself for treatment. She had come from the rural countryside to the big university hospital complex seeking help for her many somatic complaints. Her back hurt continually, her head throbbed with intermittent pain, with any exertion her legs ached, and nausea often confined her to bed. She was given a medical workup by the internists and referred to psychiatry as being free from demonstrable pathology.

When I saw Julia in psychiatric consultation, I recognized that her physical symptoms were in large part caused by her underlying anger and unrewarding life. She continually berated the doctors who were unable to cure her symptoms. Any male with whom she had contact was cut apart with vindictive anger, and this was my clue in trying to help this most unhappy woman. She was not angry at women—the male of the species alone was her mortal enemy.

Julia was assigned a female therapist, and a good relationship was established. Until now, no one had ever taken the time to sit and listen to her. As she expressed her anger to the therapist, the somatic symptoms which had been incapacitating her showed good improvement. Her primary rage was directed against her husband. He was called in for interviewing and marital therapy was begun. Wife and husband were seen together by both a female and a male therapist.

Now we began to realize the extent of marital discord. Conflict was extreme. During the interviews, Julia would berate her husband for all his supposed inadequacies. She accused him of being a miserable failure as a father (they had somehow managed to conceive two children) and inadequate as a provider, and he was messy and lacking in normal intelligence.

Above all, Julia would accuse Max of being a dominant male who had confined her to a housewife role, paying little attention to her in the process. He was hardhearted and more interested in the latest football game than in listening to her describe her newest medical symptoms. She would tear him apart, destroying any remaining vestige of self-confidence she perceived. There wasn't much left. Max had been literally destroyed as an adequate human being.

Max's method of fighting back, however, was just as destructive. He was a master of the passive-aggressive. The more his wife became upset and the more she hurt, the more relaxed and at ease he would appear. If she developed physical symptoms, he would exhibit a gleeful smile. This behavior and pretended comfort by Max would drive his wife wild, encouraging her on to new heights of vindictive rage. There was no evidence of any affection within this relationship. Sexual contact had been abandoned for nineteen years, each partner being too stubborn to give in to the other.

Because of their close association for twenty-four years, these two knew exactly how to hurt one another. Each sensed the weak spots of the other, taking advantage of them at every opportunity.

The source of much of this conflict was rooted in mutual role dissatisfaction. Max, from the earliest days of the marriage, had been angry because he was expected to be the sole breadwinner in the family. He was uneducated and untrained, and earning a living was a real strugle—often necessitating his taking two jobs when the children were young. He hated the hard physical work available to him. Resentment welled within him as he thought of Julia's supposed dependency and laziness. He genuinely felt that Julia was a pampered woman who had taken advantage of him as a man. He felt society had given all the advantages to women.

Julia, on the other hand, resented being trapped in a housewife role which included little freedom for her. The marginal economic earnings of her husband meant there was not enough money available to do much out of the home. She felt stuck with all the cooking, cleaning, and unrewarding maintenance tasks. The early burden of child care had fallen almost entirely on Julia, a role she resented deeply. It was her husband's fault that the children were conceived because he was, after all, the one who had wanted sexual relations. She punished Max by withholding sex until he refused to ask for sexual contacts. Julia was convinced that Max had all the privileges because he was the master and could leave home and engage in supposedly rewarding work.

It would seem that such blind adherence to structured roles which were so mutually abhorrent could be resolved with sharing and compromise. Sometimes they are, but this was not to be the case in this situation. Communication was too poor, and an insurmountable amount of anger had accumulated during twenty-four years of struggle. After this couple had engaged in a reasonably long period of treatment, termination was recommended, although little improvement was evident in the marital situation. The same patterns in the relationship between Julia and Max continued to exist. Julia did retain her improvement in terms of having fewer physical complaints. All suggestions on our part that maybe they should consider divorce were rejected adamantly by both partners. They were mutually dedicated to marriage in order to preserve their status in the community.

Why would a couple like this stay together for twenty-four years—and probably for close to another twenty-four as well? Were they satisfying masochistic or sadistic needs? Would they be unable to stand the loneliness without their mate to fight with? Were they bound together by anger and a desire for revenge? Probably all of these things were involved, but I think most important was their complete inability to conceive of alternatives. They both felt trapped by marriage in a society which inculcates male and female role behavior in a thousand different ways; yet they could conceive of no feasible means of escaping this destiny.

Neither Julia nor Max perceived this role behavior as rewarding, but it had become an integral part of their personalities. As a young couple, they never had the advantages of a well-publicized feminist movement to help them set up alternative methods of relating which could bring about more sharing and equality. Perhaps if Julia had been able to combine work outside of the home with her household chores and if Max had been able to work at only one job and do his share of child and house care, they could have avoided such extreme anger and dissatisfaction. They had learned their traditional role lessons all too well, however, and at their point in life, they could in no way envision any other manner of living.

Conflict is usually not this extreme, at least for this long a period of time. But exist it does, forming the environment in which many of our young are raised. What influence is women's liberation having on this historic conflict between the sexes? Is it possible that the feminist movement can help prevent the serious role antagonisms that developed in a couple such as Julia and Max, or will it only increase dissension and antagonism, serving to sharpen the battle lines? These are questions with no uniform answer. It does seem that the influence will be quite different for individual people, again depending on personalities, upbringing, and adaptability.

There are factors in women's liberation which are apt to increase this historic conflict between the sexes, making it even more difficult for women and men to relate with some degree of harmony. Some dedicated feminists are working for an even greater polarization between the sexes. They are girding for combat, proclaiming men to be the enemy with whom no socialization is allowed. Thinking tends to be in black and white terms, men being bad, women being good. The following quote from *Gold Flower*, a radical feminist newspaper is representative of this segment of the movement:

> Anyhow, it seems that all along men have just wanted to hunt and be wild and run around and kill things and women have always tried to change that and make them civilized and loving like women which is not their nature.[1]

This simplistic reasoning with its sweeping generalizations inevitably leads to dreamlike fantasies in which men and women can live in separate worlds. To continue the quotation:

> John Paul Getty ought to build a mammoth terrarium in the Pacific and all men could have free one way passage and slaughter each other to their hearts' content and leave us women to build our Amazon nation.[2]

Much of this language is of course not to be taken too literally, but it does reflect the deep antagonism some feminists feel toward men. This quite hostile segment of the feminist movement cannot just be dismissed as a small minority. It is too strong, loud, and influential for that. Moreover, behind the anger and strident language resides a degree of insight and truth which it is important not to neglect.

Not surprising, then, part of a movement which teaches such anger and hate could be intensifying the historic conflict between the sexes. It is not unusual to talk with young women whose anger toward men has been so intensified by the messages of this polarizing segment of women's liberation that they can in no way relate intimately to men. Their fear and rage are too massive. Some feel this represents a problem for them, others do not.

There are also forces in women's liberation which might help reduce the degree of conflict between the sexes. These are definite, strong forces with a high degree of potential for helping women and men relate on a less conflictual basis. My work with people leads me to feel that this is a potentially much stronger influence of women's liberation than the more polarizing elements previously discussed.

These forces for ameliorating conflict center around the potential for reducing conditioned role behavior. The role prescribed behavior we are inculcated with can lead to anger, fear, and conflict as it did with Julia and Max.

If women weren't taught to cook, sew, and clean house for men, as well as satisfy their sexual needs on demand, they might not be so angry. Will women be so dissatisfied if they can grow up with more freedom to choose their own destiny, without feeling coerced into a role they deem unrewarding, and if they can look forward to more equal opportunity in the business and professional world?

Men might not be so angry if they could mature without feeling they had to be sexually and economically aggressive, climbing over others in an effort to reach the top. Many men could be more comfortable if society did not structure a virile role of dominance and lack of tenderness for them, and how peaceful it would be if they were not taught to strive for masculinity by fighting wars and hunting lions in Africa.

Fear of the opposite sexes' real or imagined power is one of the greatest sources of conflict. Women often fear the economic and political power of men, and they are taught, and often believe, that men are emotionally hard with little capacity for love and affection. They learn men are strong, striving for dominance and "success," and wanting to get ahead at all costs. Above all, women are taught that men are sexually aggressive, out to get whatever sexual satisfaction they can from a woman.

Men fear the dominance and control of women in the home, a control they often perceived their mother having in the parental family. Outside of the home women are expected to be weak and thus need special laws and privileges. And of course women are feared because of the manner in which they are thought to gain control over men by withholding sexual pleasure until they gain some ulterior purpose. Women are expected to cry and manipulate to gain their ways, again a stereotype which is certainly not flattering.

Yes, women's liberation has the potential to reduce conflict arising from such prescribed role behavior and misconceptions about the opposite sex. Is this not one of its primary messages— allow each of us to develop in our own ways to the height of our potential, without artificial and unnecessary limitations which are imposed by concepts of traditional role behavior? Can we not realize that both women and men have suffered under a system which has taught such stereotyped role behavior, a system which has resulted in much anger and conflict between women and men?

Writing in *The American Journal of Psychiatry*, Dr. Virginia Abernethy shows an understanding of this conflict-reducing potential of feminism. After examining how a decrease in female-male stereotyped behavior can benefit marriage, she writes:

> Men as well as women can derive greater satisfacton from a marriage in which both partners are allowed a full range of human expression—from competence and rationality to passivity and tenderness. Both men and women are, by turns, tough and soft. By accepting these needs in each other, they can be friends.[3]

It is quite possible that conflict between the sexes really serves no one. I think we will find that ultimately what works in the best interests of one sex will most likely be advantageous for the opposite sex as well.

Chapter 4

The glory of a man is knowledge, but the glory of a
woman is to renounce knowledge.   **Chinese proverb**

Intellectual
or Career Success

"I'm sick of people thinking I'm just a dumb blond."

With this, Carol began to relate her lifelong struggle to attain
self-respect and dignity. Carol was indeed a gold-haired
blond, but she was anything but dumb. For some confused
reason, she had been labeled as a "dumb blond" by her classmates in high school and the misnomer became entrenched in
her self-concept. Much of her energy in the years since had
been spent in proving she was an intelligent, capable woman.

Carol was the innocent victim of a subculture which devalues
the intellectual capabilities of women. Her family openly discouraged higher education, stating that she would never use it
anyway. Her impressive physical attributes had been emphasized, and she was repeatedly told that she was lucky for there
would be no trouble finding a man to support her. The implied
message was to use sex and her bodily charms in meeting the
vicissitudes of life. Anger and frustration welled within Carol as
she matured and recognized the role society had cast for her.

Carol detested women—for not only had her own intellectual
capabilities been minimized, but the capabilities of all women
had been denigrated. Unfortunately, she had in large part
accepted what she had been taught about women.

"I never had any close girlfriends . . . couldn't stand them.
Women are so shallow . . . all they want to do is trap a husband
and raise babies. They talk about the most superficial things.

I've always related better with men. Women never seem to be doing anything interesting or have any real concern about the world. What a way to waste one's life."

Thus Carol conceptualized her own sex. It was certainly not a flattering view, and Carol was always fighting similar feelings about herself.

Carol said she related better to men. What this really meant was that she at least related to men while just ignoring women. Her relationships with men were full of struggle and conflict.

"Sure I'm competitive with men . . . have to be. Men have all the advantages. A man's life is much easier than a woman's. It's the women who has to change her way of living. A woman has to be twice as good as a man to get anywhere . . . otherwise we are passed over and the man is advanced."

"I told you about my job—how I'm continually ignored while my husband receives promotions. Everyone assumes that his job is more important than mine even though we do much the same thing. What a constant insult that is to live with."

"And the men at work—I'm a dumb broad to them . . . some sexy looking gal to flirt with and try to seduce . . . the affronts I have to put up with. Yesterday I presented a report on that meeting I went to. One of the men came up afterwards and said I would have done a better job if I'd had a good fuck the night before. He would like to get my clothes off, that's all. It's a man's world, all right."

Carol felt constant humiliation as a women. Her anger at this carried over into the marital relationship.

"Ted and I have been married close to nine years now. Sometimes I wonder how we've managd to make it for this long. It's been a stormy course. We have our good times, and then it all seems worth it . . . but then we fight something terrible and threaten to leave each other. I suppose we won't, or we would have by now."

"What are the main things you fight about?"

"Sex is the worst by far. I don't like sex. It's ridiculous and stupid. You know, the human body is ugly. Why if a creature from Mars existed and came to earth, he would think women were positively funny with their bumps and knobs, and men with that crazy thing in front."

"The worst is when someone likes me just for my body. This

infuriates me no end. I feel like that dumb blond kid in high school . . . no brains, just big tits and a tight hole. When Ted keeps after me for sex, I end up feeling the same way—like he doesn't respect me as an intelligent person."

A constant source of irritation to Carol was her husband's greater job success relative to her own mediocre advancement. They had started out in the same area of the business world; in fact, they had met in a office where both were hired as accountants. Carol and Ted each had a college degree in business, but Ted's promotions had come with relative ease in the large company while Carol had to struggle for every little victory. She was deeply resentful of Ted and what she saw as his easy road to attainment, even though he personally had nothing to do with the job discrimination she was experiencing.

Ted's fault lay in his lack of support and understanding for what Carol was experiencing. He failed to see the obvious sexual discrimination against his wife, and at times he would make derogatory comments about Carol's abilities. He would especially use this when Carol withheld sex. He knew how sensitive his wife was about her intellectual abilities and how much he could hurt her in this area.

Carol continued to talk about her marital conflicts.

"Another thing that gripes me is the way Ted expects me to run his errands, like I'm some sort of maid or servant. I never have liked the housewife role, and it's a constant fight to get Ted to do his share. He would just as soon leave everything for me. And money . . . why I earn my share, but he thinks he can control the way I spend it. I'd like my own bank account, but he says that's too complicated. He never fails to remind me that he earns more than I do, but if it weren't for this damn prejudice against women, I'll bet things would be different."

It was only after Carol and I had known each other for some time that she could tell me about her one-night affairs. They were a source of confusion and shame to her, and she desperately wanted them to stop.

"I suppose we haven't talked much about my relationships with other men. I told you that I don't enjoy sex very much, but I get myself into the craziest situations. I don't even know if it is sex. I have no feeling of wanting to screw these men. It seems to happen more when I'm angry."

Carol stopped at this point, probably waiting to see what my reaction would be before she continued.

"What seems to happen when you are angry, Carol?"

"You can guess already. Last week I decided to seduce my boss. I don't know why, but it seemed like a way of getting even. You know how I hate being treated like a sexy blond. Well, that's exactly what this new boss at work has been doing. I decided to show him that I could wrap him around my little finger . . . him and his damn presumptuous airs. Masculine dominance, shit . . . I had him in bed the next day. But it sure was no fun for me, and then I wonder why I did it. It doesn't make any sense, does it?"

I had to agree with Carol; her behavior didn't make a great deal of sense. She had periodically turned to these one-night seductions to handle her anger at the way some men were treating her. She already recognized how self-defeating and unrewarding this pattern was. This was a deep secret from her husband, and she couldn't stand the thought that he might find out.

It was at this time that Carol began to talk about women's liberation, or in her own words, "those women who write like I feel." She didn't join any type of feminist group, for women were still not particularly to her liking and she was no "movement joiner." I never did find out how she came to be influenced by the feminist movement, but it was probably through scattered reading in magazines and from publicity by the news media.

At any rate, Carol began to talk more like a feminist. Her spirits perked up as she began to realize that the future could bring some important changes her direction. She correctly sniffed the changing atmospheric currents, and she was the right women in the right place at the right time.

"Things at the office are changing. Management has started looking for women to fill some executive positions. It's about time, and I'm damn angry they had to wait until public opinion forced their hands . . . but I'm not going to let my anger spoil my chances for advancement. I've waited a long time for this. I applied for this new executive training program for women at work, and I think I have a good chance of being accepted. My work has always been good, and I think I have the abilities."

Change for Carol was slower than she had expected. She seemed to expect overnight advancement.

Management did accept Carol in an executive training program. There were several evening school courses to take in addition to on the job training. This meant months of hard work for Carol, and she applied herself with diligence. Her substantial intellectual abilities came to the fore, and the company was impressed with her progress.

Eventually Carol was promoted to an executive position. She was pleased as she reported her success.

"Well, I made it . . . new salary and a new office of my own. You know, I think things have finally changed so that it won't be as much of a disadvantage to be a woman in the company."

Carol was right. Evidently her company was short of women in management positions, and they were under public pressure to show off some women in more top echelon positions. Carol was a logical candidate, and she was highly motivated in this direction. At last she had a chance to prove that she was no mere "dumb blond." She was also accurate about her abilities—they were real as proven by her progress.

Some remarkable things happened to Carol as she became more successful. She began to like herself better, and she even said a few kind things about other women. Most noticeable was the effect on her relationship with her husband. As she became more secure about her talents, she had less need to be defensive and angry around him.

"Ted and I fight less now—not that everything's all right, for I still have to clean up after him . . . but it doesn't make me as angry. We've worked out an arrangement where I do more of the housework which Ted hates, and he does more of the repair work and takes care of both cars. It's not what I'd like, but I have to be a realist. 'Those women who write like I feel' have got me convinced that complete sharing in a marriage is the best arrangement, but Ted won't agree to all of that. He goes part way when it's convenient for him."

"It does sound like you're willing to change more than he is, Carol. But say, I've been wondering if sex has changed any for the better with you and Ted? You haven't mentioned it for some time now and other things seem to be running smoother."

"Sex will never improve much for me. I try, but I really get nothing out of it. I've been reading what 'those women' say about the female body and how we've been conditioned to find all sorts of imperfections with ourselves. I suspect they are right, but my figure still seems unattractive. I don't even enjoy taking my clothes off. I know men find me sexy and attractive, and I can seduce them with ease. But none of this seems to make any difference.

"I have changed my approach to Ted, however. We've been getting along better, and I don't keep turning him down. This isn't great, but it seems the best I can do.

"One thing pleases me. I doubt that I'll ever feel like seducing a man again just because I'm angry. This never did add up, and I suppose there is no need to get even with men anymore. 'Those women who write like I feel' describe men pretty well, and they helped me realize that letting some chauvinist guy screw me isn't going to help in any way. I suppose it relates to having more respect for myself as a woman. Who knows, maybe someday I'll like women enough to have one as a friend."

That indeed would be the day the earth stood still—but change is always measured in relative quantities, and Carol had done her share compared to where she started.

In a sense, Carol rode on the coattails of the success of women's liberation. She never was active in any social change movement, and she never campaigned for women's rights. She had accurately perceived the job discrimination against women in the business world long before this was popularized, and she was the pawn of a culture which conditions women to mistrust themselves and other women in terms of intellectual accomplishment. But a changing social climate in regards to women, especially as it permeated into her firm, benefited not only her business career, but also her personal life and feelings about herself.

My contact with Carol ended as she became more confident of her success. Problems remained—but she was happy at this time, and I think the future bodes well for her.

The current feminist movement is the embodiment of women's hope for a more equitable position in our culture. For many women this does not represent mere wishful thinking but accurately reflects the reality of their present life. Carol is one living example of the type of women who are undergoing a marked improvement in their lives as the feminist movement continues to permeate our society.

There is no doubt that women's liberation is being successful in achieving some of its goals. This in no way implies that further effort is not needed as this is patently not the case. While being cognizant of early societal changes, most feminists sense that this is only a beginning, and no relaxation of pressure is indicated. In fact, the opposite seems to be the case. The attainment of each new success seems to be a source of new motivation for increased vigor and openness in pursuing goals.

Early obvious success is helping women achieve a sense of confidence and power. Women are beginning to feel and say, "See, we can make demands and people will listen to us. We do not have to continue submitting to what we feel is an inferior position. We are not the weak and ineffectual creatures society has labeled us as being."

One of the areas most noticeably affected by women's liberation is the whole career-job-work situation. It is an area where impact is seen on a day-to-day basis as the public media proclaim the newest hiring of a woman in a previouly all male field or the latest pay raise for women is remarked upon. Or we read about yesterday's governmental suit against such and such an industry for alleged discrimination against women in promotional procedures, or we hear a debate on the pros and cons of removing weight lifting maximums for women in industry.

Important as these changes are, these represent only the more measurable part of the situation. The scope of this issue is far more broad and complex as it involves the very psyche of women. It has to do with the expectations of society, with role structuring, and with incentives and rewards. And it has to do with our basic concept of what woman is, or as society has approached it in the past, what woman ought to be.

What woman ought to be or should become—how reprehensible a concept! Yet this is exactly the situation women have faced for hundreds of years (and men too). Woman has been given a pattern for her life, a pattern which allows precious little in the way of individual freedom. Oversimplified, the channeling is that of sweet, passive schoolgirl—underpaid secretary—

submissive wife—dutiful mother—loving grandmother. The structure has been enforced through a legion of pressures, some overt, others more subtle and covert.

Yes, there have been individual women who have chosen to escape this route and march to a different drummer. Some women have chosen not to marry, others have followed a creative life in the arts, music, or writing, and some have become successful executives, politicians, or professionals. But these have been few and far between, usually individuals with a great deal of courage and ego strength. And what price have they paid? There is recent suggestion that an increase in anxiety and continuing doubts as to one's femininity has all too often been an accompaniment to such daring individuality.

To become a successful career woman, competent in her own right, has rarely been part of the idealized image a woman has learned to strive toward. In 1975, a report on the educated woman by the Group for the Advancement of Psychiatry stated that most people, women included, believe marriage and motherhood should be women's primary goals and that other aspirations, although acceptable, were not to be taken very seriously.[1]

It can certainly be no surprise, then, to learn of the small number of women who have up until now entered the professions. We read that in 1972 "only seven percent of physicians are women—only three percent of lawyers—one percent of federal judges—four percent of full professors—seven percent of scientists—one percent of engineers—two percent of business executives—four percent of top federal civil servants."[2]

One of the more damaging psychological effects of this conditioning process is the difficulty many women have in coming to terms with intellectual success. It is common to talk with women who are motivated to avoid achievement, at least in certain areas. Professional success or intellectual achievement is all too often viewed as a negative or at least questionable goal. Success outside of the home is seen by many women as a male arena, one to be shunned and avoided. A recent study by Horner from the University of Michigan supports this position. She found that over six times as many women as men fear that academic achievement could have negative implications for them.[3]

Jonathan Swift wrote: "I never knew a tolerable woman to be

fond of her own sex." Many women are conditioned to the point where they mistrust professional women and their work. Their ego structures seem to have accepted as fact the male's supposed intellectual superiority. Women become prejudiced against other women. A widely quoted study by Goldberg in 1969 supports this view. He concluded that nonprofessional women are indeed prejudiced against professional women.[4]

Why should some women fear and mistrust success in academic or professional fields? The answer does not seem especially difficult if we examine some of the messages women are given. Women are consistently told that if they are too successful professionally, they will be less feminine. They fear being unattractive to men.

Sexuality plays a large role in women's fear of success. Women worry that if they are too competent men will find them less desirable sexually. I repeatedly talk with female graduate students who are concerned about their sexual attractiveness and functioning as they become more academically successful.

This touches a pervading mythology present in our culture. Sexual competence is often associated with adherence to stereotyped sex roles. It is a continuation of the club-wielding caveman dragging the helpless female philosophy. We commonly associate sexual prowess with the strong, dominant male and sexual responsiveness with the passive, yielding female. To depart from our traditional role is to invite fears of our sexual abilities and attractiveness. This is probably as true for the male as it is for the female.

Sexuality is susceptible to the conditioning process, and psychological expectations do influence how we function. Thus some women do have trouble in the sexual area as they become successful professionally. They associate orgasmic response with the traditional feminine role of passivity and lack of worldly accomplishment. Masculine dominance is thought to be necessary for sexual completeness.

Some men likewise experience sexual difficulties if their traditional masculine image is threatened. An erection is felt to be dependent on strength, athletic abilities, dominance, and other trappings of the masculine stereotype.

These observations find support in the literature. Dr.

Constantina Safilios-Rothschild, a professor of sociology, writes:

> Therapists should become increasingly aware (of the need to treat) an unconfident husband whose masculinity is threatened by his wife's professional involvement and even more by her success. Or the counseling of a husband who must equally share with his wife all housework and childrearing by sacrificing part of his leisure or a few hours of work.[5]

In a fascinating article in the *American Journal of Psychiatry*, Dr. Virginia Abernethy reports a study which suggests that female dominance may lead to an asexual quality in male-female relationships.

> Primatological, ethnographic, and psychiatric data suggest the hypothesis that male dominance facilitates male-female copulatory behavior while female dominance inhibits it.[6]

Women's liberation is doing much to counteract sexual difficulties associated with departure from typical sex role stereotypes. By giving women, and now men, a new set of messages regarding the suitability of "sex-inappropriate" roles, psychological expectations can be influenced. Sexual doubts and fears can be ameliorated for those who opt for a life pattern different from traditional norms. It is important to reassure women that their attractiveness as women, their sexual desires, and their desirability will not be curtailed by new choices. Dr. Constantina Safilios-Rothschild also writes:

> On the contrary, they (therapists) can assure these women that the assumption of rewarding, satisfactory, and fulfilling roles will tend to increase their attractiveness and desirability as well as their libido."[7]

It is repeatedly emphasized to girls as they are maturing that men will not find them appealing or attractive, and will most certainly not marry them, if they become too successful. To not marry, to not obtain a man, is usually seen as the epitome of failure. One's worth as a woman seems to be inextricably bound up with the man she can attract and permanently keep. Many women appear to accept this message without seriously questioning its validity. One's self concept as a woman is thus negatively associated with achievement. Is it any wonder that myriads of women choose to not compete seriously with men in the intellectual or professional arena?

Women's liberation is challenging all of these stereotypes regarding woman's role. Feminists are encouraging women to strive for satisfaction in work outside of the home and to welcome success in traditional male areas. They are directly counteracting the previous cultural message that creative and challenging work for a woman is only proof of her inability to attract a man who will support her. Maybe women who choose a career instead of marriage will no longer be looked on as incapable of sustaining a close love relationship with a man. For the women's movement is saying most clearly and most loudly, "Women—be proud of your intellectual creative, and professional abilities and feel free to develop them to their furthest extent! No longer allow yourself to be ruled by cultural conditioning which has told you women should not achieve!"

The women's movement is providing moral support for those who are challenging the tightly knit role structuring of society. Women no longer have to feel peculiar because they perceive inequality within the system. There has been a tendency to view problems fitting into traditional role structure as personal hang-ups. Women can now realize that instead of these problems being their own unique emotional difficulties, they are often shared by other women and reflect real problems in our society. Women are gaining support and justification for their anger at inequality and inferiority of position.

The women's movement is a godsend for those not wanting to marry and raise a family. Marriage and sacred motherhood, those bastions of virture and goodness, are being subjected to a withering barrage of criticism. Marriage is attacked as being a form of enslavement for women, a prime breeder of servitude and inequality. It is seen as being one of the basic institutions society relies on to keep woman in her place.

Children are infrequently attacked as such, but rather woman's freedom to choose whether or not to have a child is emphasized. Modern birth control techniques are consistently presented in the feminist literature, usually with a great deal of thoroughness and competency. Abortion on demand has been one of the women's movement's trademarks, one of the goals women have worked the hardest to achieve. They are jubilant over the recent Supreme Court decision which in effect legalizes abortion during the first six months of pregnancy. Feminists are claiming that this decision would never have been rendered if it were not for their having waged the continuous war to legalize abortion.

The woman who desires neither marriage nor children is thus given real encouragement. She is reassured that this does not make her abnormal and that there are other rewarding, worthwhile goals to pursue. She is not inferior because of a primary emphasis on career and intellectual achievement. Women's liberation is indeed doing a great deal to bring about a new set of messages for women.

On the more measuable, practical front of career and job opportunities for women, the movement is having a noticeable impact. Inequalities in our present system are being exposed and publicized to such an extent that their continuation is difficult to justify. Almost daily we hear of new careers being opened to women as job discrimination based on sex slowly disappears. For the first time we hear of women becoming commercial airline pilots, truck drivers, and loggers.

We see professional schools actively seeking qualified women applicants. Any quotas for admission to professional schools based on sex which have existed in the past are rapidly dying under pressure engendered by women's liberation. In 1976, we read that, "The professional areas of dentistry, law, medicine and veterinary medicine recorded the largest increase in women students."[8] This survey of student enrollment at one of the nation's largest universities shows a doubling of its female enrollment in medical school since 1968. Law school noted an even more dramatic increase as women increased their percent of enrollment from 6 percent in 1968 to 28 percent in the fall of 1975. The article attributes this increase to a change in social attitudes where women want more ambitious careers.

Some engineering schools are beginning to realize that female engineers are in demand, and they are encouraging women to enter the field. Stanford University's engineering school has recently publicized a new recruitment program to find women students.[9]

Promotional opportunity for women is running at high tide as previous discriminatory practices are brought to light. Many companies are searching among their own women employees for potential management material as they feel the heat of the government breathing down their necks. Carol's situation which was discussed previously is a case in point. She is a prime beneficiary of this recent change as she is given a well deserved opportunity to advance in her firm.

A recent governmental victory in obtaining a large financial settlement against one of our largest corporations for promotional discrimination against its female employees is being heeded by other companies. In fact, it has reached the point where capable women are in such demand that pirating of the ablest is becoming a problem. A company executive states, "Sure we're interested in women, but so are lots of other people."[10]

Newsweek explored the increasing role of women in management in an article during April of 1975. They found that more and more women were finding a place at the corporate directors' table. They state:

> The drive to enlist more women directors is getting so intense that the relatively few women with business experience are heavily recruited.[11]

Companies compete with each other to announce the splashiest headlines concerning their most recent opportunities for women. Much of this is of course flatulent rhetoric designed for favorable publicity, but undoubtedly some of it is true. This can and does lead to some rather humorous situations. Recently a large firm in St. Paul devoted a major part of its annual report to extolling its fair and equitable treatment of women employees. The pages at the end of the report contained a collection of photographs of all the officers and high managerial personnel. Significantly missing was the presence of even one woman among this group of executives.

Recruitment of women employees is probably at an all time high. In some areas a woman will have a better chance in obtaining a job than a man with the same qualifications. This is especilly true for college graduates. In an article analyzing the demand for women college graduates, a newspaper article states,

> Many businesses, prodded by the government, are now actively recruiting women for top-ranking jobs. Many are actually paying a bit higher salaries for qualified women and minority members than they are for white males.[12]

A recent report from a Midwestern private college states that many firms recruiting on campus are specifying women and only rarely if at all men. The report goes on to announce that while the initial pressure to hire more women came from the federal government, this is changing. Companies are now realizing that women are very effective and some companies are no longer trying for just the minimum number of women. Several companies came to this particular campus stating that they were primarily interested in women. Only women were invited to visit their plants and enter their management trainee programs.[13]

Another placement director from the College of Liberal Arts at one of our largest universities feels that women could easily be placed in many traditional men's jobs. He states that the demand for women in traditional masculine areas such as industrial sales and management trainee programs is on the increase.[14]

Universities and colleges are currently under a great deal of governmental pressure to increase the percentage of women on their staffs and faculties as well as to raise their salaries. The discrimination they are trying to rectify is real. University faculty women consistently receive lower pay than their male counter-parts, the most recent survey showing a 17.5 percent discrepancy. Furthermore, the percentage of women in higher academic positions is small. By last count, only 17 percent of the faculties of category I universities were female.[15]

The federal government, through the Department of Health, Education, and Welfare, has threatened to hold up federal contracts (and money) from universities where discrimination on the basis of sex is found. This has resulted in a proliferation of so-called affirmative action programs which are attempting to meet national guidelines. Universities openly advertise positions which they are reserving for women. For many high-level positions, a male cannot be hired unless an extensive effort to hire a woman has been undertaken and failed. Furthermore this effort must be documented in writing by submitting a list of women to whom the job has been offered but who have refused the position.

The strong protesting hand of women's liberation has been instrumental in forcing much of this initial change. The improvement in career opportunities for many women is real, and some, like Carol, are seizing this opportunity and making the most of it. Female students on campuses realize they have a new freedom to enter many hitherto forbidden areas, and many are taking advantage of this situation. In addition to the previously mentioned areas of medicine, law, engineering, and dentistry, other areas are experiencing penetration by women.

It is reported that Business Administration is witnessing a dramatic influx of female students.[16] A university newspaper states that "Women are swelling the ranks of freshmen who plan to go to graduate school."[17] Career opportunities in Army ROTC programs are drawing increasing numbers of women.[18] The American Chemical Society reports, "New woman chemists will earn more than their male counterparts for the first time this year."[19] Indeed, women can increasingly plan on a career with less fear of rejection and a new sense of opportunity.

Let us now turn to Becky. She is the embodiment of some of the basic conflicts we have just covered, as well as some that will be treated in the near future. However, being flesh and blood and a complex, unique individual as all humans are, she will not fit neatly into stereotyped categories in order to illustrate this book. If we look closely and tenderly at Becky with all her contradictions, problems, and strengths, I think we can gain an increased understanding of how an individual woman can be helped by the tenets of women's liberation.

Becky presented herself to my office approximately one year

ago. Her initial complaint was quite clear—she was a third year graduate student in a Ph.D. program in philosophy, and for some time she had been unable to study. During that initial hour with her, I realized she was one of those special people to whom I am immediately drawn. She was attractive, vivacious, sincere, remarkably intelligent, and quite verbal. She was wrestling with certain philosophical problems concerning life and death and was capable of serious abstract profound thinking. There was nothing superficial or inane about Becky, and one never had to worry about being bored in her presence. She was fun and exciting to be with, the type of person one continually learns from. She appeared to be one of those chosen few destined to go through life from one success to another. Yet her life had not been following this course, and she was disappointed in herself.

Becky presented her story in a logical, consistent fashion, almost as if it had been rehearsed—yet one could sense the intense emotion as she related.

"Doctor, I'm going to be twenty-nine years old next month, and I don't know what my life is all about. Several years back I thought I knew, but now confusion and lack of meaning seem to be my lot. My life is going in circles, round and round in a frenzy of doubt. I think about my life, ponder and reflect on its direction, analyze my problems and get nowhere. For almost six months now, I have been unable to concentrate on my work. Studying remains undone, papers never get written, and I have put off taking my exams."

Becky sighed and slowly continued.

"Recently this has become so bad that I have been avoiding teaching my classes. Teaching has always been a highlight in my lire, really one of my first loves. Now I can't even do that. I sit at my desk and force myself to study, but the words won't sink in. The phrases blur, and I pace back and forth in the room. I am thoroughly disgusted with myself and don't know where to head.

"You don't know how difficult it is for me to be here. It never occurred to me that I would end up in a psychiatrist's office. I have always been the capable, efficient one, handling my own life and listening to other's problems. And now I don't know what direction to turn."

"Becky, you mentioned that teaching has been a central part of your life. Have you had much experience teaching?"

"For four years I taught overseas in France and Luxembourg where my knowledge of French and English enabled me to get various positions teaching high-school students. This was such a happy part of my life . . . I really liked my students and enjoyed going to school. Now I have a teaching assistantship at the university and have two undergraduate classes. At first I was enthused about teaching these classes. The students are fun, and I have been able to support myself while getting a Ph.D. But now I am afraid to face my students."

"I'm curious why you came back to school if you were so happy teaching high-school students?"

"I've often wonderd myself. I know it sounds as if I made a mistake, but it was something I had always planned on doing and the time seemed appropriate. Mom never could understand why I went away to college. She thought I would marry some local boy and raise the grandchildren she always wanted. I'm an only child, you know. Life for mom has been lonely, all alone out there on the farm for most of the day. I remember how lonely I was as a child. The farm was so large, and Dad always seemed to be busy in the field. I never had playmates except at school. Mom was about the only one to talk with, and she just kept telling me how alone life could be—sort of feeling sorry for herself, I guess. She always cautioned me against marrying a farmer. 'Marry yourself a town fellow and be happy' was what I grew up on.

"Mom was always afraid of education, especially for a girl. She could never see where it did much good. But I always did so well in school, and Dad was proud of this. When I graduated at the head of my high-school class, Dad was about as happy as I've ever seen him. My teachers at school were encouraging, and I was able to get a scholarship at several colleges. Mom could never understand, but she didn't try to interfere. She just hoped it wouldn't make me unhappy. After all these years it looks as if she's right. I've really been miserable this past half-year."

Becky paused, sort of drifted off into space, and quietly cried. They were tears of loneliness, tears of frustration, and tears of remembrance for her earlier life. She was deeply in touch with her feelings and needed no urging to continue. Gradually she turned her face in my direction and for the first time recognized me as a person. Our eyes met, and I saw beauty and strength in this woman. Soon she smiled through her tears and continued with her story.

"It's been a long, long time since I cried. Crying was always for someone else, for Mother and those with problems . . . but not for me. Anyway, I went away to college and had the time of my life. For the first time I was surrounded by people and my behavior changed. Parties and a gay night life were my steady diet, and sex was free and easy. School was fun, but I put little effort into it. Still I learned, and my grades were excellent. I earned several honors, and my professors thought I should apply for graduate school. I wasn't ready then, but I knew that someday I would be back. I had the ability for an advanced degree, and this goal became a part of me."

During the next several interviews, Becky and I explored her social life. Her recent sense of loneliness and isolation was quite real and had left her in a panic. As it turned out, she had been withdrawing from her old friends. The reasons for this gradually emerged, and they centered around serious doubts concerning her worth as a woman.

"For some time, doctor, things went well socially. Overseas I lived with a professor, but then he broke things off. He said I was too domineering and just too damn capable, that I threatened him sexually. I didn't worry much about this at the time, but recently it has been bothering me. Am I really just a domineering, controlling career woman that no man will take? The other day one of my best girl friends said I always appeared so capable so much in charge of things. People have always seen me as aggressive and efficient. Men in my department are nice to me, but they always keep a distance. They come to me for advice, but they almost seem afraid of me. I began to feel that people couldn't like anyone who seems so competent, and I gradually stopped seeing my friends. And if it's this way now, what will it be like when I have a Ph.D.?"

Thus Becky's fear of obtaining a Ph.D. gradually unfolded. No wonder she couldn't study. In Becky's mind, obtaining a Ph.D. represented the pinnacle of success, but on another level it symbolized failure as a woman. The closer she moved toward

her higher degree, the more sharply fears paralyzed her functioning. Career success was seen as loss of desirability as a
female. To be overly aggressive and capable would turn men off
sexually and create a distance in social relationships. After all,
hadn't men told her she was too domineering and strong?

Becky's fear of loneliness seems to have come from her early
years on the farm where she was isolated. She greatly feared
being like her mother, even though there was little similarity.
Mother's early fears about men not liking Becky if she became
too educated had returned to haunt her . . . and if men didn't like
her there could only be years of aloneness ahead. A tragedy,
yes, for a woman to have to think in these terms, but one that is
quite common in our society.

Becky was strong, capable, talented, and aggressive—there
was really no question about this. However instead of these
being negative qualities, they were really a positive part of
Becky. She combined these elements of her personality with
other qualities, and the resultant mixture was pleasing and
attractive. The problem was how to convince Becky of this.
Group therapy seemed to be the answer. I also recommended
that she read some of the recent material written by feminists.

I placed Becky in a group composed largely of other graduate
students. Some of the other women in this group were
struggling with problems similar to hers, and Becky was sharp
enough to pick up on this almost immediately. The men in the
group were a most capable bunch, being quite proficient in their
own fields. Several were having problems with doubts about
their masculinity, and you will meet at least one of these men
further on in the book.

One man in particular was instrumental in helping Becky. He
was having difficulty finding a woman to relate with in an
intimate fashion. His problem was that he could really only
respect capable, intelligent women who were successful in their
own right. How he hated superficial women, and how he would
rail against women who were only in college to find a husband.
He was immediately attracted to Becky, and she gradually felt
his honesty and sincerity. For the first time in her life, Becky began to realize that there were men who really wanted an intelligent, successful woman. As she began to talk about her

fears of rejection and loss of femininity and sexual attractiveness if she were too successful, the others were able to reassure her. "Yes, some men are probably threatened by a capable
woman, but they are really not worth worrying about" was the
atmosphere in the group. And it certainly doesn't make sense to
give up one's strivings for fulfillment as a professional person.

Becky gradually began to like herself more and to accept her
more aggressive, capable side as an integral part of her personality. She even began to study and to again find joy in her
teaching.

One group meeting, Becky talked about her latest boyfriend.
"I haven't talked much about Jim in group, but we have been
spending a lot of time together. Last week he asked me to marry
him, but he wants me to give up my career and have children.
You know, he really doesn't like the idea of my earning more
money than he. I thought a great deal about this during the
week, and last night told him no. He accused me of being
antimarriage, and maybe I am—at least to a man who restricts
me. I've been reading some of the women's liberation literature
recently and they're right on. I don't see why a woman should
have to give up a career in order to follow her husband around
and play up to his ego. I realize now that my profession is more
important than that."

Finally Becky's anger spilled out . . . pent up rage at men who
have told her she was too capable or intelligent and at a society
which teaches women to be fearful of success. Her pride in
herself and her abilities had noticeably increased. No longer
would she give up a part of her greatness in order to buttress up
some fragile male. Her inherent strength had finally risen to the
surface.

I had one final interview with Becky following a three month
summer vacation. She burst into my office with happiness and
confidence etched into her face. The summer had been a good
one. She had studied with more pleasure and efficiency than
ever before in her life. She had taken the oral preliminary exams
for her doctorate and had passed with flying colors. She was
beginning to work on her dissertation and had a topic she
was really enthused about. Her final comments were about
marriage.

"You know, doctor, I have a hunch that someday I will get married. But it has to be to the right man, to someone that will repect me for my success and not be threatened by me sexually. And if I should never marry, well, that will also be O.K."

I really doubt that Becky could ever have made this transition without the help of outside support. She needed some definite reassurance that professional and intellectual success need not mean failure as a woman and resulting loneliness. The publicity concerning this problem in the culture, the recent writings of feminists, and the group support all helped her in this regard. The early pride her father showed in her high-school success was undoubtedly a positive element in her character structure. Many women are so damaged by early conditioning with no counteracting influences that they are probably destined to go through life suppressing their intellectual abilities in order to feel confident as a woman.

Chapter 5

There's nothing in the world worse than woman,
save some other woman.   **Aristophanes**

Sexual Stereotypes in Literature and Language

Language and literature reflect the values by which a society lives. They are instrumental in the formation of personality, particularly in the sexual area with its susceptibility to outside influence. Literature affects our sexual identity and behavior by presenting us with ideas and models to identify with. Language conditions the way we conceptualize ourselves and others.

An examination of language and literature can thus provide an understanding of the stereotypes molding women's self-concept and identity.

To be a woman is to be thought inferior in our culture, especially in comparison to the male of the species. This is a basic, salient view which permeates our cultural mythology.

In Genesis II, 21-23, we read:

> And the Lord God caused a deep sleep to fall upon Adam, and he slept: and he took one of his ribs, and closed up the flesh instead thereof;
> And the rib, which the Lord God had taken from man, made he a woman, and brought her unto the man.
> And Adam said, This is now bone of my bones, and flesh of my flesh: she shall be called Woman, because she was taken out of Man.

Women have been considered a second-rate member of the human species cut from Adam's rib—an afterthought creation of Lord God—who somehow could never quite measure up to the superior male. Too many women have received a message during their conditioning that they, as women, are beneath men just because they are females.

Examples of the female of our species being viewed as innately inadequate or inferior permeate history. It is known that many cultures insisted their kings sire male offspring, encouraging them to leave wives who produced only female children. Historically, female babies were often killed during certain difficult periods, leaving the supposed superior male children to survive. Many religions make an obvious point of valuing the male over the female, and in the process give young girls definite negative messages concerning their own femaleness. And does not a Jewish Orthodox prayer for men state, "I thank thee, O Lord, that thou has not created me a woman?" In fact, many people are so accustomed to living with this myth that they do not experience it as a problem.

Not all women sense a prevailing notion that they are second-class citizens, again showing that we are a remarkably diverse group of people and that universal generalizations are not applicable. Some women experience no particular feelings of inferiority and find no evidence that the culture in general views them in this manner. At times one meets women who regard their femaleness as a definite advantage, an innate superiority over the hapless males—and they manage to find confirming evidence in the general culture to support their view. It is, after all, usually possible to find whatever "discernible trends in the predominate society" one is looking for.

While many men assume and accept the above myth that woman is indeed an inferior creature who was created from his body in order to serve him and make is life more comfortable, other men view woman as a superior being and assign her tremendous power. These men are apt to feel that woman is exalted to a high plane from which she then demands subservience and obsequious behavior from her male subjects. Woman is thought to occupy the throne of power from which she rules with an iron fist. [This topic will be explored later.]

Perhaps more common in the male is a mixed attitude in which man's fear of woman's power is combined in a confused manner with his feeling that she is an inferior species. In *The*

Adolescent written in 1874, Dostoevsky, with his usual uncanny, almost frightening insight into the depths of human personality, has given us an excellent example of this.

> Just got to the theater, or go out for a stroll. Every man, for instance, knows what it means to keep to the right, and when two men meet they step out of each other's way—he to his right, I to my right. But a woman just forges straight ahead, without even noticing you're there, taking it for granted that you'll jump out of her way and let her pass. I'm willing to yield to her because she's the weaker creature, but why should she take it for granted and consider it my duty? That's what's insulting! I always snort with disgust when I meet one of them—And, after that, they dare to come and yell at us that they're oppressed, that they demand equality—What equality is she talking about when she tramples me underfoot or fills my mouth with dust.[1]

The myth that woman is an inferior creature is here in our culture for any woman to accept who so chooses. The tragedy is that so many individual women have accepted this view and incorporated it into their personality structure. Our Western literature has tended to perpetuate this myth and keep it all too vigorous and healthy. It is commonly recognized that many authors have a distinct antifemale bias. They range from St. Paul to Nietzsche, from Tolstoi to George Bernard Shaw. Even Shakespeare does not come off well as far as equality of the sexes is concerned.

Sigmund Freud has been well worked over by just about everyone recently, and the feminists are no exception. Many attack Freud's concepts for which they have little understanding, much in the fashion of Don Quixote attacking his famous windmills. But then even Freud's most ardent disciples cannot exactly dare to claim that he was fair in his treatment of women.

Although many entertaining quotes from our literature are available which demonstrate this antifemale bias, I have chosen one by Shaw because his wit and language are supreme. In the play *Man and Superman,* Tanner is talking to Ann.

> Even then you had acquired by instinct that damnable woman's trick of heaping obligations on a man, of placing yourself so entirely and helplessly at his mercy that at last

he dare not take a step without running to you for leave. I
know a poor wretch whose one desire in life is to run away
from his wife. She prevents him by threatening to throw
herself in front of the engine of the train he leaves her in.
That is what all women do. If we try to go where you do
not want us to go there is no law to prevent us; but when
we take the first step you breasts are under our foot as it
descends: your bodies are under our wheels as we start. No
woman shall ever enslave me in that way.[2]

Shaw does not present a flattering view of woman.

In *Sexual Politics,* Kate Millet illustrates in detail how the sexual
stereotype of male supremacy and the inferiority of women has
been woven into the fabric of our literary culture.[3] The four
main objects of her analysis are works by Sigmund Freud,
Henry Miller, D. H. Lawrence, and Norman Mailer.

This leads into a topic that is difficult to dispute. Until
recently, most material written about women has been authored
by men. There have been a few notable exceptions such as
Margaret Mead, Simone DeBeauvoir, and Helena Deutsch, but
even they do not date back very far. Basically, women have only
been able to read about the female sex as revealed in the pages
of male authors. Women have had to see themselves through
men's eyes, a condition leaving much to be desired. This is as
true in serious works of psychology, sociology, or philosophy as
it is in the equally important area of fiction. It seems crucial for
women to have the opportunity to read works by other women
where a female viewpoint is expressed. Although important in
all facets of life, this would seem particularly important in such
areas as pregnancy, childbirth, motherhood, marriage, female
reactions to careers, and importantly, female sexuality.

In no other area have the effects of men writing about women been so disastrous as in woman's sexuality. It is only within the past few years that we have even begun to realize the extent of misconception and confusion that surround the thinking
on the nature of sex in women. How we could have gone so long
without seriously listening to women talk about their own
sexual nature is beyond comprehension. In the past, we did not
even allow women the right to have sexual feelings. As we came
out of the Victorian age, women were told that yes, it was all
right to have sexual feelings in moderation, but they still had to
fit them into a male framework. Those of us who have been

listening to women trying to fit their sexuality into their total personality have realized problems that have arisen from the basically prejudiced and inaccurate information they have been given.

Marriage manuals are a literary genre important to examine in this regard. Often consisting of a mixture of folklore and stereotypes, they are a source of abundant misinformation about sexuality. They are literally more fiction than fact. Female sexuality has especially been presented with misinterpretation and distortion, largely due to male authorship of marriage manuals in the past.

For years, women have studied these manuals in a sincere effort to learn more about their sexual nature. Attempting to force their sexual feelings and behavior into the prescribed patterns has frequently led to confusion and discouragement.

Some common myths perpetuated in marriage manuals include the superiority of vaginal orgasm, the need for mutual orgasm, and the theory that masturbation will hinder a woman from enjoying sex with a man. Oral sexuality is often singled out for special castigation. A male physician writing in 1971 on marriage and sex states, "To people of normal inclinations, such perversions (oral sex) are disgusting."[4]

The stereotype of female passivity in the sex act has been taught in marriage manuals for generations. Reading from a marriage manual which advertises it has sold over 670,000 copies, we find that:

> In practically all species the male is sexually the more ag-gressive and active, while the female is primarily receptive and passive. This difference is expressed even in the very character of the respective sex cells.[5]

The message to women is clear but full of misconception: depart from the passive, receptive role in bed only at severe risk.

Similar misconceptions are numerous in the sex literature, and at times they precipitate a woman's visit to a therapist's office. Assuming the sex manual's mythology to be fact, the female reader can be tormented with self doubts and bewilder-ment as she realizes her own sexual nature does not fit the dic-tated pattern.

"I'm a nymphomaniac, doctor. That's all there is to it."

With these rather dramatic words, Sally began to relate what prompted her first visit to a psychiatrist's office. She had been married almost four years, and sex had gone well initially.

"Felix and I were very compatible for a long time. Sex was fun, and we both wanted it on about the same schedule. But then my sex drive gradually increased. I don't know why—it seemed like something I didn't have any control over.

"At first it was fine. Felix responded with more sexual excitement, and I think he enjoyed my growing responsiveness. But my God, doctor, it's reached the point where I want sex almost every night."

Sally blurted out these last words with obvious pain. She was truly concerned and confused about the growing nature of her sexual drive.

It developed that Sally was naive and inexperienced about sex when she first married. As her experience grew, she became more comfortable with her body, and the inherent potential of her sexual being asserted itself.

"Felix would tease me about wanting sex so often, saying that I was wearing him out. I think he was rather proud of me in spite of his joking. But this past year or so I have wanted sex more than Felix, and I know that isn't normal. He stimulates me manually when he isn't up to intercourse, but I wish I could be rid of this extra sexual energy.

"Actually, it was all right until I read that marriage manual. I didn't recognize the problem until then. But that doctor pointed out how men have more sexual drive than women, and how they have to restrain themselves in order to please their wives. It made me feel so abnormal, wanting sex more often than Felix. I've been so ashamed of my problem since then that I haven't been able to tell Felix what I read."

Sally was certainly the innocent victim of misinformation perpetuated in some of our sex literature. Her sexual drive was healthy and normal, and her fears of being a nymphomaniac were completely unrealistic. Females frequently do have a greater sex drive than their mates, a pattern which should in no way be looked on as abnormal. Some sexual compromise may be necessary in the marriage, but Sally and Felix had already arrived at their own solution. Clearing up Sally's worry about her sexual drive was relatively simple, and her fears of abnormality subsided.

The stereotype of the greater sexual drive in the male has commonly been presented in marriage manuals. While more prevalent in previous decades, it is still with us in the 1970s as demonstrated in the following quotation.

> The fact remains that nature has equipped the average human male with a more intense sex drive than even the sexiest female.[6]

Women have been saddled with the concept of nymphomania for generations. Seldom, if ever, is it a relevant theory, being used mostly as a negative slur against women with a strong, active sexual drive. The corresponding concept for males, satyriasis, is seldom used and actually unknown to much of the public.

Sexual drive during pregnancy is also subject to inaccurate generalization in many marriage manuals, a situation which reminds me of Holly.

I saw Holly for about eight months in therapy. In general, she was a rather insecure young woman who had troubles with her self-confidence. Holly was pregnant when I started seeing her, and about midway in therapy she began expressing the difficulties this was causing in her sex life.

"You know how I've had troubles with sex, doctor. We've talked about it enough. First of all I wasn't confident enough to respond much sexually. Then this changed, and these last few months Gene and I have had a good sex life. But now my sex drive is way beyond what it used to be. Gene says I'm insatiable.

"Here I am, six months pregnant and I've got more sexual interest than ever. I couldn't mention it to my obstetrician. He'd think I was loony.

"I'm worried. This book Gene and I have on marriage says a woman's interest in sex wanes when she is pregnant. But the opposite has happened with me. Could something be wrong with my hormones? What if it means something's wrong with my baby?"

This increase in sexual drive during pregnancy experienced by Holly was perfectly normal. True, some pregnant women find their sexual interest waning; but others find an increase or no change at all. It is very much an individual thing.

Holly, however, was insecure. She was especially susceptible to whatever she read. Inaccurate sexual information about women had caused trouble for her on several occasions. As Holly realized her own sexual response was different from what her marriage book said was normal, she developed fears about her body and her pregnancy. Although her lack of confidence played a large part, she too was a victim of myths perpetuated in the literature about women's sexuality.

The scene does appear to be changing as women are writing and publishing more. Womn's liberation, while not the only force working in this direction, is probably one of the most instrumental and influential. Writings by feminists about women have appeared with such frequency recently that it is literally impossible for one person to digest them all. They cover a wide range of topics: from politics to birth control, from psychology to sexuality, from marriage to career, and from discrimination and inequality to medical care of the female body. Any list will necessarily be incomplete and undoubtedly out of date, but some have already become classics. These include *The Feminine Mystique* by Betty Friedan,[7] *Born Female: The High Cost of Keeping Women Down* by Caroline Bird,[8] *Sexual Politics* by Kate Millett,[9] *The Female Eunuch* by Germaine Greer[10] and *Our Bodies, Our Selves* by the Boston Women's Health Course Collective.[11]

The effect is noticeable and salutary as women begin to have an opportunity to visualize themselves as seen through the eyes of other women. The literature, as is true of any other field, ranges from the downright inaccurate to the most excellent, well thought out positions. It is now possible to refer interested women to many outstanding works written by females. This is a truly valuable, and basically only recent, addition to our culture. It can only lead the average woman to have a better understanding of her own nature and an improvement in her self-concept. It is one effective way of destroying a myth.

Running parallel with women writing more about women is the recent emphasis on women's studies classs in our school system, particularly at the college or university level. Women's liberation groups are frequently instrumental in pressuring administrations to establish these classes. One of their main arguments is that women must counteract the historic negative view of the female sex that has predominated in our literature. Now, more positive identification models are needed so that women can learn to respect themselves and other women more. It is also hoped that men will develop an increasing respect for women, including their past achievements and future potential.

Typically these classes include the study of women who have been sucessful writers in the past even though their contributions have been largely unrecognized by the main cultural body.

Women currently prominent in their fields are studied and at times invited to speak personally to an audience in the area. By having actual living examples of competent, successful women available for students to learn from and identify with, it is possible women will more fully realize that they do not have to accept an inferior status in life. Woman's historical role and her current patterns of reaction and behavior are studied in order to gain a better understanding of forces tending to mold her lifestyle. The psychology, sociology, philosophy, and physiology of women are also delved into in some depth. We have indeed entered the era of women studying women in order to gain a better understanding of their own nature and counteract negative sexual role stereotyping.

There is another element which contributes to the sexual stereotype of woman as an inferior being. This is the tendency of our culture to view women who depart too radically from traditional role prescribed behavior as being odd or even mentally ill. Somehow they are thought to not be as emotionally well adjusted as "more normal" women who choose to stay home and tend their children and husband. The strong, independent, assertive woman who has a great deal of confidence in herself has often been looked on with suspicion by other women and by the neighbors. "She must have some pretty serious emotional problems or she would have been able to find a husband a long time ago" would be a typical comment about her.

Drawing heavily on myths, often as revealed in literature, Phyllis Chesler in her well known book *Women and Madness* has done a good job in demonstrating how the independent, confident woman is often seen as emotionally ill when there is no evidence for this.[12] She goes on to argue that mental health therapists operate by reinforcing these cultural stereotypes in their patients. In general this would be countertherapeutic to the individual patient, and I think most therapists are more

sophisticated than this. However, there are undoubtedly therapists who operate in this fashion as they themselves are caught
up in the validity of role performance stereotypes.

Feminists have been attempting to make more explicit our
historic, negative, inferior image of women by examining lists
of adjectives which we normally associate with females versus
those we would typically relate to males. There is, of course, no
list of terms which we would all agree describe one sex versus
the other, but some degree of general agreement can be found
concerning certain words. Controversial adjectives found in the
feminist literature describing women are thought to be passive,
submissive, weak, emotional, warm, dependent, soft, childish,
silly, loving, timid, maternal, irresponsible, wily, illogical, and
understanding. Men are not as often described but tend to be
seen as aggressive, hard, nonemotional, violent, strong, responsible, logical, dominant, independent, and achievement oriented.
These lists do contain more than a grain of truth; they capture
much of the popular imagery in the United States regarding the
personality of woman versus man as presented in our language.
We are of course dealing with cultural myth which exerts such a
powerful impact on the formation of personality.

The image of woman, as does that of man, contains a mixture
of more or less positive and negative qualities. It is frequently
remarked on that the more positive elements of the female
stereotype such as love, understanding, and warmth do not lead
to any great degree of achievement as defined by our culture.
The stereotyped image is that of the warm, tender, passive
woman who will do great at housework and maternal functions
but certainly not have much success in career, artistic, or political endeavors. Woman is thought to lack the strength,
responsibility, logical thinking processes, and aggressiveness for
achievement in such undertakings. Feminists are quick to point
out that this results in woman being held in an inferior position
where she is regarded as inadequate and second-rate. Again, the
point which makes this all seem pertinent is that so many women have accepted this view of their own nature—and so many
men have concurred and encouraged woman to continue thinking of herself in such a fashion.

Women's liberation is attacking this sexual stereotype
regarding the basic nature of woman's personality on two

fronts. Feminists are attempting to affirm and emphasize the more positive elements in woman's image as well as to convince women that they do not have to accept the negative qualities society has imposed on them. This double approach is sound and desirable, but frequently one does not find both messages in the same author. Indeed, some feminists will extol one approach while criticizing the other. Both lines of attack are clearly discernible in the feminist literature, however, and they do seem to be helping some women develop a more positive self-concept. concept.

Women are being told that warmth, emotion, tenderness, gentleness, and understanding are rich, rewarding qualities which have previously been assigned to an inferior status in our male dominated culture. The message is to be proud of these traditional feminine personality traits as long as one guards against their leading into any type of subservience. Especially to be guarded against are traits such as passiveness and weakness which have historically been taken advantage of by males in order to achieve their dominant position in society.

Some radical feminists rail against any of these so-called feminine traits and encourage women to cast them aside, the argument being that they have never served women very well. These are the women who are attempting to achieve equality by identifying with all the worst features they find in the supposed aggresssor—man. I personally have little sympathy with this view as it is hard to see how many women or for that matter, many men, could be helped by attempting to stamp out human warmth and understanding. I do realize what they are trying to guard against—the subservience and inferiority of women. There are, however, sounder ways of achieving this goal. The feminists who are working to achieve greater recognition for the so-called female principle would appear to be in a better position to help women improve their self-concept and feelings of worth and dignity.

The other spearhead of the attack on woman's stereotyped image as an inferior species is rather universally supported in the women's movement. We find women being encouraged to be stronger and more aggressive. Women are now told there is no inherent reason they need be passive door mats, sitting on the sidelines holding the hands of their successful husbands—or that they are somehow not logical or strong enough to enter politics and assume positions of authority and power. The word is out to women—"You are not weak, ineffectual, illogical, dependent creatures who need to be taken care of by big, strong men. Do not allow the myths of our culture to influence you into believing that you are indeed a second or third-rate creature because females necessarily lack attributes of courage, strength, fortitude, and consistency." There is so much positive and accurate in this message that I think even women's liberation's most ardent enemies will be forced to admit some soundness in this approach, however begrudgingly it may be offered.

Another manner in which feminists are attempting to attack this historic negative image of women is by an analysis and publicizing of certain words which are in common usage and negate woman's value. An excellent example is the word "forefathers." Some feminists have begun to use the word "forepersons" in order to emphasize the role of women in our legacy from previous generations. Our past is not just a chronicle of men and their wars and fiascos and their inventions and achievements but includes, or should include, women as well. It is remarked upon with some degree of regularity and a great deal of accuracy that we have almost totally ignored the role of women in the successes and foibles of our collective past. It is felt that use of the word "forefathers" with the emphasis on the "fathers" is symptomatic of our ignoring the role of women and consigning them to the background.

At first this may appear humorous to many people as "forefathers" is such an established and accepted word in our culture. Most people have used the word automatically without giving a second thought to it for most of our lives. Any serious thought that somehow "forefathers" will be replaced by "forepersons" in common usage is I suspect doomed to failure. But it is not a humorous situation, and the word we actually use is not the main issue—it is rather the assumptions and patterns of past thinking as they reveal diminution of woman's value that are important. And if analysis of individual words can help expose traditional methods of thinking which are less than rewarding to women, why then let us go ahead.

Use of the words "man" and "mankind" in the collective sense to refer to both women and men is inimical to many women in the movement. Again, with a great deal of legitimacy, they feel that use of these words symbolizes our culture's negating of woman as an equal member of the human race. Other such words in this group include "man-made," "manpower," "chairman," and "humanity." They all symbolically ignore the importance of women. Other words such as "mailman," "fireman," "milkman," and "policeman" reflect more how women have been excluded from certain occupations.

Part of the inferior image of women involves the area of physical pursuits such as athletics and pride in developing strength in one's body. Traditionally such endeavors have been reserved for males, and girls who have inclinations along these lines are referred to as "tomboys," a rather derogatory term which questions a girl's femininity. Feminists are quick to point out that this is just one more way in which women are conditioned to remain in a weak position in society.

There is now encouragement for women to break out of this preformed mold and develop their interest in sports and other physical activities. It would seem eminently reasonable that a woman need not think of herself as unfeminine or inadequate as a female because she prefers to play basketball or soccer instead of knitting or bridge. The feminist literature is emphasizing physical fitness for women, and of late, there has been considerable interest shown in women developing skills of self-defense such as karate. It adds up to one more way in which women's liberation is encouraging females to avoid the weak, passive role with all of its inferior connotation and instead adopt a more outgoing, aggressive approach to the world.

"I really don't like myself very much, almost as if I've failed as a woman."

Thus Patricia began to relate her general discouragement with life and with herself. She was a most distinguished looking twenty-two year old woman who had graduated from college about one year earlier. Now she was working at a job far below her abilities as a secretary in a large law firm, a job she truly hated. Her complaints during that first visit were not centered around her job problems, however, but were related to the negative feelings about herself.

"I've been so down on myself. Everything I do seems to go

wrong. My roommate and I had a big blow-up last week, and she screamed that I was selfish and ungiving and not at all sweet and feminine. That hit where it really hurt, and I cried for two days. Finally she came into my room and apologized, saying she had been angry and didn't really mean it . . . but she's right—I have been inadequate as a woman.

"It's hard to understand. All my life I've been taught that a woman by herself is third-rate, that she needs a man to legitimize her in this world . . . almost as if there is a stigma attached to being a female. I've fought against this, and yet I go into a panic if someone says I'm not feminine.

"My roommate and I talk about this a lot, and she says I should act more dependent and feminine and play up to a man's ego . . . be sweet and don't challenge a guy on anything. She does this and it works for her, but somehow it's not a part of me. It isn't that men don't like me. I've had three marriage proposals already, but always from the wrong men. I seem to attract men I don't like."

Patricia was born into a traditional family and had one older sister. Her father was a relatively successful business man, and Patricia adored him. Mother was a typical housewife and had devoted most of her adult years to raising two children. Now she was home alone during the day, moping around in a bored, depressed fashion. Patricia admired her father, but her primary identification was with mother. To a large extent she had adopted her mother's conventional attitudes regarding the value of a woman—a woman is taken for granted and has very little worth by herself.

Patricia learned there was only one possible role for a woman—to be a wife and mother. She could conceive of no alternatives. No woman who had been successful and competent on her own had been present for Patricia to learn from as she matured. The women she knew as a child, especially her mother, had obtained much of their value from the man they married. To not marry would leave a woman helpless and inadequate. After all, doesn't the sexual stereotype teach that women are the inferior sex?

This is one facet of Patricia, the part that was readily observable. In some ways this sounds like a cultural stereotype, and that is exactly what it was . . . except that Patricia was a living example of this stereotype, a not uncommon position for American women to be in. If this had been all there was to Patricia, she probably would have married, had children, and lived a reasonably content life. She would have obtained self-worth and value from her role as a wife and mother.

Something else gradually emerged during the interviews, another segment of Patricia's personality which she had been largely unaware of. It was the part of Patricia which did not want to get married and be subservient to a man, an unconscious realization that she would never be happy doing housework and running errands for her children and husband. It was also the part of her which was resentful at the helpless position women in her family were supposed to occupy.

The problem was that Patricia had been unable to recognize this latter part of her value system as she lacked independent strength and confidence in herself. Her worth as a woman was dependent on potential marriage and motherhood, a life pattern she was unconsciously avoiding. How could she part with a theoretical attachment to a traditional life when this meant giving up her main sources of learned confidence and meaning?

This is exactly what precipitated Patricia coming into my office looking for help. She had already begun to subliminally realize that a conventional, stereotyped role as a woman would be too restricting and unrewarding for her, and she was suffering from resulting self-doubts. She was feeling unfeminine and had a distinct dislike for herself. Her roommate's derogatory epithets only verbalized what Patricia was already feeling.

While Patricia was outwardly relating to men with the goal of marriage, she was at the same time choosing relationships where marriage could in no way ensue. Listen as she talks about her relationships with men, and I think you will be able to perceive their self-defeating nature.

"I met this wonderful man two weeks ago when I was in that new bar across from where I work. He was pretty aggressive, coming up like he did and buying me a drink. But at the same time he was respectful and considerate . . . and is he handsome. I couldn't resist him, and ever since we've been seeing each other on a consistent basis. We hit it off well together.

"You know how much I like a man who respects me and tries to make me happy. The greatest part is that he satisfies me sexually more than any man ever has. He is experienced and knows exactly what to do to excite me. Why he seems more interested in satisfying me than in pleasing himself. He isn't out for a quick rub as many men are.

"There is one trouble, however. He has been married for about ten years and has two children. But his wife is a bitch and has been in and out of mental institutions. She's in the hospital now and is due to be released any day according to her doctor. Doug feels that this time he will leave her for sure and ask for a divorce. I know you think I'm repeating a pattern, but Doug is different. He is trying to work up the courage to leave his wife when she comes home from the hospital, and I know he is thinking of marrying me."

About three weeks later Patricia was talking somewhat differently about her newest boyfriend.

"Doug and I don't see each other much these days. I really miss him, but he has to spend some time with his wife. She does need him, and she gets upset if he leaves for the evening. We had lunch together the other day, and he was happy to pour out all his problems. He trusts me so much that he can tell me all about his sexaual problems with his wife. According to Doug, she's really frigid and not at all responsive like I am. It can only be a matter of time until he ditches her. He just has to work up his courage to leave his wife."

For some time following this interview, Patricia did not mention Doug. When I asked her about him and how their relationship was going, she was evasive and quickly changed the subject. Then one day she stormed into the office and raged for the full interview.

"Well, doctor, it happened again, and if you dare say 'I told you so,' I'm going to leave. Doug said he was thinking a lot about our relationship and how much fun we had together—but he feels so obligated to his wife and kids that he can't leave. To think I thought he had more courage than that. Why as soon as his wife leaves the hospital and they are back together, he gets all affectionate toward her. He said he missed me a lot, but I know he wasn't even thinking about me. That relationship is over for good, and I hope I never see him again."

The pattern Patricia talked about was that of falling in love with married or committed men. This was a constant predilection of Patricia's, and she zeroed in on married men as a well-trained golden retriever does on a pheasant in the field. The outcome and final disposition of these relationships was easily predictable in advance by a neutral observer, but Patricia was a main participant and not an uninvolved spectator. Patricia was still not ready to realize the significance of her predisposition in relationships with men, and she had to repeat the pattern one final time.

Norm, the next man in her life, was a distinct improvement. At least he was divorced and not married. The trouble with Norm was that he was so embittered toward marriage from the disaster of a recent divorce that he was not ready to become committed to any woman . . . but Patricia was determined to try. To make a long story short, she tried for approximately three months and finally gave up in a last desperate death struggle. For she was fighting to hang on to something that had actually died some time back—her theoretical commitment to marriage and a home and children. When this last relationship ended, Patricia was finally ready to come to terms with her new identity and forge a more rewarding life for herself.

As Patricia finally gave up her conflictual drive toward marriage, she faced the fundamental task of building her self-esteem based on new values. This was not as difficult as it may sound, for she already possessed the prerequisites within her personality structure. It was a matter of helping Patricia recognize and then appreciate these latent strengths and values which already resided within her. Women's liberation was a great help at this point. "I contacted that women's organization you suggested, and they seem like a nice group. It feels great to meet women who aren't obsessed with marriage and the need to have a man around all the time. I never had a chance to talk with this type of person in my younger years."

There is no question that Patricia gained a great deal by associating with some so-called "liberated women." She became good friends with several peers who were outspoken in their criticism of society and the role allotted to women. She identified with some successful career women and began to feel more pride in herself. A developing awareness of her own strengths and worth as a person independent of any relationship with a male was soon perceptible.

These new feelings of confidence led Patricia into improving her miserable job situation. In her job as a secretary, she had been working far below her abilities and educational training in sociology. She had been content to "put up with the situation" as long as her motivation was to mark time while waiting for the right man to come along. This was reinforced by her lack of confidence in her own career abilities and her somewhat typical female feeling that women should not be strong and aggressive and strive for a responsible job. Now her goals and ambitions were changing, and she was developing a better sense of self-worth. Obtaining a job in her field as a social worker was not too difficult, and before I had much time to digest this, she was doing a great deal of responsible work.

During one of her last sessions, Patricia started talking about her earlier views of marriage.

"You know, I must have been crazy to put so much emphasis on marriage and children. I guess that's all I heard or saw when I was growing up. Why, I realize now that I never wanted to be married and be tied down. I must have been unconsciously choosing men and relationships that were bound to end in disaster . . . how I went from one to another with no realization of what was going on."

During the last interview, she related the new direction her life with men was taking.

"I really don't hate men. There was a lot of bitterness there for awhile, but most of it has disappeared. It's not men's fault that I was conditioned in such a fashion. This whole role thing is stupid. I'm with women's lib all the way on this point. I've been dating again recently, and it's really fun—far more fun that it ever used to be. I seem to enjoy being with men and not having to always worry about marriage. Both the man and I can be far more relaxed. But it has to be a certain type of man before I will spend much time with him . . . a man that is liberated from traditional role values himself and motivated toward equality. I enjoy sharing and doing things on an equal basis . . . no games to play, just honest communication."

Since Patricia and I terminated our regular sessions, I have continued to have sporadic contact with her on a friendship basis. She periodically sends me a report of the latest project she is working on, and we have met once or twice for coffee. She

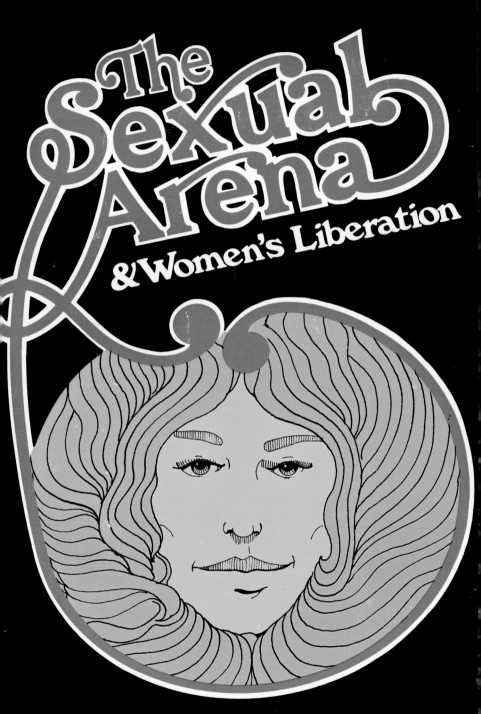

The Sexual Arena
&Women's Liberation

Edward J. Bardon M.D.

often sends me a long letter describing how her life is going. There is no doubt that Patricia has different feelings about herself as a woman than those she was raised to accept. Any feelings that woman is an inadequate, ineffectual creature who needs a husband to give her identity and take care of her have long since disappeared. All of Patricia's problems with life have not evporated, but she approaches them with more self-esteem and confidence in herself as a female. She can even smile and say, "You know, a guy at work the other day said I wasn't very feminine with the independent lifestyle I've been leading. This time I didn't even get depressed and go into a tailspin but shrugged it off as just so much male chauvinism."

Chapter 6

All witchcraft comes from carnal lust, which is in
women insatiable.   **Kramer and Sprenger,**
                                    Inquisitors, Malleus
                                    Malificarum, c. 1486

Sexual Messages

The female of our species and carnal desire is an enthralling
topic which causes imaginations to soar and edicts to flow.
Legends and myths proliferate as males preach on female
sexuality. They range from virgin birth to female lust and
witchcraft, from woman using sex to seduce man in the Garden
of Eden to the complete denial of sexual feeling in women, and
from woman's inherent sexual insatiability to the necessity for
vaginal orgasm. Through the ages of recorded history, few have
been inclined to allow individual woman the basic right to
determine what her own sexual needs are and then express and
satisfy them in her own unique, individualized fashion.

Now women's liberation is on the scene, and at last we have
women holding forth on the nature of female sexuality. This is
a great improvement, but confusion of purpose and message is
nowhere more evident than in the response of women's liberation to sexuality. It is here that we run into diametrically
opposed views among feminists, each claiming that they are the
true believers and that their approach will be best for women.
One segment teaches increased heterosexual activity and freedom for women and it places emphasis on woman's inherent
right to sexual pleasure and orgasm. Another vehement group
of feminists are furious at this position and in general feel that a
withdrawal from sexual activity is needed because any type of
heterosexual contact is exploitative of females. A third core of
women's liberationists are so angry and vindictive toward males

that they espouse a general movement toward female homosexuality.

There are many manifestations of this confusion in individual women. I frequently talk with young females who just plain don't know what type of sexual pattern they want for themselves or what type of sexual response, if any, they want from men. They are influenced by the vituperative conflict raging around them on how women "should" respond sexually. They listen to feminists who say one thing, they listen to feminists who say another thing, and they listen to their families who promulgate still another position, losing track of their own individual inclinations and desires in the process. Confusion and inconsistency of behavior are natural results, and this is often characterized by wide variations in sexual thought and behavior within the same individual.

There still seems to be an open field day for all and sundry who wish to tell woman how she will or ought to respond sexually and what her sexual motivations and moral values should be. Many "experts" enter the contest and perform vigorously on the field with their outspoken ideas concerning the "fundamental nature of female sexuality." They range from Freudian disciples to Masters and Johnson, from Dr. Reubens to "J," and from Germaine Greer to Ann Landers. The poor individual woman often continues to be lost in the process as no one seems content to just let her have her own responses which might not (and probably don't) fit into some feminist's or researcher's pet theories. Is it any wonder that so many women are confused and angry at the many conflictual messages they are receiving regarding the nature of their sexuality—messages which never seem to quite fit their own unique personalities?

When one has listened to literally hundreds of women describe the intimate details of their sexual desires and responses, it seems impossible to escape the conclusion that female sexuality (and indeed male sexuality also) is a most complex subject that defies any accurate generalizations. The physical and emotional and psychological and social have such an intriguing way of interacting with each other, producing an almost infinite variety of delightful reactions such as one finds in a colorful kaleidoscope. It is useful and practical to dissect out one facet of sexuality such as the physical which Masters and Johnson have done and then strive to elucidate as much factual information about it as is possible—but in so doing, it is crucial to remember that in the individual human being such an artificial dissection is not possible and one cannot divorce the physical or the social from the rest of the personality.

Mary is one such woman who was caught up in a maze of cultural confusion regarding sexuality. She came from a fairly traditional background and had a reasonable amount of sex education which concentrated on teaching her the "proper" sexual role of women. Being intelligent and perceptive, Mary very early in her life recognized that this so-called education was more brainwashing than anything and that it was not particularly suited to fulfilling her needs. She was perplexed and angry that society should teach values and behavior patterns which almost totally ignored her own sexual needs and desires.

Mary was easily influenced by her first college roommate who taught her that girls should be liberated and rather promiscuous, satisfying their sexual needs whenever the opportunity arose. A brief fling at this left her unsatisfied, and she began reading widely about the sexual nature of woman. Settling down to one boyfriend seemed appropriate, but now Mary came under the spell of those who preach the necessity of orgasm, single orgasm at least and multiple orgasm if possible. Mary tried to mold herself to the pattern and meet the expectations of the books she read and the women she heard speaking. During one session Mary finally exploded.

"I'm tired of everyone telling me how to behave sexually. All my life I've heard do this and don't do that. No one really seems to care what my needs are except my boyfriend Rob. He tells me to relax and let come what may. He is the first one who has let me be myself and not tried to force a whole set of expectations regarding my performance. It is so comfortable to experiment and find out what I really am and what my own sexual nature is apart from what all the books say it should be.

"I guess it's my fault for letting so many people tell me what to do sexually, but you know something—it's hard for a young woman to not listen to all the people writing and talking about sex. I am so sick of reading that I have the potential to have multiple orgasms and to satisfy a whole team of men. My anger has been coming out at my liberated girl friends who keep saying that I will lose my independence if I become involved with only one fellow. I have quit reading the letters from my family because mom keeps saying that I should be a 'good' girl. She just wants me to be miserable and repress all my sexual nature. Why have so many people tried to tell me what to do with my own sexual energies? It's much less confusing if I just listen to my own body."

It would be most unfair and inaccurate to place the responsibility for all this sexual confusion on women's liberation. Much of this maze was present long before the advent of the women's movement, and it is an outward reflection of serious problems in the way our culture has conceptualized the female of our species. Feminists have become aware of these basic attitudes toward women and the way they relentlessly lead to sexual problems. What has happened, however, is that feminists have adopted a wide variety of approaches in trying to solve these realistic problems, approaches which are frequently mutually contradictory.

The feminist movement contains a great deal that is of potential sexual benefit to the individual woman, but there are also many pitfalls for women such as Mary who can get lost in the confusion and axe-grinding. Some women are using the women's liberation movement to support their own idiosyncratic approach to sexuality, seeking reassurance for their own behavior by attempting to proselytize and make converts. Women who show a missionary zeal in espousing lesbianism or celibacy are examples of this. There is a remarkable and significant difference between an attitude which allows every woman the freedom to develop and pursue her unique approaches to sexuality no matter how unusual they might be and an attitude which attempts to persuade others to one's way of thinking and behaving. The latter position is an anathema to freedom, a futile attempt to coerce others through a dictatorial approach to sexuality. If women can be aware of these difficulties and not allow themselves to be persuaded into adopting a particular feminist's view of sexuality, many can gain a great deal from some of the issues raised by women's liberation.

> I just laid there in bed feeling so angry at the discrimination against women that I couldn't respond sexually.

There are several ways in which women's liberation has the potential to help women in the sexual area. The first of these that I have chosen to explore is the manner in which resentment and hostility between women and men can have a deleterious effect on sexuality. Women's liberation has been especially helpful in emphasizing that anything which oppresses women and holds them in an inferior position will have a negative influence on the sexual act. Women are stating that sexual relationships often turn out to be bad trips because they feel unequal and exploited in their general treatment by males. The woman who is angry about being treated as an unequal by her lover is apt to have a destructive experience in bed.

Anything which can help women feel and be more equal in her relationships with men will most likely have a positive effect on her enjoyment of sexuality. There are some exceptions, of course, most notably masochistic women who derive their sexual excitement from being humiliated and hurt. This type of woman can become totally unresponsive sexually if she is treated as an equal and not subjugated. We see examples of this clinically, but they represent special problems and are probably not frequent enough to alter the general tenor of this discussion.

Anger and hostility are often the key to lack of sexual response. How many wives lie in bed feeling humiliated and bitter as they are having intercourse, feelings which have arisen from anger at the way they have been treated during the day? This is a theme which comes up repeatedly in the feminist literature and in talks with individual couples. The complicating problem is that this anger and resentment can have such a multiplicity of causes, varying from one individual to another. One common pattern is the woman whose anger is basically related to feelings of being treated unequally as a female and at being forced into a rather conventional life pattern.

Amy and Van are a married couple who exemplify some of these statements. Four years of marriage had passed when they first consulted me for general marital problems which were at the point of forcing a breakup in their relationship. Much of their mutual hostility was related to their sexual life which had become progressively worse during the past year or two. Both Amy and Van agreed that sex had gone well during the early part of their marriage. These were happy times to look back on, and they were perplexed as to what had gone wrong in their relationship.

Their life together had been fun and rewarding and sex was frequent and exciting. Both were college students when first married, and they had found a great deal of meaning in mutually working and supporting each other. As both were busy with school and jobs, they developed a system to share the housework. College graduation for Amy and Van occurred at about the same time, and both were glad to be done with formal schooling and the necessary papers and tests.

Following graduation, Van felt that because Amy was pregnant, she ought to stay home and be a traditional housewife. Amy acquiesced to her husband's strong feelings without ever realizing the serious psychological difficulties this would bring about. Van was trained in advertising and business and thoroughly enjoyed his field. He obtained a job with a small, independent advertising firm, and was soon able to assume a significant amount of responsibility. His job was exciting and rewarding, and he was in daily contact with many interesting people. His life was adventuresome, and he was ready to come home at the end of the working day.

Amy's life, however, rapidly took a different course. She found little of an exciting nature to do at home, and she was bored beyond her tolerance. Following the birth of their son, Amy was even more tied to the house. Van was a conscientious, responsible, and compulsive father, and he devoted a great deal of time to caring for his infant son. He insisted that Amy not have babysitters during the day as they would not provide adequate care for his offspring. For the same reason, they rarely if ever went out at night. Without realizing what was happening, Amy developed more and more resentment at the pattern her life was assuming. Part way through the sessions, Amy began to realize what some of her anger was about. Listen as she talks.

"I feel trapped, like I am caught and have no way out. Van has such an exciting life, and mine is so dull. I really envy his being able to leave the house and have a job he likes. I always enjoyed working and earning some income, but now I have to stay home and take care of the baby. It's not the child's fault, but I have even grown to resent him and all the demands he makes on me.

"Do you know, Doctor, these visits to your office are the only time all week that I get out of the house except to go shopping? It doesn't seem fair. Here I am a college graduate, and I have nothing to do. I wonder why I spent all those years struggling through school. I guess I'm pretty angry at Van, but then that doesn't seem fair because he tries to be a good husband. He helps me around the house whenever I want, and he does such a good job of being a provider."

As I was seeing Amy and Van together, Van was present in the room as Amy spoke. He heard what Amy said, and as this theme was explored during the following sessions, he gradually realized what Amy was resentful at.

During another session, the connection between anger and sexuality became more explicit. Again it is Amy who is talking.

"Last night Van and I were in bed making love for the first time in weeks. You know how I have been refusing to have anything to do with sex for some time now. Well, as I was lying there, I suddenly realized how bitter I was at Van and how I resented letting him use me sexually. I never used to feel used sexually. Maybe it has something to do with the way I feel trapped at home. Could that be why I have been so unresponsive sexually?"

Most assuredly, Amy had realized an important connection in her life. The validity of her observation was demonstrated when her sexual responsiveness and enjoyment returned in conjunction with a change in her life pattern. Although somewhat compulsive and overly conscientious, Van was a reasonable person and had no fundamental wish or need to be unfair to Amy. As Amy recognized what she wanted out of life and became assertive in setting up a more rewarding life style for herself, Van proved to be quite helpful.

Surprising as it may seem, Amy knew little of women's liberation and the type of issues being raised. If she had, maybe she never would have allowed herself to be trapped into such an unrewarding pattern. Amy desperately needed someone to help her realize that she would not be a bad mother or an inadequate woman if she found herself a rewarding career outside of the home. We talked about women's liberation during some of these sessions, and Amy began to tune in on some of their messages and explore some alternative lifestyles for herself. She never became an ardent feminist, but Van and Amy did set up a more mutually satisfying marital pattern. It was perhaps easier for them than for some other couples because they had the precedent of their early marriage when they were both in college and shared the income producing and housework responsibilities. Also Van was in no way adverse to childcare or routine house maintenance. Amy and Van worked out an arrangement whereby through judicious use of childcare facilities and more sharing between them, Amy was able to return to work and spend time outside of the home. Her feelings of being trapped disappeared along with most of her anger toward Van. Sex again became mutually rewarding and satisfying to Amy and Van.

Amy clearly represents one type of woman whose sexual problems as well as lifestyle difficulties are readily helped by women's liberation. It is almost as though the feminist movement was conceived especially to help Amy. The type of sexual problem she presented (that is lack of responsiveness and enjoyment) is a common one, but unfortunately most such sexual and marital problems do not have this simplistic or storybook type of finish. Life is generally more complicated.

Underlying resentment at one's treatment as a woman and resulting sexual dysfunction as elucidated by women's liberation can take some curious and perhaps unexpected directions. Lucille and Peter are such a couple.

On the surface, Lucille and Peter presented with much similarity to Amy and Van. They had been married about three years and their present complaint was a very poor sexual relationship. Things had gone from bad to worse in the marriage and they were barely talking to each other when I first saw them. Each had separately considered having an extramarital affair, but both rejected this as something they did not want.

Both Lucille and Peter were motivated to avoid open conflict, and they were quick to point out that they had never had a fight. They of course meant an open fight, for both were great combatants using more passive techniques. They were afraid of open hostility and could not communicate in any realistic fashion concerning areas of disagreement. Lucille especially had a tendency to withdraw and avoid looking at any problem which might be upsetting to her.

After we had met for several sessions and opened up some communication regarding their sexual problems, Lucille began to recognize her anger at Peter. During one particularly memorable interview, she recognized how she had been expressing her anger in the sexual area.

"I have always known that it was important to Peter for me to enjoy the sexual act. When sex was going well between us, Peter would spend a great deal of time trying to excite me. I used to enjoy this as he was so tender and considerate—but for some time now I have just been lying there letting Peter use me. I wanted to hurt Peter, and I knew this would get to him. I could sense how my total unresponsiveness was hurting him as I lay there in bed absolutely still. But I never said no to Peter . . . he could use me whenever he wished. I don't think I was particlarly aware of what I was doing."

I asked Lucille if she knew why she was so angry at Peter, but she could not come up with much during that session. During the next interview, however, she was more in contact with the sources of her bitterness.

"I realized I have been angry at Peter for some time now, almost back to the early part of our marriage . . . it has built up during these last two years. When I married Peter, I was expecting a traditional marriage. My family is very conventional, and Mom has always been happy in her role as wife and mother. She never had to work outside of the home, and Dad has always taken good care of her. I guess I expected the same sort of relationship, but Peter and I never talked about this. We must have assumed we were thinking along the same lines.

"Well, shortly after our marriage, Peter began to put pressure on me to have a career. He had been reading a lot of stuff written by those damn women's lib types, and he began to feel that a woman would never be happy staying at home and having children . . . but this is what I wanted. I remember Peter once telling me that he was afraid I would become resentful toward him if I was stuck at home. It's sort of paradoxical, but I became angry at him for just the oppoite. He was so influenced by other women he talked with and by what he was reading in those women's magazines that he never found out what I wanted. But I never told him either. Peter has been fearful of my being too dependent on him, and he keeps encouraging me to be independent.

"I always wanted a man to support me while I stayed home and took care of things just like with Mom and Dad. I think Peter's really scared of that responsibility. I never wanted a job, but Peter kept insisting that I find an interesting career. My heart isn't in it, though, and I develop more anger every day. At one point he bought me a copy of *Open Marriage* and insisted I read it and then go through it page by page with him. He is so concerned that we each have our own independent career and friends and this is not what I want at all. I want to stay home and have children and not be forced into some stupid liberated lifestyle."

So goes life with its delightful unpredictable responses. I cannot report as favorable an outcome with Lucille and Peter for their communication was too poor to permit much change in their basic marital pattern. When last seen they were continuing to express their anger in subtle ways, and their sexual relationship was remarkable for its lack of mutual enjoyment.

Another major way in which women's liberation is helping women sexually is by teaching them to have more comfortable contact with and better appreciation of their own bodies. The importance of female masturbation is often singled out for special emphasis. It is noted how masturbation has been discouraged or how the act has terrified women in the past. The following is an illustrative quote.

> Woman Is: masturbating like crazy and being terrified that you'll go insane, be sterile, turn into a whore, or destroy your own virginity.[1]

The women's literature is now popularizing what counselors who have been willing to listen to their women clients have known for a long time. An active, healthy, guilt-free sexual exploration of one's body including masturbation can be helpful in establishing a lifelong pattern of sexual enjoyment. This is as true for women as it is for men.

The old, outdated concept of masturbation being a sin is being replaced by the active encouragement and teaching of masturbation in sexual awareness groups and sexual therapy clinics. Less and less often do we now encounter guilt associated with masturbation as more of our population seems to realize the normalcy and desirability of masturbation for both sexes. The Kinsey studies demonstrated a significantly higher percentage of masturbation to orgasm for males compared to females, 92 percent versus 58 percent. This was approximately twenty years ago and contemporary evidence indicated that the gap is narrowing because of an increase in female masturbation.[2]

The feminist literature is abundant with references to the desirability of masturbation and the way it can help a woman know her own body and discover what will turn her on. A most excellent example is the following:

> Masturbation is not something to do just when you don't have a man. It's different from, not inferior to, sex for two. It's also the first, easiest, and most convenient way to experiment with your body.[3]

This paragraph is followed by a detailed anatomical description of the clitoris and its essential role in female sexual response. Many methods of masturbation are then suggested in this excellent sexual course for women and in other women's books. They include such things as masturbating by rocking back and forth on a basketball, climbing up a rope or pole, using gymnastic parallel bars, active stimulation with feathers and other soft materials, employment of various types of water streams and pressures, and of course information on the use of dildoes and electric vibrators. *The Sensuous Woman* by J. is a widely circulated book which is illustrative of this point of view.[4]

Women's liberation is trying in general to help women establish better contact with their bodies, masturbation being only one facet of this. Quite correctly, feminists have perceived that women have tended to be isolated and alienated from their bodies as shown in the following quote.

> Woman Is: feeling basically comfortable in your own body, but gradually learning to hate it because you are: too short or tall, too fat or thin, thick-thighed or big-wristed, large-eared or stringy-haired, short-necked or long-armed, bowlegged, knock-kneed, or pigeon-toed, something that might make boys not like you.[5]

Women have been taught shame and guilt in regard to the human body and its normal processes and functionings. Feminists write that they have learned to abhor and despise the parts of their body, and only with great difficulty can they begin to like and appreciate their limbs, breasts, genital organs, body configuration, and so forth. Furthermore, women have been taught that they must be the beautiful sex, and in the process they have adopted all sorts of impossible beauty standards.

There is a great deal of legitimate anger as women begin to realize they cannot accept themselves as they are. They are taught to purchase various and sundry cosmetic products and devices to somehow achieve a "more desirable" standard of beauty. Women write that the standards are impossible, that women end up feeling deficient and insecure with their bodies— their nose is too long, or their breasts are too small, or their hair has split ends, or their buttocks sag, or their legs don't have the "proper" type of curves, or their hips are too big, or their body structure is too large, or they smell wrong, and on and on and on. They are bombarded with advertising and cultural pressures to buy and use all types of mechanical breast supports, girdles and buttock molding devices, razors to shave off "excess hair," false eyelashes, deodorants for all the body's openings and crevices—in short, any conceivable device to change their natural body toward a so-called more acceptable norm.

Indeed, we have even entered the cosmetic surgery age where women can and do have their breasts made larger or smaller, their buttocks corrected for normal sag, their faces lifted and made more "desirable," and their noses surgically corrected to achieve a more Anglo-Saxon form. No wonder so many feminists are enraged about the "beautiful sex" role women have been taught to assume. There is no question but that feminists are correct in stating that this cultural conditioning process has produced a great deal of body dislike and insecurity in women. The evidence surrounds us in the public media, in women seen clinically, in general observation of women in our culture, in reading of personal accounts, and in some research studies done.

There may, however, be a tendency to overdo this problem. Yes, many women feel insecure about their bodies but many other women do not. Some women are proud of their bodies and have no particular wish to change its configuration. They accept normal bodily functions and possess no particular degree of shame or guilt about their body. They feel attractive and in general are in good contact with their physical self. How common are such women? I do not know, but it is always a delight to meet and communicate with them, certainly not an unusual occurrence. This would seem 'a reasonable goal for women to aim towards, and women's liberation can have a significant impact on helping some women achieve this comfort.

Bodily insecurity and attempts to adhere to a cultural norm are not unique to the female but are also found in the male. This is seen in such things as so-called penis lengthening devices, muscle building apparatuses, girdles to hold in abdominal muscles, toupees, and other devices to build more masculinity. In the past, our culture placed more emphasis on women being the "beautiful sex," but this may now be changing.

The feminist's messages in regard to the female body are useful in clinical work. It has been helpful on numerous occasions to refer to these writings in working with a woman who is having difficulty appreciating her body. This is a subject which frequently comes up in group therapy situations, and I find almost universal support and approval for the women's liberation position on the female body. Increasingly the young women that come to my office are demonstrating a more positive awareness of and contact with their bodies. There is a new sense of comfort and security in this area. One senses that the general cultural mileu in regard to teachings about the female body is changing for the better, a good part as a direct result of the women's movement.

How could a man ever like a girl with small breasts?

The history of Jean is appropriate at this time as she can demonstrate how some of these problems affected an individual woman. Jean was a twenty-one year old computer programmer at one of the area's large electronic firms when I first met her. She had been dating sporadically for about two years and had recently found a man she really liked. It was difficulty in relating to this man which precipitated her seeking help. Her career work was excellent, and she had reasonable goals which she was successfully pursuing.

After spending several hours with Jean, I noticed that she

began to develop some trust and could relate more directly to the anxieties which had engulfed her.

"This is hard for me to talk about, but if I am to get any help I guess it's necessary. Clayt and I really get along well. We seem so much in love, and Clayt has been mentioning marriage. We want to spend all our free time together, and I can hardly stand to leave him. No, there is nothing wrong in our relationship as you suggested. I'm very sure of that . . . we have too much fun together. It's that I can't respond physically to him."

Jean broke off here and turned her head to look out the window. She was blushing and too embarrassed to look directly at me. She had talked around this problem for several interviews without being able to directly deal with it. I sensed that she was now ready to discuss her problem as her motivation to bring about some type of change was very high. The ground work had been set, and now I could only wait. After several minutes of silence, she continued talking, but her eyes remained averted.

"Clayt and I have been sleeping together. It seemed right because we were so much in love. I thought it would be O.K., but I froze when he began undressing me. I am so ashamed of my shape that I make him keep the lights off. I have never let him see my body. We've tried several times now, and Clayt seems to have a good time. He runs his hands all over my body, and although he doesn't say anything, I know he must be disappointed with me."

"Why should he be disappointed in you?"

Jean's discomfort was intense at this point, but she carried through.

"My breasts are so small, and I know men like large breasts. My body is ugly. Since I was fifteen, I have worn falsies, but they make me feel like a fake. I can't marry Clayt feeling this way. All I can do is lay there terrorized. I want so much to enjoy it, but I am too anxious."

There it was. Jean had learned to detest her body, and she had developed intense insecurity surrounding her degree of breast development. Her dislike for her body and lack of confidence were paralyzing her sexual functioning. She knew with a certainty that she had found the right man, and she realistically did not want her sexual problems to destroy their relationship.

There was a huge discrepancy between the reality of Jean's physical presence and her conception of herself. Jean was not ugly—in fact she was beautiful. She was thin and her breast development was small. She was lithe, supple, pert, and athletic in a most graceful way. She had more the figure of a fashion model, the type so many women could be proud of. Many men would find her intensely attractive and exciting. As she aged, there would never be a problem with obesity or sagging breasts. Her physical structure was that so commonly seen in longevity. And yet she felt ugly and ashamed of her body. What had happened?

Jean was talking about some of her experiences in living with her girl friends.

"I like the girls in the house. We all have a good time together, and I have known some of them for over a year now. But I get so jealous of the well-endowed girls. Some of the girls with big tits have the habit of walking around the floor in their bras. I get so furious that I can hardly talk. It's almost as if they are making fun of me. Why should they have so much and me so little? It isn't fair. I can't even undress in front of my roommate. She has never seen me with my bra off."

"Have any of the girls made derogatory remarks to you?"

"No, and I know I must be oversensitive. But what is a girl supposed to do? You wouldn't understand because you're a man, but that is what women hear all their lives. All the magazines, all the advertising, all the jokes about small women. The way the boys in high school talked . . . I could have killed them. They used to tease me and ask me when I would develop. I pretended to ignore them, but their comments hurt. It reminded me of when I was younger."

Jean stopped here, and I sensed that she wanted me to ask her what had happened when she was younger. She had developed more trust now and could look at me as she related difficult material.

"Well, as you know, I have two older sisters and a younger brother. My sisters matured, and then they would tease me. I could never tell Mom because I was too ashamed. I was thin as a bean pole, and my sisters would say that no man would ever be interested in me. One time they held me down and pulled open my blouse in front of my brother. He was too young to know what was happening, but I have never forgiven my sisters."

Jean had indeed been hurt on several occasions as she grew up. Her negative body image was fixed long before she met Clayt, and she "tuned out" any positive comments she now received about her appearance. It was easy for me to reassure Jean that she was a very attractive woman and that her small breast size did not have to be any particular problem unless she insisted on keeping it one. Jean listened carefully to what I had to say. This helped, but it was not enough. Jean needed support and encouragement from her peers, both women and men. She had been hurt by both in her developmental period. Now she had achieved a greater degree of comfort in herself and could talk more openly about her problems. Because of these factors, I placed her in group therapy, a situation she could not have handled any earlier because of her acute sense of shame and embarassment.

For some time Jean remained relatively quiet in group. She listened carefully as others discussed rather intimate problems. Her trust developed as she sensed that this was a "safe" atmosphere in which others would not hurt her as she had been in the past. One session she related her negative feelings about her body, especially the concern over her small breasts. This opened up a general discussion as other members of the group had similar concerns about their physical attractiveness. One girl related, with a great deal of embarrassment, that she grew up feeling her legs were too crooked and that she had been teased by some of her peers during earlier years in school. She had been unable to wear dresses for fear her legs somehow did not measure up to par. Another girl in the group was concerned about being slightly overweight, and she off and on felt pessimistic about her body. One man told how he was sensitive about not being particularly coordinated or athletic, a subject of acute self-doubts as he grew up.

Jean received very immediate and honest positive feedback from her peers in the group. Her physical appearance was so pleasing and her body was such a well integrated whole that other group members looked askance as she talked about her "ugly" body. One fellow told Jean how he had been having sexual fantasies about her and how attracted he was to her. Two of the girls expressed envy toward Jean's physical structure, especially the girl who felt she was overweight. Most important, no one teased or laughed at Jean.

For the next session, one of the women brought in some feminist literature she had been reading concerning the impossible standards of beauty which are imposed on women in our culture. She read some of the shorter articles out loud, and the other group members had a positive response to the idea that this can bring about an over-abundance of bodily insecurity. They tended to feel that this can be a problem for men also, but that probably it is a larger problem for women.

Following these sessions, Jean experienced a noticeable increase in pride and confidence in her body. Much of her sense of shame left by the back door, and she reached a point where she could joke about the way she used to feel. All of her sexual problems did not disappear overnight, however.

"Things are much better with Clayt when we are in bed. I actually enjoy him looking at my body, and I laugh when I remember how I used to need the lights out. He really digs my body, and to think that I never used to believe him. We play a card game to get undressed. The loser has to remove one piece of clothing, and we go on until all our clothes are off. But I still don't respond much sexually. The old panic and fear are gone, and I enjoy the physical contact but nothing happens. I think it is similar to what you said recently, Linda. You know, about being inhibited sexually. It's hard for me to participate and do anything myself—as though I expect Clayt to do it all and that isn't very exciting for me. My upbringing sounds similar to yours, Linda. Somehow I learned that a girl should be passive sexually and this is hard to change. You were telling how it helped you to climb up on top of your boyfriend and do it that way, that this made it easier for you to get excited. I'd like to try that and Clayt encourages me, but I just can't bring myself to do it. It seems somehow wrong."

Jean had been brought up in a fairly traditional way and had learned typical female sexual role patterns which were now inhibiting her functioning. She had not only learned to think of her body as ugly, but she had also grown up feeling alienated and out of contact with her body. Traditional female passivity had been impressed on her as a moral "good."

Jean was not alone in the group in this regard. Some of the other women had similar problems, and this was an opportune time to have a full group discussion regarding the importance of every individual discovering what approach to sexuality works best for them. The women were able to express their anger at being conditioned to play a passive role sexually and to not feel free to play a more active, participating role. Group members were able to discuss ways to achieve a greater awareness of their own sexual selves, including masturbation. This all had a marked influence on Jean who was able to integrate these concepts into her sexual functioning. She gradually developed a greater degree of sexual comfort and active responsiveness.

Chapter 7

Women must humanize the penis, take the steel out of it and make it flesh again. **Germaine Greer**

The Pursuit of Sexual Happiness

Women and the capacity to enjoy heterosexuality to its fullest potential is indeed a topic to tempt the imagination of most mortals. One widespread interpretation of the women's liberation movement is that it stands for an increased sexual freedom, a permission to partake of and enjoy sexuality in a way which has traditionally been forbidden to women. While we will later meet feminists who radically depart from this position, it is a view which is commonly held and expressed by those in the movement. Many women whom I meet are positively influenced by this new attitude toward sexuality, and it is important to understand this position.

Feminists who espouse this position argue that women did not develop on earth to merely function as a sperm receptacle for the supposedly more active, dominant male. Women should now seek and demand an equal role in sexual relationships, and sexual pleasure should be developed as one of life's most precious benefits. Victorian woman with her sexual guilt and nonresponsiveness is the symbolic representative of much that is evil in the sexual past of contemporary woman for she is the embodiment of female passivity and subservience to the male's sexual needs. Guilt is no longer seen as an appropriate reaction for women seeking sexual happiness.

Thus one part of the feminist movement gives permission, and at times orders, to women to partake with pleasure of the sexual act. This is a message which is strong, aggressive, and full of hope and promise. It is heard and listened to by countless women, and in many instances it is having a most positive impact on the sexual life of the involved participants. I suppose we cannot give women's liberation the total credit (or total blame if one is oriented in this direction) for the recent increase in sexual freedom and permissiveness for women. There have been other forces in our society working in this direction, but certainly the women's movement has been one of the most powerful and influential. As long as this position that women can enjoy sexuality more is seen as a suggestion and not a commandment, it would seem to be a long overdue and welcome addition to the messages of our culture. When it is taken as an absolute, however, it can and does lead to difficulty in some individual women. June is such a person.

June had been married for about sixteen years when I first met her in my office. Her husband, Sam, was not particularly impressed that there was any problem in the marriage, and he was reluctant to come in for joint sessions with June. I thus saw June alone, but only for a few interviews as her problems were not deep rooted and cleared up rather rapidly.

"Doctor, I've been feeling depressed and down for about five months now. I mope around the house, and I haven't got the energy to even meet friends for lunch. The kids have been bugging me, and they tell me I am irritable and crabby. But I have so much trouble sleeping at night that I can't be friendly during the day. And my appetite is terrible. Why I lost five pounds last month. Food just doesn't taste good anymore. I guess I have the 'blues.' I saw my regular doctor, and he said I was depressed. He thought you might be able to give me some medication."

Yes, June was depressed but not severely so. She had retained a good sense of humor and could still laugh at herself. Her past history revealed no previous depressions or emotional disorders and until recently she had been leading a full and rewarding life. What June needed was not medication, but an attempt to find out what she was depressed about. The second interview produced the following:

"You asked me about my marriage. It has been good, with its ups and downs. We fight at times, but I don't think it is any more than our friends. But I have been worried about sex. I have rarely been very active sexually. I never used to worry about this, but then I started reading some of those articles on sex in the women's magazines. They say that a woman should enjoy sex as much as her husband, and I never did. Sam always gets so excited, and I guess I'm supposed to do the same. One of the last articles I read gave a list of six ways a woman can increase her sexual enjoyment. Well, I tried but the feelings never changed. Something must be wrong with me as a woman. I realized during the week that this is what I have been worried about. I can't seem to put it out of my mind. What is wrong with me that I can't enjoy sex like other women? Is it something really serious?"

"No, I don't think it is that serious at all, but can you tell me what your sexual life was like previous to the past few months?"

"I never thought it was all that bad. It's just that I never became very excited. Sex seemed enjoyable to me, especially the part where Sam and I would be so warm and close together. I always liked the sense of him inside me, and it made me feel like a real woman. It was like I was giving Sam something, and we would both feel so tender and affectionate. We would be together like this for hours, and often I would wake up in his arms. Sam said this is all very normal, but I worry he is just saying that so he can have his own pleasure . . . at least this is what some of those articles are warning about. But this never seemed to make sense because Sam is willing to do whatever I want. He has been really trying to excite me with all the tricks I read about recently. Sam says he doesn't care one way or another, just whatever pleases me. I know what I used to like, but now that seems so inadequate."

June's earlier enjoyment of sexual contact with her husband was real and normal. It is the type of sexual response one frequently hears from women, and it was easy to reassure her that she had every right to enjoy sex in her own way. June was merely frustrating and depressing herself in trying to change a sexual pattern which had previously been so rewarding and meaningful to her. Her depression cleared quite rapidly as she began to realize that she was no less a woman because of her somewhat quiet enjoyment of sexuality.

One might reasonably ask why June allowed herself to be so readily influenced by what she had read if her sexual life had been all that good. Is it possible she had an underlying propensity to doubt her feminine nature? Could there have been marital conflict present which did not emerge during the interviews? These are good questions, but unanswerable as I deliberately chose to not delve deeply into them with June. Her depression and physical complaints cleared nicely, her past history was excellent, and I saw nothing to be gained by bringing up these issues.

Some feminists will argue that women such as June who enjoy such a traditional passive type of sex are merely showing the end product of a propaganda type of social conditioning. This might be true, and I would not argue against this position. It might also be true, however, that June represents the type of woman where traditional role conditioning in regard to sexuality and inherent biological and genetic potential are in close harmony. We have no fixed answers as to why individual women respond as they do sexually. What is certain is that there is a wide variety of response patterns, and that to try and label one as more healthy or normal than another is a most foolhardy exercise. The most important question would seem to be whether or not the individual woman is satisfied with her sexual functioning. This in no way implies that people should not try to increase their sense of sexual enjoyment, as long as it can be done with a spirit of fun and exploration. The danger and the trap come when individuals feel they ought to change their sexual patterns in order to meet someone else's standards. This is the basic conflict that June ran into, one that is a common problem for American women.

A quote by psychiatrist Saul Rosenthal from the University of Texas Medical School is germane at this point.

> Where perhaps in a previous generation they [the wives] would have been pleased to be passive recipients, they are now aware that sex is something that women are supposed to enjoy. The more they read in the popular press, the more inadequate and unfeminine they feel personally. They often avoid sexual encounters after a period of trying in vain to increase their sexual enjoyment.[1]

Along with giving women permission to enjoy sexuality and thus possibly alleviate guilt, the feminists movement is attacking the sexual role concept which states women should be the passive partner sexually. At first glance, it might appear that the freedom to enjoy sex includes or assumes an end to sexual passiveness. This is definitely not the case, and it is useful to separate out these two connected but different concepts. In some women they go together, but in many other women they are distinct entities.

It is common for some women to be the passive sexual partner and yet enjoy sexual relationships to an intense degree. This type of woman perhaps waits for the man to approach her and initiate sexual contact, and she is passive once she is in bed with her lover. Typically she will wait for and expect the male to excite her, meanwhile doing little if anything to actively excite the male. In a sense she chooses to do whatever her partner wishes, and she takes no responsibility herself to determine the course of sexual events. There are of course infinite variations on this pattern, but they revolve around the central theme of the woman functioning as the receptive partner, while the male initiates and excites in an active fashion. Some women are intensely excited with this type of sexual relationship, and they would not wish it differently. Sexual enjoyment and sexual passivity can be and definitely are closely associated in many individual women.

Some segments of the feminist movement do not like this. They write as though they expect all women to take a more active and aggressive role sexually. This is a very positive message for many women, but for others (such as June), it is destructive and out of tune with their personalities. As we have seen so often, one has to properly fit the shoe to the individual foot for whom it is intended. Messages to women must be sorted and fitted to the individual woman in question in order to avoid being destructive. Thus to say, as the feminist movement is inclined to, that women in general will be better off if they take a more active aggressive role sexually is simply a grossly inaccurate simplification. Some women experience just the opposite. They attain a happier, more enjoyable sexual life as they switch from an active role to a more passive one.

Women's liberation tends to equate sexual passivity with submission to and subjugation by the male. In many women this is a valid observation, and they are one type of women who are apt to benefit from adopting a more active approach to sex. They have learned subservience to the male, and they have carried this over into the sexual area. Feminists feel women have been trained to respond to the male and not to initiate sexual contact, a rather indisputable point in regard to many women. This is seen as unequal and humiliating to the woman, a further proof of her inferior position in our culture. Sexual passiveness is seen as dependency and a lack of power, a condition breeding anger and contempt for the male.

Women who initiate sexual contacts and function quite actively once in bed are sometimes called castrating to men. This is a derogatory slur hurled by men who are so insecure that they feel threatened by a sexually active woman. Women need not have to ask permission or obtain male approval in order to function in an aggressive manner sexually. There is no reason for a woman to feel guilt for initiating sexual activity if this is a role she chooses and is comfortable with.

Psychiatrist Natalie Shainess feels that sexual self-assertion by women is discouraged because of the traditional tendency to interpret it as a rejection of femininity.[2] Feminists have helped to create a new emotional and intellectual climate in which female sexual assertion and femininity are not seen as contradictory. Perhaps one of the most widely read books which has helped to create this atmosphere is Germaine Greer's *The Female Eunuch*. With great insight into both female and male psychology, she states "Men are tired of having all the responsibility for sex; it is time they were relieved of it."[3] We shall have occasion to examine this male reaction in some detail in one of the later chapters.

A few feminists are now writing their personal sexual experiences, with an emphasis on women being an equal and active sexual participant. Some of these personal accounts are intimate and reveal an active pursuit of sexual pleasure.[4] These are positive messages for many women and they have the potential to help numerous women achieve a more satisfying sexual life.

The rise of modern civilization, while resulting from

many causes, was contingent on the suppression of the inordinate cyclic sexual drive of women because.[5]

The "female orgasm" is a subject of recent intense interest and discussion as women finally claim sole ownership rights. The feminist literature insightfully points out how only recently have women felt the right to a "personal orgasm." In bygone generations, the woman tended to gear her sexual functioning to that of the male and her orgasmic response and potential was seen as secondary to that of her partner. No longer does this hold true, as countless feminists emphasize women's right to have an orgasmic response in the sexual relationship.

Vaginal orgasm versus clitoral orgasm is a topic of current interest. Since Masters and Johnson demonstrated so convincingly that they are physiologically one and the same, women's liberation has embraced this new knowledge and adopted it as one of the largest stars on its flag. Countless articles refute the traditional Freudian emphasis on the female attaining an orgasm with vaginal penetration and correctly show how this tyrannized many women. The clitoris is achieving a new degree of importance. Women seem to be now depositing as much energy and importance onto their clitorises as men have traditionally placed on their penises. The biological sexual insatiability of the female now comes into the forefront as feminists ask:

> When does a woman finish now? She can take one man after another, one orgasm after another (not that she will or needs to, but she can).[6]

In her book *The Nature and Evolution of Female Sexuality*, psychiatrist Mary Jane Sherfey states that the penis is an exaggerated clitoris. She examines what she feels is the inherent insatiability of the female and states that civilization came about in order to control and somehow handle the inordinate demands of female sexuality.[7]

How are individual women being affected by all this? Authors' viewpoints vary. Psychiatrist Natalie Shainess considers women to be caught between classic analytic concepts which tend to deny orgasmic potential to females and Masters and Johnson's work which interprets orgasm as strictly a mechanical thing available to all.[8]

Psychiatrist Elizabeth Stanley in an article entitled "Can Women Enjoy Sex Without Orgasm" states,

> Finally, it must be stressed that our performance-oriented culture has created a widely held but false belief that anything short of a 100% orgasmic response in a woman represents sexual inadequacy. This, more than any other factor, has made women unsatisfied with nonorgasmic sex.[9]

Along a somewhat different track, widely read feminist Dana Densmore states, "Most women don't have orgasms at all, and very few always have them."[10]

Most of the women with whom I talk have integrated this new knowledge and freedom concerning their orgasmic potential and clitoral sensitivity quite well into their personalities. Young women especially seem to adopt whatever seems to best fit into their own unique personalities. They thus can have a most positive reaction and use this information to improve their sexual life. The potential for this is certainly there if women can avoid some of the pitfalls of increased pressure to attain multiple clitoral orgasms.

Yes, like other therapists, I do see women who are having problems because of this new sexual awareness and knowledge. Some are confused by the transition and feel caught between conflicting sexual values. Others do have difficulties because of the increased pressure on the female to attain a minimum of at least one orgasm per sexual contact. Seldom do I meet a woman who feels a driving need to attain one orgasm after another and satisfy countless men sexually within her insatiable capacity.

At this point I do think of Bonnie as she is quite memorable, if rather unusual, in her approach to women's liberation and sexuality. I suspect many feminists would not care to claim her, but she claimed them with an astounding fervor.

Bonnie came to my office stating that she was the completely liberated woman. She was a twenty-six-year-old career woman in a downtown business office, and *The Female Eunuch* by Germaine Greer was her constant companion. She would carry this book with her and often refer to it in the course of presenting her story, much as Chinese people are taught to carry and quote from Chairman Mao's *Little Red Handbook*. Her initial words were about the women's liberation movement and how it was influencing her life.

"I have been liberated now for two years. You must understand that this isn't any problem, even though this is what some of my friends say. I'm lonely, and it seems that I can't get it together with one person for any length of time. But women's liberation has helped . . . none of this marriage and slavery crap for me. What I need is a totally equal relationship. I feel so liberated sexually. This book has helped me (pointing to her Bible, *The Female Eunuch*). Why I'll bet I have twice as many orgasms as I used to with no more of this feeling that I have to sleep with only one man. I've slept with five different men this last week."

Bonnie went on and on about how liberated she was. It was only with great difficulty that I was able to get some idea of what brought Bonnie in looking for help. She was an active, energetic woman, and her constant verbal outpouring was truly staggering. There was little chance for me to get a word in edgewise, and Bonnie didn't seem to listen when I did. She was too intent on proving to the world how great it was to be "liberated." Gradually some of the pieces of her life fit together.

Bonnie was truly lonely and alienated from people. Her intense activity and almost compulsive talking were in part an attempt to avoid looking at her sense of isolation from the world. For complicated reasons which I never fully understood, Bonnie had developed a feeling that people and the world were always rejecting her. She had grown up a loner and was proud of the independent manner she had adopted in meeting life. Her upbringing had been conservative and moralistic, and there were many messages that sex for a woman was an evil and dirty thing. Her father was described as narrow and judgmental, and he taught Bonnie a whole list of "thou shalt nots." As Bonnie matured and went through adolescence, he regularly admonished her to keep a safe distance from boys or she would "get a reputation." On the few occasions when she did date, Bonnie was accused of being an immoral woman. She was literally threatened with hell and damnation, even though her behavior had been immaculately chaste.

Bonnie reacted against this moralistic upbringing by swinging widely in the other direction when she became a young adult. She had been promiscuous for years, and she had never been able to establish any sort of lasting relationship. Her life was the world of one-night stands and brief affairs. Now she found a justification for this behavioral pattern in women's liberation.

Bonnie had a great deal of justifiable anger at her overly strict and forbidding childhood. She was furious at the negative sexual messages she had learned during maturation, and she was spending her life fighting these early injustices and trying to undo past insult to her sexual being. She had a great need to talk about her "liberated sexual behavior," and she would do this in an "I'll show the world I can do anything I want" tone of voice.

"I call myself a fuck-freak. I like it as often as I can get it and as hard as possible. Thank goodness the world has changed so that a woman is free to be aggressive sexually. I used to have trouble approaching a man, but since reading my book and joining the women's liberation group, this has been no problem. We women realize that men have had all the fun. Now it's our turn. Too long have women had to sit back and wait for the man to take the initiative. We weren't even supposed to enjoy sex. Why I enjoy sex as much as any man I've ever screwed, and I can climax over and over. Thanks to women's lib, I know I have more sexual capacity than any man. I've taken four men in one night and satisfied them all."

Bonnie collected orgasms. During another interview, she talked about her "cruising."

"Some of the women in my lib group taught me how to cruise. We're tired of men being the only ones who can initiate sexual activity. Now I can approach a good looking guy at the bus stop and directly ask him if he wants to come to my place and fuck. Some of the men really do a double-take and walk away as fast as they can, but about half of the men accept and we have a great time. At first it was hard to approach a man I'd never met, but now it's easy. It just takes a bit of nerve. It really helps to be liberated."

Not surprisingly, Bonnie felt the world to be lonely and isolating. Bonnie never gave herself a chance to experience anything different, and she set up one rejection after another. Her so-called "liberated" lifestyle was in many ways a false type of liberation in which she remained emotionally distant from the world and perpetuated her loneliness. There was little I could do to help Bonnie. She had adopted a life-pattern which she felt was "liberated," and she in no way wanted to hear any suggestions that maybe part of the responsibility for her loneliness was her own. Bonnie was basically too busy proving to the world that she could have as much fun sexually as any man, and she had become sort of a female Don Juan. My relationship with Bonnie ended when it became apparent that there was little if anything that she wanted to change in her life at this time.

Ginger presented quite a contrast to Bonnie's "liberated" sexual behavior. She had much of the same loneliness and isolation, but she feared and hated men with a passion. Our first meeting proved to be quite interesting.

"I wanted to see a male psychiatrist because men give me so damn much trouble. I hate everyone of you—you're all male chauvinist pigs—and you're no different, sitting there so smug and superior like. I suppose you have me undressed already. Every man thinks this way as soon as he meets one of us. He just can't wait to get his hands into our pants. Well, what the hell are you sitting there looking so surprised for? Why don't you say something?"

And with that, Ginger gave me one of those threatening, hostile glances which is calculated to wither you on the spot. Before I had a chance to reply, I was caught up in another deadly barrage.

"I can see already that you don't like me. I expected that before I came. I suppose you're sitting opposite me so that you can look up my skirt. Men never like me as a person: they just want to get their rocks off inside me. My roommate said that I don't give men a chance, but that's bull shit. [I was puzzled how any man could ever get close enough to touch her. He would have to be a most daring soul.]"

Quickly I saw my opportunity to get a word in and distract Ginger from her man-hatred. I asked her about her roommate and their relationship. These were my first words to Ginger, and I hoped they were in fairly neutral territory.

"You can't get off that easy. I'm not stupid you know. You just want to change the topic because you know men are lousy, and you can't defend them. I came here to talk about men and sex, and that's what I'm paying you for. And don't you forget that I've hired you, and that puts me in the driver's seat.

"I suppose you are wondering why I hate men and sex so much. Well I'll tell you if you'll shut up and give me a chance. And quit leering at me like all the men in the office. I came to see you because my relationships with men aren't the most friendly. [I could believe that.] This wouldn't present any problem except I have to work with the shits all day. If you must know, it's interfering with my work. I have a good job, and I don't want to louse it up. I make good money, and I have a lot of control over the men under me. But they've started complaining to the higher ups—the word is out that I'm a bitch just because I keep the men in their place. I suppose if I were all sugar-sweet and took my clothes off for some of them it would be different, but I don't give them a chance to see anything. For awhile, I went braless so that my breasts wouldn't be molded into some attractive shape for men. Then one wise clown in the office came up and said that he liked the way my sexy nipples stuck out."

By now some of the surprise element in Ginger's rather unique presentation had worn down, and it was apparent she was going to talk about men and sex as she had announced. I asked if she had always been so angry at men.

"I don't know how you can assume I am angry at men. You've only known me fifteen minutes, and already you are making conclusions. That's the trouble with men. They are not rational like women.

"I did have a lover once, if that's what you mean. You can be more direct you know. I'm not embarassed by sex. . . . I've just had my fill of it. When I was twenty-two, I lived with this guy for close to eight months. I let him screw me whenever he wanted, not that I got anything out of it but the clap. To think that I supported him . . . used to buy his drugs and everything. Not that I minded, for I was always more capable than him. I could earn more money in a day than he did in a week. He just sat around the house smoking dope while I was off at work. Not that we feminists mind being capable and supporting a lazy guy. [My first hint that I was dealing with a feminist.] Well, believe you me, did I let him have it when I got the clap. He moved out on the spot. I was so damn angry at being used by him that I had a few one-night stands with guys I picked up in the bars.

"That's when I started being active in women's liberation. I was marching for abortion on demand and met some gals that had been used by men. They're my friends now. We all agree that independence is just too damn important to risk it by screwing with some guy. We're not going to let men get the upper hand. I haven't taken a man since, and I'm not about to start now. I tried making it with one of my new girl friends, but that didn't turn me on. I'm not some sort of queer, you know. That's all you psychiatrists think of.

"I suppose you're wondering what I do for sex. [It really hadn't occurred to me, but I knew I was going to find out now whether I wished to or not.] Well, you must know that a woman doesn't need a man, especially if she's liberated like I am. [Oh, wouldn't Bonnie love to hear this.] We have a clitoris, and it's every bit as good as your penis. It may not be as big, but it's much more sensitive. This penis envy crap that you psychiatrists teach is just a way of putting women down. And this vaginal orgasm myth. . . I never could climax with a man in me, but my electric vibrator does wonders. But don't you get any mistaken ideas. I never need to put it inside me like some phallus. Women don't need some guy's penis to have a good time. I always make certain that I am well satisfied so that those creeps at work can't get to me."

It was nearing the end of the hour. If I was ever going to find out what type of trouble Ginger was having with the men at work it would have to be now. After all, she did say that is what brought her in. I gathered together all my courage and tried once more.

"Ginger, can you tell me how the men at work get to you?"

"I knew you'd ask me that. You just want to hear about my problems. It makes you feel superior if you can think that a woman can't handle the responsibility of men at work. Well, let me tell you, I'll take care of those complainers at work. We women are every bit as capable as men, and don't you dare to imply otherwise."

Well, I had tried. You can't win them all. Ginger went on

about her vibrators for another five minutes, and then the time was up. When I told her that we would have to stop, she let loose.

"Time's up! What do you mean the time's up? I pay you good money to come here, and you haven't even heard why I came in to see you. Why you just sat there like other men do when I talk. Some fat job you've got. Genetically inferior and you get all the top jobs. Why you're probably just trying to figure out how you can seduce me."

With that Ginger left my office. As you might guess, I haven't heard from her since. Exactly what brought her into my office is conjecture, but a good guess is that her massive anger and sexual mistrust of men were making it difficult for her to function efficiently at work and that possibly the owners of the business she worked for had cautioned or threatened her.

Ginger and Bonnie are two women who have adopted life patterns which are dramatically different and conflictual with each other. Yet each one is an active member of women's liberation, and each considers herself to be a "liberated" woman. These two rather extreme interpretations of the feminist movement battle with each other over who represents the "correct" sexual approach, and they spare no words in condemning each other.

The towering antimale feminist approach to sexuality is exemplified by Ginger. She is certainly not alone in her inter-pretation of women's liberation, for, as five feminists have clearly stated, "We no longer compete only for men; we also compete as to who needs men less."[11]

In this antimale sex approach, the sexually liberated woman is attacked as pursuing false goals—she should be saving her energy to help fight male oppression. In order to be free of men and assert female independence, it is deemed imperative to do away with heterosexual needs. Thus a woman who is able to arrive at a position where she doesn't need a male sexually will be better able to avoid structuring her life around a man. As men are the common enemy, it becomes imperative to not fraternize with them. At times celibacy and lack of any sexual outlet are recommended as a means of helping define one's self as a woman. The exact mechanism as to how this will occur is not spelled out.[12]

Perhaps this is a more radical feminist viewpoint, but it is one that has been fairly well publicized recently. The sexual freedom of the sixties is condemned as being exploitative of women, and the seventies are now to say goodby to the sexual revolution. Women are now urged to achieve independence from men by avoiding them sexually. Feminist Germaine Greer is seen as the archenemy, and she is attacked with a vengence which used to be reserved for an onslaught against the male.

What's more, the whole tone of 'The Female Eunuch' is shallow, anti-woman, regressive, three steps backward to the world of false sexual liberation from which so many young women have fled.[13]

Behind this passionate outburst against the enjoyment of sexuality, one senses a great deal of personal hurt and anger. It is possible that women such as Bonnie who have pursued such an extreme in sexual liberation eventually wake up feeling used and abused by men. Often they then react in the opposite direction, again in an extreme fashion, and rail against the groovy, free-swinging, sexually liberated role which did not work for them in any rewarding way.

You can sense the disappointment and rage in statements such as the following:

The generation of women who only a few years ago saw themselves as the vanguard of a sexual revolution between women and men suddenly find themselves plagued with all the problems of their grandmothers—loss of interest in sex, hatred of sex, disgust with self.[14]

Further on in her article, the authoress states,

Most women, I suspect, have given up on sex, whether or not they have informed their husbands and lovers.[15]

Thus the controversy among feminists rages, with biting insults being hurled back and forth. Two extremist positions, as represented by Bonnie and Ginger, battle for control over the sexual mind and body of women. One camp tells her in no uncertain terms that to be an independent, liberated woman she should forsake marriage and actively pursue sexual pleasure with a variety of partners, collecting as many orgasms as possible along the way. The other sector emphasizes that freedom from male domination can only be achieved by a refusal to engage in sexual relationships with men. One senses that the hapless, individual woman and her own unique reactions are all but ignored in the process. After all, who has the time or inclination to listen to the common woman and how she is actually responding to all these various forces? Extremist groups are usually so busy promoting their own intolerant ideas that they show little concern with how their viewpoints are actually affecting individual people.

Between these two rather extreme positions on sexuality, there is a wide middle ground which has enough latitude to comfortably encompass large numbers of American women. These are the women that are enjoying heterosexuality within the framework of a regular or committed relationship or else on a selective basis with several different partners. Often they are using some of the recent teachings on women and sexuality by feminists to increase their participation in the sexual act. Although I see women who are living examples of extreme positions, such as Bonnie and Ginger, I discern no major movement to embrace such radicalism.

What I do perceive happening is a tendency for women to adopt more of an intermediate approach to sexuality when confronted by some of these far-out sexual ideas. Some women go through quite a period of confusion, however, in trying to sort out a reasonable approach to sexuality for themselves from amongst the more radical messages which are thrown their way. This is especially true if the woman in question is young and in a state of flux regarding her sexual approach to the world. Often this confusional state is of brief duration as the involved woman quickly realizes that such an extreme position has little personal reward for her. There are other individual women where a longer, more troublesome period of time is required to sift out a rewarding personal approach to sexuality.

Kitty is such an individual woman. Mistrust of men and difficulty in relating to them brought her in seeking help. Kitty's father died when she was a young child, and she had only the vaguest recollection of him. She is the youngest child in the family and was raised with her three sisters in an all-female household.

Men were a strange and unknown factor to Kitty. She had no close contact with them as she grew up, and when I first saw her at the age of twenty, she possessed no experience in relating intimately to male peers. Kitty was naturally perplexed about sexuality, and there was considerable fear and misunderstanding present. Her upbringing at home had not been particularly antimale or antisexual. Rather, men and sex were just not mentioned. Kitty's fear of the unknown came to the forefront as she began exploring relationships with men in her own age range. Furthermore, she was easily influenced by antimale and antisex feminist literature which she had come across.

"I've been reading how men take advantage of women, especially sexually. I guess we are just a play-toy, and no man takes us seriously. This makes me so damn mad that I won't let a man get near me. The other day I had this blind date, and he tried to kiss me . . . but I know what he wanted. He wanted to go all the way and just use me. Women are subjugated and treated like slaves, and I'll never let any man do that to me.

"The women I've been reading about must have had a lot of experience. They seem to know what men are like, and they say it's important for a woman to remain independent. And sex makes you dependent on a man, puts you in a situation where you will be crapped on. A woman always ends up the loser in a sexual relationship. But I don't know what I am supposed to do with my sexual feelings. That fellow I had the blind date with was sort of nice. It's too bad he tried to kiss me."

"Has any man ever hurt you, Kitty?"

"No, and I'm not going to let them get close enough to try. Why should I open myself up to be used sexually when basically women don't enjoy sex anyway? But it does seem rather confusing. Mom said my dad was nice to her. And things she said to me and my sisters led us to feel that she must have had a good sex life. Ann, my oldest sister, and I have been talking about that recently.

"Ann doesn't seem to feel hurt or used by her husband. We talked about sex the other day, and Ann said I was crazy to feel that men just use women sexually. She doesn't interpret women's liberation that way at all. She seems to dig sex and wouldn't want to go without it. But all those women writing that sex with a man is so degrading and subservient must be writing from experience and know what they are talking about."

Kitty's mixed feelings about men thus came up for discussion. She wanted to relate to men, but she didn't want to be used and hurt. She had little experience of her own, and this left her extremely susceptible to other women's comments and experiences. Kitty needed to have some direct experience of her own in relating to men, but this was difficult as she was so terribly frightened and confused.

I felt that group therapy might be a good place for Kitty to explore her confused feelings about men, and she was enthused about the idea. This would provide a setting in which she could discuss her feelings directly with other women and men, as well as gaining some practical experience in relating to men. I was forming a new group, and Kitty seemed like a logical addition. It was a most interesting group of people that were gathered together. Two of the men and one woman in the group were divorced. One woman was having serious marital problems and difficulty taking care of her three children. There was a young man near Kitty's age who hated women and a woman several years older than Kitty who was very conflicted in terms of how she wanted men to respond to her. In short, every group member was having real difficulties in relating to the opposite sex.

During the first meeting, a regular male-female battle developed with everyone's hostility at the opposite sex spilling out. Some of the women felt men were an unrealiable group of bastards, and they took out their anger at the men present in the room. The men retaliated with their views that women were seductive and then castrating, but above all, too controlling. Hostile words were the order of the day, and I began worrying that Kitty would have her anger and fear of men reinforced.

As is frequently the case, the second group meeting was quite different. Members had relieved themselves of their pent-up emotions during the initial gathering, and now they could settle down to work on some of their own personality problems. Kitty was mostly an observer during those first few sessions, but she listened intently as the others talked. It was apparent she was learning many new things which would eventually help her work out a meaningful approach to sexuality. As she heard some of the other women talk about their sexual experiences, she gradually realized that not only do women have sexual desires, but sometimes they put considerable sexual pressure on men to satisfy these needs. She was most surprised as Beth talked.

"Since Ed and I were divorced last year, I've been dating rather heavily. I'm not sure I want to marry again, but I sure as hell have no intention of going without a man. Last month I dated this character about three or four times, and you know he never made one sexual advance. My clothes stayed on for three dates, and was I frustrated. I thought he must be some sort of a queer.

"Well, the last date was something. I remembered what you were saying, Kate, about women's liberation preaching that a gal can take the sexual initiative. I maneuvered him up to my apartment after the show to serve him a drink, but while I was out in the kitchen I stripped off all my clothes. It was really something to walk out nude with his drink and watch his reaction. I thought maybe he was just shy with women, but he did a real double-flip. He yelled at me to get my clothes back on and he got out of there as fast as he could. Boy, was he scared. I'll bet he was a homo or something."

Jim, the twenty-two year old fellow with so much anger at women, couldn't let this one pass.

"You women are so damn confusing. I'm darned if I can figure out what you want. Just last week, Beth, you were bitching at the way men were looking at you sexually . . . as though they were undressing you on the spot. You said this is one of the things women's liberation is going to do away with . . . how you were going to eliminate all those uncovered women in movies and advertisements, and how you were tired of men using you as a sexual object. You complain if we make sexual advances and you complain if we don't. And damn it, I'm tired of looking at your underpants. Sure they're sexy and pretty, but you could wear a skirt long enough to cover your underwear."

Jim seldom missed an opportunity to let out his underlying

anger at women, but the group was used to him by now. He was genuinely confused, however, by how women wanted to be treated.

Kitty looked overwhelmed at the directness of Jim's attack, but she evidentally understood some of the confusion he was experiencing for she nodded her head as he spoke. Actually, members of this group had become good friends during the weeks in spite of the anger which periodically flared up. Kitty and Jim had especially become good friends, perhaps because they were close to the same age and shared so much confusion in relating to the opposite sex. They listened most carefully to each other during the group sessions.

During the next session, Kitty began relating what she had thought about during the week.

"Beth and Kate, you run around calling yourself liberated women and seduce every man in sight. Sex to you is fun and exciting, and you've worked out your own pattern which is fine. Other feminists complain because men lust after them, and they advise not relating to men sexually. Jim, I can see where you would be confused. But if you weren't so damn angry at all of us, you would realize that women are individuals and want different things. This is what I've been helped to understand. I don't have to mold myself into a pattern that some angry feminist is spouting off. I have my own needs to consider. It's been good listening to you men in the group talk. I've gotten to know you as human beings, and I realize how strange men have been to me. Somehow, I don't feel as frightened of men any more.

"And this women's lib thing. Every one interprets it in a different way. My sister Ann feels that she is a feminist, and she is married with a child. She thinks women's lib has helped her have a better sexual relationship with her husband. She thinks these extreme positions are for the birds. I just don't feel as confused about men any more. I know that I want to set up as good a relationship with a man as I can, and I'm confident about this. My mom and dad had a good thing going until Dad died."

Kitty had made her way through the confusing, conflictual messages regarding men and sexuality to which she had been exposed. Her confidence was a bit premature, for much would depend on the type of experiences she had as she began to relate heterosexually. But she would probably never again take very seriously the extreme statements on sex and women's liberation to which she had been exposed. She now realized that she liked men and that there was no reason she had to avoid them sexually in order to be "liberated" and remain independent. On the other hand, women such as Beth and Kate who considered "liberation" to be the equivalent of seducing every man in sight left her with a great deal of antagonism and anger. She was not at all oriented in this direction, and she would never become indiscriminately promiscuous.

Kitty could hardly wait to tell the group about her first sexual experience. Her spontaneity was a joy.

"Well, guess what happened? Brad and I finally made it to bed. And to think I once swore that I would never let a man touch me. It was really fun, just as some of you have been telling me it would be. And I wasn't shy or awkward or embarrassed or anything. I wanted it, and I guess that makes all the difference.

"You know, my sister Ann has helped me the most. We've had these long talks about sex, and she tells me how women's liberation has helped her enjoy sex with her husband more. All those old feelings about a woman needing to be passive in bed have disappeared. She enjoys reading about sex and trying new things, and I've learned from listening to her. I felt so spontaneous and free with Brad. This is what Ann says, that women have as much right to sexual pleasure as men, and do I dig that. To think that women used to feel that their primary duty was to satisfy their husbands . . . what a bunch of propaganda that was."

This was a red-letter day for the group. By now, everyone had become interested in Kitty and they were excited over her happiness. Kitty was indeed in a carefree, laughing mood as was the rest of the group, and it was good for us all to have carnival-like spirits. For this was to be the group's terminating session, and goodbys had to be exchanged. Kitty could not resist one final commentary on her sexuality.

"I know some of you, especially Kate and Beth, have tried to convert me to a more free-love position, but this isn't me. I owe a lot to you, however. You have made me realize that sex can be fun and enjoyable, and I don't know that marriage is for me either. I really do value my independence, and I sure don't want to end up taking care of some man. Ann has a good marriage, but she puts up with some stuff that I wouldn't want. I guess the future has to remain a big unknown."

And with that our group ended. It had been a fun group, and we were all sorry to part . . . but it was time for us all to be on our own way in life. Kitty indeed faced an unknown future, but she had arrived in that large, rather nebulous middle ground concerning her sexuality and she was comfortable.

Chapter 8

You're not a radical feminist if you don't sleep with women.

Anne Koedt

Homosexuality

Female homosexuality, or lesbianism, often comes up for discussion in reference to women's liberation. Are they connected in any fashion, and if so what is the nature of their relationship? Is the women's movement indeed a breeding ground for female homosexuality? Are innocent young heterosexual feminists seduced into a fate worse than death? Must one sexually love other women in order to be a proper feminist? Is lesbianism the ultimate answer to male supremacy and women's historic inferior role in society? Are lesbians really sick people, or are they normal healthy women who are leading the fight against male chauvinism? And so the questions continue to flow, reflecting the confusion and disagreement surrounding the relationship between women's liberation and lesbianism.

The crucial element to realize is that lesbians are far more interested in women's liberation than the feminist movement is in female homosexuality. Cries of outrage and denial from the homosexual community will not alter the basic realities of the situation. Most of the feminists with whom I talk have little or no interest in homosexuality other than perhaps a passing curiosity or an anger at lesbians who try to claim the feminist movement for their own.

Some lesbians write that they are really the vanguards of the women's movement. They state that they have done away with sex roles long before there was a women's movement, and they also point out that they have no need for men. Bisexual women are often attacked as copping out on the feminist movement because they lack the courage to leave men completely.

Why should lesbians be so interested in women's liberation? This is not a difficult question to answer when we realize some of the problems a homosexual faces in our society. Female homosexuals seem to desperately need a movement. They are outcasts in our society and they have been treated with such fear, disdain, and prejudice for so long that their self-image suffers. To be a homosexual in America is to suffer from humiliation, degradation, and constant affronts to one's ego. Recently a homosexual individual was talking to me about loneliness and self-doubt in a most poignant way.

"I don't think you can ever realize how much homosexuals suffer as they go through life. This is especially true as we grow up and begin to worry that we are different. Everyone says we are queer, sick, or somehow dangerous to others. We have nowhere to go for support, no place to turn where we can be reassured that we are O.K. and that we are basically just like anyone else except for our sexual nature. We are not only outcasts in society but also in our religions and even in our families. It helps now to realize that there are others like me and that I am not some type of freak."

Homosexual women often seek a movement to help them feel legitimate. They would like to ride on the coattails of women's liberation's success. You can sense this need in some typical statements that homosexual women make: "Women's Liberation needs lesbianism. Lesbians need women's liberation. We are all sisters."[1]

Many of these statements have a missionary zeal as lesbian women try to bolster their own egos by seeking converts. We read that it is necessary for a woman to show her love toward other women by sleeping with them or that a feminist is somehow oppressing women if she does not seek them sexually. Some claim that feminists cannot be heterosexual because they must devote all their energy to loving women. Indeed, some homosexual women write that they are angry because the women's movement is trying to ignore them in order to appear respectable and gain advantages in society. They conveniently ignore the fact that many women are involved in women's liberation but not at all interested in turning homosexual in order to prove this. Such propaganda rhetoric is not unlike what heterosexual society does in applying pressure on homosexual individuals to mend their ways and join so-called "normal" society.

Some women are attracted to both movements, and they combine them in their behavioral pattern. By and large, these women would be homosexual whether a women's movement existed or not. The feminist movement helps them feel a freedom to express their homosexuality and avoid the usual connotation of it being an abnormal activity. It gives permission to love another women and not feel guilty in the process. There is a great deal of emphasis on "the sisterhood," and women are encouraged to like and accept other women. One of the best illustrative quotes regarding this that I have run across is as follows:

> The mutual respect and love of the lesbian for another woman is especially meaningful at this time when all women are beginning to realize their sisterhood, and to liberate themselves from personally and socially binding sexist assumptions. Since a lesbian is freed from emotional, economic, and erotic dependence upon men, she affirms by her life the fact that women have worth in and of themselves, that women are not "completed" by acquiring a husband, and that women may need to defy the socially prescribed female role in order to create healthy, fulfilled lives for themselves.[2]

Julie portrayed many of these ideas.

Julie was a thirty-two year old woman who was apathetic and withdrawn from life when I first talked with her. Her normal interest in work had waned considerably, and she was finding it hard to go about her daily life.

"I have no enthusiasm. I can barely muster up the strength to get out of bed in the morning, and I routinely go through the day. Here it is, the middle of summer and I don't even get outdoors. Normally I am a real nature bug; camping, canoeing, hiking, and all that stuff. But, gosh, for these past several months none of this appeals to me. I pretty much sit and mope around the apartment when I'm not at work. I haven't been seeing anyone."

It took little time to discover what Julie was reacting to. She already knew what the problem was, and there was no need for me to play detective. A simple question as to what had gone wrong several months ago opened up her train of thought.

"My roommate moved out on me. I don't know what happened, but we had been quarreling something terrible. She said she couldn't stand it any more, that we were finished this time for good . . . claimed I was too jealous and possessive of her, and I suppose I was. I was always afraid of losing her, and she used to delight in threatening to move out when we would fight. But at the last minute she would change her mind and stay—until this last time. I miss her, and yet I'm angry at her for abandoning me.

"Sure, I'm homosexual. It's no secret, and you've probably guessed by now anyway. We were lovers for close to three years. It was the best relationship I've ever had, and I wanted it to last forever. But in my heart, I knew it couldn't. Betty, that's her name, was basically too promiscuous. I wanted her for myself, and she always said that was too restricting for her. I knew she would go out and cheat on me with some other woman, but sometimes I would pretend to not know in order to keep peace between us. Other times I would explode. That's what we fought about the last time. I guess it's my fault for being so jealous and chasing her away, but I couldn't seem to help myself.

"Don't misunderstand me—homosexuality is not my problem. Sure it causes me difficulties in society, but I'm a confirmed lesbian. I know some psychiatrists think we are abnormal and try to change our sexual patterns, but I've heard that you are different. One of my friends recommended you because you helped her without trying to convert her to loving men. That's what I want—someone to help me set up a better relationship with a woman without throwing all this heterosexual crap at me."

That was a fair request, one that I could certainly live comfortably with. I was pleased that Julie could set some ground rules of her own. It was a promising sign for the future.

Julie knew she was depressed because her lover had moved out. What she didn't realize was the extent to which she had been tyrannized by this woman. Julie felt that her jealousy of

Betty's sexual relationships with other women was wrong, that somehow she must learn to live comfortably with a lover's lack of commitment to her as a person.

As Julie realized during the next few sessions that she had a right to an exclusive relationship with a woman if this is what she wanted, her anger toward Betty became more overt and her depression tended to clear. Now the problem was to help her set up a new more rewarding and lasting relationship with a woman of her choice. This was somewhat difficult as Julie was basically a quite shy and retiring woman, and approaching other women was not easy for her. Moreover, her ego had suffered many blows as she matured and she lacked self-esteem and liking for herself. She needed to be more self-confident.

As we explored some of Julie's past history, she began talking about her parents.

"I get so angry at my parents continually asking me when I'm going to get married. Here I am, thirty-two years old, and I haven't been with a man for years . . . they still think I'm going to get married. You'd think they would have wised up by now, but they are too busy fighting with each other."

Julie stopped here and looked at me, evidently seeking permission to talk about her parents. We had avoided Julie's upbringing at home because of her request to not mess around in her sexual development. Now she wanted to talk about her parents.

"Why don't you tell me about these fights, Julie."

"Dad is an alcoholic—has been ever since I can remember. And Mom is a martyr—always feeling sorry for herself and what she had to put up with from Dad. Dad is nice when he is sober, but watch out when he starts drinking. That's when he starts slugging. Mom has been beat up bad a couple times, but she never does anything about it. She complains a lot about Dad, but she'll never leave him.

"Dad used to travel a lot for his work. Often he would be home only on weekends. Now I realize he was doing this to avoid Mom, but she would always say he was out drinking and carousing with other women. She would talk with me when Dad was gone, telling me how terrible he was and how he used her sexually. Mom always said men were no good, just wanted to use us women for sex. She warned me repeatedly to not marry someone like my dad. I grew up thinking sex was dreadful. They would fight something terrible about sex. When Dad got drunk, he would holler that Mom withheld sex to punish him and that she was a cold fish.

"I remember this one vacation trip. Dad had rented a small cabin and the walls were paper-thin. Their screaming in the next room must have awakened me. Evidently Mom was refusing to have sex, and Dad was trying to force her. He finally hit her in the face, and Mom cried herself to sleep. I remember lying awake all night thinking what brutes men were. I swore I would never let myself end up like Mom, being beat up and tyrannized by some man.

"I guess that's partly why I've turned to women. Men are so damn controlling and aggressive. I know now that Mom did her share to cause these fights, but it doesn't seem to make any difference. It's like so much water over the dam. Men never seem to care about the other person. They're just like my dad— selfish and inconsiderate . . . and how they force women to take care of them."

During another session, Julie began to relate some of her early sex experiences.

"I never knew I was a lesbian when I was young. This may sound strange, but I never even knew what one was until I got a little older. All I remember was the anger and disgust at men. The only early experience I can remember was picking up a men's magazine with nude pictures of women. The women's bodies looked so smooth and beautiful, not so coarse and hairy like men.

"It took me a long time to try sex with a man. I guess I finally did because this is what women are supposed to do. I had several experiences, and they were all disastrous. Nothing happened. Men just used me and I got nothing out of it. There was no sense of excitement, actually more of a revulsion. I felt so dirty. All I could think of was Mom and Dad and their sexual fights. After the first time, I rushed home and scrubbed my whole body. Another time this guy forced me to go down on him. I nearly vomited. The men didn't care at all for my needs.

"It was after these experiences that I began to suspect that maybe I was homosexual, but I didn't know what to do about it.

I might still be confused and frustrated if I hadn't met Louise. We became good friends and used to go camping together. I had no idea she was a lesbian, but we would sleep together in a small tent and one thing led to another. My first sexual experience with her was beautiful but confusing. For the first time in my life, I was sexually excited with another person. It seemed so natural and peaceful — nothing at all like it had been with those men. Louise never pressured me to do anything . . . she just let me go at my own pace.

"We would spend hours in bed together, just playing with each other. It wasn't at all like men who are always rushing— just in and out leaving the woman unsatisfied. Louise really cared about me and how I felt. She was so understanding and gentle with my body. A woman has a more natural sense for what pleases and excites another woman.

"When I was with Louise, it was all so good, but when we were apart, I felt confused and strange. I kept wondering if I was doing the right thing. Guilt I guess you call it. I knew what I liked and wanted now—what gave my life pleasure and meaning. But I was also raised in this society which teaches that homosexuality is sick and bad, and my Catholic religion says it is a sin. I had quite a period there where I was really discouraged. I was a worthless sinner."

It had taken Julie many years, but she gradually felt less guilty and more certain of her homosexuality. The assaults to her self-esteem were serious, however, and she had many residual scars from this when I saw her. It was in this area of helping Julie like herself better that we concentrated much of our time and energy.

Julie had a well-established homosexual life pattern when she became interested in women's liberation. As the feminist movement was publicized and gained strength, she became aware of a strong attraction to many of its ideas.

"I realized several years ago that women's liberation was verbalizing many of the things I was thinking. It felt good to have a movement I could belong to and meet other women who sensed some of the same things about men. We all want to avoid submission to a man and to lead a life where we are not under their authority and control. I want an equal relationship where I don't have to put up with the same things my mom did. To be trapped into a marriage where a man can force you into having sexual relations and beat you if you don't would be terrible.

"Many of my feminist friends are saying that marriage is not for them. They have had bad sexual experiences with men, just like I did. They say that men are clumsy and don't understand a woman's body. Why, that's what I feel. And the movement talks about loving women. They say that for too long women have been jealous and competitive with each other—never respecting other women enough. It's time for women to realize that we have a lot in common and much to gain from being considerate with each other."

As Julie became less shy and more confident, she became more involved in women's liberation. The movement provided a great deal of reassurance to love another woman and gave her a ready source of female friends who had similar ideas. Her feeling that a woman does not need a man and that she can function independently in life was repeatedly confirmed. Her underlying hostility and mistrust of the male sex was echoed by many of her feminist friends, and she gained support for her experiences which had taught her that women are more gentle and kind and easier to relate to without structuring a dominant-submissive pattern. My relationship with Julie was terminated when she gained more self-esteem and began to realize that she could set up the type of committed relationship with another woman which she desired.

"What is a lesbian? A lesbian is the rage of all women condensed to the point of explosion."[3] An unabating rage at the male sex is often seen in the homosexual woman, resulting in a kinship feeling with women's liberation. Julie had a great deal of this underlying anger, but hers was not as extreme as one finds in some other homosexual women. In fact, homosexuality, both female and male, is frequently the resulting life pattern for those angry at the opposite sex. Thus a retreat to one's own sex is often a mechanism to avoid relating to the opposite sex. It is fascinating and enlightening to witness both female and male homosexuals saying the same thing. The other sex is controlling, power hungry, dominating, and definitely inferior. All problems can conveniently be blamed on the failings of the opposite sex. Thus lesbians are fond of saying that men are incapable of true love because they are selfish and inconsiderate, that they just want their egos fed, and that they strut around waiting to be admired. As you might expect, many gay men state the same thing about women.

As we continue to explore the links between women's liberation and lesbianism, we are led to the general area of sexual roles which lead to inequality. Certainly, the feminist movement places a great deal of emphasis on avoiding relationships which leave the female in a submissive or subservient position. Homosexual women feel they have the ideal manner of doing this; simply avoid men and relate to women, especially sexually. Julie adopted this behavior as the primary means of handling her impossible relations with men.

Women quarrel among themselves as to exactly what constitutes a "lesbian." Some homosexual women feel it involves a life pattern of involvement with almost exclusively women, while others apply the term only in the sexual sense and leave room for relating to men on other levels. But there is general agreement among these women that turning one's sexual energy toward other women is an ideal way of avoiding the supposed inequality that occurs in all male-female sexual relationships.

Women who are attracted to both women's liberation and homosexuality tend to assume that there is a built-in inequality in heterosexual relations because of the stereotyped manner in which society conditions roles for women and men.

"A male-female relationship almost automatically involves problems of inequality since in our society the male is defined as inherently superior to the female."[4] Homosexuality offers a way in which these women can have love and independence at the same time. Restricting dependence on the male is avoided. The woman can thus avoid feeling that she is giving in and being taken over by her sexual partner. Because there are no ready made rules as to who is dominant and aggressive and who is to be passive and submissive, lesbians feel that homosexuality provides a better basis for equality in sexual relationships. Lesbianism can affirm to a woman that she is complete without acquiring a husband. She does not need someone else, that is, a male, to protect her and provide for her earthly care.

As we have seen in the case of Julie, many homosexual

women feel that a woman knows best how to sexually stimulate another woman. It is believed that a male can sexually mix up a woman in bed because of his lack of sensitivity and understanding of the female body. A great deal of emphasis is placed here on clitoral sensitivity versus vaginal sensitivity (or vaginal insensitivity as many would say), and arguments at length are produced to show that a woman does not need a phallus to climax.

Julie also showed us how women's liberation can help reduce guilt in the homosexual woman. By receiving the stamp of approval to love other women, lesbians who have spent many years feeling isolated, sinful, and worthless can begin to build their self-esteem and sense of individual dignity which is so essential for every human being.

Is all this too optimistic or ideal? For some homosexual women I suspect it is, but for others these things do seem to work. Again, as we have seen throughout this book, it depends on the individual woman involved. Certainly homosexual love is not as utopian as many lesbians would have us believe. Relating to any other human being in a sexual manner (or for that matter, nonsexual also) is a complicated process which can be beset by interpersonal difficulties. Sexual problems between lesbians most certainly do arise, and often they involve problems of submission and dominance and resulting inequality. Stereotyped role behavior is not unknown in the homosexual world. It may merely take a different form.

A pertinent quote from the women's liberation literature illustrates this problem.

> And though sisterlove is something we've experienced and know is wonderful, sex and love with other women seems to have the same problems as sex and love with men. "Sex is really a problem," we agreed.[5]

The connection between feminism and lesbianism can cause sexual developmental problems for some young women who are not basically homosexual. On occasion, the political and sexual messages examined in this chapter play an instrumental role for the young female struggling to attain sexual identity. In a fascinating article entitled "Pseudohomosexuality in Feminist

Students," Dr. Zira Defries examines this issue in some depth. She states:

> For some students in the (feminist) movement, the various expressions of sexual behavior advocated either implicitly or explicitly—in particular the encouragement of open expression of homosexuality—pose difficult problems.[6]

Using case histories, Dr. Defries demonstrates how feminism can lead some susceptible women to experiment with homosexuality even though they are fundamentally heterosexual. This can and does provoke considerable anxiety and sexual confusion, even though a fixed homosexual orientation is not necessarily developed.

Childhood experiences and parental relationships are certainly involved in the development of homosexuality. Although poor identification with mother is often involved, it is impossible to be more specific as the pattern varies so much from one woman to another. Dr. Defries feels that family background and early developmental factors have predisposed the women she has written about to "tilt" toward homosexuality. Although a strong contributing factor, the feminist movement is not the total cause of female "pseudohomosexuality."

Individual women must sort their way through this confusion. The connection made between feminism and homosexuality has validity for a few women, but it can cause problems for others when it is taken as a dictate with universal applicability.

Chapter 9

American women are a privileged group. . . .
Beneficiaries of a tradition of respect for women which dates from
the Christian age of chivalry (and) the honor and respect paid to
Mary, the mother of Christ. **Mrs. Phyllis Schafly**

Traditional Woman

"What does that E.R.A. sticker on your door mean?"

Emily blurted out the words before she was even seated. We had not met before, and her opening question was to set the tone for our initial introduction. Actually, I think she already knew the answer and was only registering her shock and dismay at discovering the small red sticker with the bold white letters so prominently displayed on the front of my office door.

A moment of awkward silence followed as I motioned Emily to the grey, stuffed chair by the window and she nervously reached for a cigarette. Using my most conciliatory manner, I carefully explained that it was a way of showing my support for the Equal Rights Amendment which was about to be voted on in our state legislature. Her reaction was about as I expected— her face tightened, her hands gripped the sides of the chair, and her eyes anxiously wandered around the room but avoided looking directly at me. I surmised that Emily was feeling she had made a mistake in coming to see me.

"Does my support of the Equal Rights Amendment bother you?"

"That's an understatement if I ever heard one. Those women who are pushing this equal rights thing are just a loud mouthed minority."

With that, Emily launched into a tirade against equal rights, "those liberated women," and anything else which smacked of women's liberation.

"Those liberated women are trying to force their opinions onto everyone else, but we're not going to let them get away with it. At last we're beginning to fight back . . . women who want a home and children are finally mobilizing and organizing their resources. I read in yesterday's newspaper about the big protest women staged against your precious Equal Rights Amendment. One of my friends was there, and she thinks we're going to win."

"What bugs you so much about equal rights for women?"

"I don't want to be drafted. Those liberated women want to take away all our advantages—men should take care of women. I want doors opened for me, and men should pay for dates. Women should have privileges. And I sure don't want to use the same bathroom as men.

"Actually, this is pretty close to what brought me in to see you. There is so much change going on . . . so many pressures on a young woman to change her value system. As I grew up, I thought I knew what I wanted, but now I'm confused. I always thought I could work or not work depending on what I wanted, but now everyone is saying a woman should have her own career. And sex . . . I always felt sex before marriage was wrong. Now my girl friends say I'm stupid and old fashioned. It's all so confusing."

We spent the rest of the hour exploring Emily's rather conventional upbringing and value system. About halfway through the hour, she became quite animated and at ease in talking as her initial mistrust evaporated.

"Decisions are hard for me to make. I was hoping you could decide some things for me. Tim, my boyfriend, wants to get married this coming summer, and I don't know what to say. Mom has always decided everything for me—from what to wear to what kind of a job to get. She thinks I'm too young to marry, being that I'm only twenty-two. Tim is so insistent, however, and I know that someday I'll marry him . . . at least if he ever earns enough money to buy me a home. Mom says a girl should never marry until the man can provide a house, but I don't want some little tract home. She thinks I should quit my job as soon as Tim and I are married. That's what she did when she married Dad."

"Have you considered working after you marry until Tim and you save enough money to buy a house?"

"That's what my girl friends say, but that is a man's responsibility . . . to support and provide for the woman. I want to be a full time housewife, and Mom thinks that would be best. I suppose you think that's out-dated, you and your equal rights for women which only means more responsibility for us."

With this Emily glared directly at me, probably wondering if I would launch into a criticism of her values as many of her friends did.

"I don't think it's a matter of being out-dated at all but rather whether your values are working well for you. You said that you are confused, and maybe we should spend some time trying to understand why this has come about."

Emily's face relaxed and she finally sat comfortably back in the chair as she realized I was not going to condemn her traditional ideas and beliefs —even if they were somewhat different from mine. We talked a bit more about her confusion and the pressures she was experiencing, and then it was time to end the hour.

By now, Emily and I—in spite of our differences or maybe because of them—were hitting it off pretty well together. We seemed to like each other, and I think our initial disagreement over the Equal Rights Amendment served to break the ice. By the end of this first meeting, we both felt free to speak what was on our minds and not hold back for fear of antagonizing each other. We could be friends and respect each other regardless of rather basically different philosophical conceptions of life. We were both pleased to arrange further meetings.

During the next several interviews, I became more aware of Emily's dependent nature. She was extremely reliant on her mother, and as her relationship with Tim developed, she became more and more dependent on him. Her trouble in making decisions was real and seemed to be a fixed part of her personality. On several occasions, Emily became furious when I explained that I could not make decisions for her, but could rather help her work out her own standards. This was especially true when Emily asked me if she should marry Tim in the near future.

In order to help Emily make up her own mind about marriage, we explored her ideas concerning men and female-male relationships.

"Tim is the type of person who will give me the security I need when he gets more established in his dad's business. He is reliable and responsible and loves to take care of me. If I wait for several years before marrying, I'll never have to work at some job outside the home. This is what Mom says is best, and I think she is right.

"I expect a man to take good care of me. I've always liked expensive things, and I have no intention of going without them once I get married."

"Does your dad treat your mom in this fashion?"

"No, Dad doesn't earn that much money. This is what Mom always warned me: 'Make sure you marry a man who is rich enough to provide all the comforts.' Mom thinks Dad is too weak to take good care of her; she has to decide all the important things. Dad withdraws into the basement every evening and plays with his model airplanes. That sure isn't the type of man I want to marry. I want a man who is strong and capable and who can protect me from the world.

"Mom takes good care of me. She was a Girl Scout leader and P.T.A. head and room-mother for several years. These are the things I want to do for my children. A mother who leaves her child in order to work is being cruel and selfish. She belongs at home where she is needed."

"It sounds as if you have some definite directions that you want your life to take. You want to eventually marry and have children. You feel that being a full-time mother and housewife will always have primary importance in your life, and you believe in a fairly typical division of labor between you and your husband. A strong man to take care of you, protect you, and give you security in the world is something you have always wanted, and now you have a man like this that will marry you anytime you wish. What puzzles me is why you should be confused when you have such a definite set of values and traditions to live by?"

Emily looked at me with a shocked expression as she was confronted with these words. I don't think she had ever realized how strongly she felt about these values. She was quiet for several minutes as she pondered the recent confusion in her life. Finally she spoke.

"Maybe I already know what I want. Perhaps you are right. I do feel certain about these things, and I have never seriously considered changing my values. They are a part of me . . . something I would not want to be without. But I get tired of people criticizing me and telling me I am old fashioned. It seems like Mom and my boyfriend are the only ones who support me, and recently even Tim has been challenging me."

Emily broke off here and again lapsed into silence. She always presented Tim as a strong, capable man who was in basic agreement with her ideas and values, and this was the first time she mentioned any conflict with him. Maybe we had stumbled onto something important.

"How has Tim been challenging you, Emily?"

"I guess it's only to be expected. All men must be this way . . . at least that's what my girl friends say."

Emily glanced out the window and nervously shuffled her feet. She was obviously alluding to sex and this caused her a great deal of discomfort. Emily rarely mentioned sex during our interviews and never in direct reference to herself. While Emily was gathering up courage to continue, I reflected on her value system and how her sexual mores would probably be quite conventional and strict. I realized that she must be embarrassed talking to me about her sexual feelings and problems. Finally Emily spoke up again.

"I know you're used to talking about sex, but it isn't easy for me. I must be old fashioned. My girl friends talk about sex a lot, but I mostly keep my peace and listen. Most of them are sleeping with their boyfriends, and they talk about how much fun sex can be. They seem so free and easy. At times I'm almost envious, but I know that sex before marriage is wrong for me.

"I've had things under good control until right before I came to see you. When I told Tim that eventually I would marry him, he was so pleased, but since then he has been pressing me for sex. Maybe that's why I got so confused. I know sex is wrong for me now, but at times I want it so bad . . . and my reluctance just drives Tim wild. He has always been considerate and respectful, but he says that since we are going to marry it is all right to have sex now. He makes it all sound so reasonable, but I still feel like he is double-crossing me with all this pressure.

"My girl friends think I'm crazy for resisting Tim. They talk a lot about women's liberation and how times are changing, even to the point where a girl can have her own sexual freedom. They tease me about wanting to stay home and raise babies, and recently they've been suggesting that Tim will grow tired of supporting me and expect me to go out and earn my own keep like other women in our liberated culture. Underneath I'm terrified that this equal rights thing will grow until it destroys all of what I want out of life."

"It sounds like you are afraid Tim will change and force you to give up what you want."

"I never used to be until this sexual pressure came up. I'm so confused. I don't know if I can trust Tim on anything anymore. I'm afraid that after we're married he will be influenced by all this change going on around us and expect me to become a liberated woman. Maybe my girl friends are right. Maybe no man will want a woman to stay home and be a housewife."

With this, Emily began to sob almost convulsively, and I tried to comfort her as best I could. She was indeed confused and probably more important, threatened to the depths of her being by forces in the society which she felt were beyond her control. She was especially panicked by her boyfriend's sexual demands and her new fear that he would no longer be satisfied with a traditional structuring of male and female roles once they were married.

As soon as Emily calmed down, we were able to continue the conversation.

"Emily, have you ever talked these fears over with Tim?"

I was greeted with a most surprised, startled look as these words sunk in.

"I never considered that. You mean I could let Tim know he is upsetting me?"

I was about as startled as Emily—surprised to discover she had never talked over her fears with Tim, the man she was to spend the rest of her life with It was difficult to believe that she could become so worried and mistrustful of Tim without ever checking to determine how he did feel.

Emily and I spent a short time discussing the necessity of her and Tim's sitting down and discovering if they really did want the same things out of life. I also tried to help Emily realize she could let Tim know how much his recent sexual demands were upsetting her and that possibly they could work out some sort of solution.

Emily seemed to be seriously pondering this as she left the office, but the subject didn't come up again for several meetings. We spent this time looking at what I felt was Emily's excessive dependence on her mother.

"Doctor, you've been saying that I expect Mom to make too many decisions for me. It makes me angry when you imply that it should be otherwise. Who else is there to make these decisions? You continually refuse even though I ask often enough. Mom has much more experience in life. She can decide these things better than I. Maybe someday Tim will be able to do this for me. That's what Mom says . . . that once I'm old enough and get married my husband will be able to direct my life."

I was getting nowhere fast. For every step forward Emily took as a result of my encouraging her to become more independent, she took another step backward. She was indeed a most dependent young woman, and I began to realize that she would probably retain this basic part of her personality throughout life. She resented any suggestion that she was adequate enough to make her own decisions.

One day Emily charged in excited and happy; she had some important news.

"Tim and I have been talking . . . your suggestion has really helped. He seems to value the same things I do, and he reassured me that changes in the society aren't going to force *him* to change his mind. He is as upset as I am about this women's liberation thing and all this equality.

"But guess what? Tim and I have been talking with my priest, and he confirms everything I've been feeling. Father Louis isn't at all like you . . . he answers my questions and decides things for me. [With this, Emily threw me what can only be described in polite language as a most hostile glance.] He says the church can give me answers, that I don't have to float through life with confusion and a lack of values."

I could tell I was going to get a lecture at this point, so I decided to sit back and enjoy it as best I could.

"Father Louis says that this equal rights for women movement is out to destroy the very backbone of the American family. He explained the crucial role of the woman in the family and how letting a woman compete in the world would only weaken or cheapen this role. He told us how important it was to raise a large family and not sin by thinking of our own lives. And then he went on to show how a man is head of the household just as priests are in control over nuns in the Church. It all has something to do with divine will being carried out in a good Christian family, but *you* wouldn't understand this I suppose."

Again I received one of those lovely glances from Emily. She was indeed having a field day as she used papal authority to challenge my belief in equal rights for women.

"Father Louis gave us some material which demonstrated how the women's liberation movement was actually supporting abortion and he said they will all burn in hell. He preached on this the other day in church, and he says many of his parishioners are writing letters to protest the Equal Rights Amendment which you support."

"It sounds like you are feeling better, Emily . . . as though you are less confused and have more direction in life."

"Maybe I am at that. It helped to talk with Tim and then for the two of us to see Father Louis. We're going to see him again in a few days."

The next visit I had with Emily turned out to be our last. She continued to gain some much needed support for her traditional values.

"Tim and I worked up the courage to talk with Father Louis about sex during our last meeting. Father Louis said I'm completely right . . . that sex before marriage is a terrible sin in the eyes of the church. He explained to us how sex is for procreation, and I think he helped Tim understand the difference between right and wrong. We're going to keep seeing him for awhile, and he's going to decide if we are ready for marriage this summer or if we should wait another year or two."

"This seems to be helping you a lot, Emily. I think you're beginning to realize that many other people in our society think like you do and that you don't have to be thrown into a panic when your girl friends challenge your ideas. Maybe you don't need to come back and see me anymore."

Emily was rather taken aback by this. She had grown dependent on me as she did on everyone else, and the thought of not seeing me anymore was initially upsetting to her. I sensed that this was an appropriate time, however, for us to terminate our contacts as she probably had little need for our meetings beyond this point. I explained to Emily that she could continue seeing me for a few more visits if she would be more comfortable in terminating gradually, and we talked this over for the rest of the hour. By the end, Emily was comfortable with stopping, especially when I reassured her that she could come back anytime she felt the need. She evidentally didn't feel this need as I never heard from her again.

The Catholic Church was able to provide Emily with reassurance and support at a crucial period in her life. With values changing and traditional standards crashing all around her she had suffered much fear and confusion. The messages of women's liberation which are so eagerly received by many women were a terrifying nightmare to Emily. Now she found a powerful voice in the culture, a religion she deeply respected, giving her absolute justifcation for her ideas and values. She was able to transfer much of her dependency onto the church, and she felt this would provide ready answers for many of the questions in her life. Certainly it provided a reinforcement for her conventional ideas of male-female role behavior, sexuality, marriage, and a woman's place being in the home. Emily could relax and probably be more comfortable with her own niche in life.

Many women will react with instinctive anger and rebellion at the life pattern Emily so dearly wanted. Other women will feel a deep sense of satisfaction and inner peace as they read of women like Emily who, in their eyes, fight to uphold the sanctity of American marriage and motherhood. One of the real joys of our society is that we are large enough and diverse enough so that people with markedly different value structures can exist side by side. There is no inherent reason we all have to set up similar life patterns or think alike on complex topics like women's liberation.

"Liberate Us From Women's Liberation" is the slogan prominently displayed by a young woman with small child in hand as she publicly protested on the steps of the state capitol. She was one in a large group of women lobbying against the Equal Rights Amendment. Many women will find this difficult to understand. Why, they ask, would women be against equal rights and women's liberation which promise them so much? I suspect the simple answer is that these antiliberationist women feel equal rights would make their life more difficult rather than improve it.

Conventional women such as Emily are certainly not uncommon in our society. The details and specifics of their personalities and value systems will vary somewhat from one to another, but they will be united in their basic belief in a traditional life for women with classic concepts of female and male role behavior. Their primary feelings of worth and self-esteem are inextricably connected with their roles as wives and mothers, and they look with puzzled amazement on women who place more importance on career and economic independence.

There is some suggestion that most female opponents of equal rights for women are white, middle-class, and married. One reads with some degree of regularity how these antiliberationist women have been successful in finding men to take care of them and have never been forced to support themselves on a woman's wages. It is difficult to evaluate this type of comment, and there may be some truth in it. I do know, however, that some of the most active antiliberationist women I have known are young and unmarried and they come from all social classes, degree of wealth having little relevance.

Is women's liberation beginning to cause difficulties and problems for these traditional women? The answer is similar to what we have run into in so many situations . . . for some women, yes; for other women, no. There are women so deeply involved, secure and happy with their conventional way of life, especially with their husbands and children, that they are little if at all affected by the feminist movement. But as women's liberation becomes stronger and more influential in bringing about change in society, traditional women are having more pressure and tension brought to bear on them. It is no longer unusual to meet a woman such as Emily who is having her life complicated, sometimes seriously so, by the messages and influence of women's liberation.

The sexual area is particularly susceptible to challenge in the traditional woman. Women have historically had their share of sexual problems, being plagued by lack of sexual enjoyment and nonresponsiveness. A major cause of this had been the conventional messages women have received regarding their sexuality. Women's liberation is now on the scene and is offering women a new set of messages which hold out the promise of increased sexual enjoyment. A connection is being drawn between woman's traditional passive approach to life and her sexual reluctance. It is also being pointed out that women can experience an improvement in their sexual lives when their self-esteem increases and they are rid of their historic inferior image. It is no wonder then that traditional women are paying close attention to feminist ideas on female sexuality, and are at times feeling threatened.

Women who have excessive dependency needs are especially apt to experience unwelcome pressures from their peers, their boyfriends or husbands, and from the public media. Women's liberation is concerned with equality and with this comes inevitably the need to be more independent and assume more responsibility in life. Many women are finding this particularly difficult, loathsome, and threatening. A recent newspaper editorial summarized this clearly:

> We recognize that some women oppose the ERA because they actually fear equality; it is, after all, easier to accept dependency when the alternative is the responsibility that accompanies freedom.[1]

One of the more pronounced problem areas for the traditional woman is the increasing emphasis and respect which are placed on a career or work outside of the home. Pressure on a woman to obtain an outside job is mounting as it becomes psychologically more difficult to attain primary self-esteem and value from the wife and mother role. This is a problem which Emily confronted head-on as she was bombarded with teasing and criticism from her liberated girl friends about her emphasis on marriage and a family. It becomes crucial for these women to have other sources of support for their traditional values if they are to avoid feelings of self-doubt and inferiority, confusion, and perhaps depression. Emily was able to obtain this support from her mother, her husband-to-be, and her church.

Many women in our culture work because of financial necessity and/or basic career interest, and the feminist movement is especially helpful to them as more equitable salaries for women and job equality are promoted. Other women, however, have neither this financial necessity nor interest and yet they are being subjected to subtle and overt pressures to have a career or job. A YWCA director was recently quoted as saying, "I fear that because women think they can't be respected for motherhood, some will feel compelled to take a full-time job even if they don't want to."[2]

The role of mother and wife as traditionally conceived has recently been subjected to a withering barrage of criticism and vitriolic disapproval from some segments of the feminist movement. This is a direct blow to the egos of women who have been raised to view this as their fundamental destiny in life. This is especially true for the women who have conceived Motherhood with a capital M, as some sort of ultimate, sanctified purity—the quintessence of life itself. Clinically, we are beginning to see women developing depression, feelings of self-doubt and worthlessness, and sexual problems as a direct result of the recent demeaning of the housewife-mother role.

A psychiatrist from the Harvard Medical School, in a recent article on problems associated with changing sex roles, has written:

> If the present desire to broaden the role definition for women continues, those women who accepted the social limitations of the 40's and 50's are in for a very hard time. While they will get considerable support for their efforts as one perfectly acceptable way to work out a life, the homemaker/mother role will be seen as only one of a number of acceptable ways to work out the sex-career-family conflict—but not the right way.
>
> This is hard to swallow if you have given up a great deal for the idea that you were achieving a kind of purity.[3]

Certainly, many people live by traditions and values which they have learned and become accustomed to. It should come as

no surprise that as some of these predominant cultural traditions and myths are challenged, criticized, and gradually
changed, some people will experience depression, confusion,
lack of meaning, and in general will flounder by the wayside. In
her recent book *The New Chastity and Other Arguments Against
Women's Liberation*, Midge Decter makes clear her abhorance at
the abandonment of tradition and woman being forced to make
up her own code of conduct, especially in the sexual area.[4] Some
of her reasoning is based on moral factors, but she also feels
women's traditional sexual values have served well. She seems
to doubt that individual women can select the positive from the
new messages in such a way as to improve their sexual lives.
She sees nothing but trouble ahead for women who adopt
feminist ideology, an ideology which she feels goes against the
fundamental nature of woman.

Ideally, each of us should be able to determine and develop
our own individual value structure and pattern of life and then
live comfortably side by side with other individuals who have
perhaps chosen markedly diverse behavioral standards. In such
a situation, we would each be confident and secure enough to
feel no threat from people who have developed different value
structures and we would sense no missionary zeal to convert or
force others into our way of thinking or acting.

However, we were not programmed to live in such secure and
comfortable harmony. Individuals of the human species are
generally too insecure to live in such a fashion, being too easily
threatened by people who think differently. One of the more
common reactions to our own lack of confidence is to make
aggressive attempts to change or coerce others into believing
and acting as we do.

As women attempt to develop their own approach to career,
marital, and sexual areas, such an insecure reaction is commonly seen. Women are now presented with a variety of
choices; there is no longer any sense of absolute right and moral
purity to guide one's decision. All individuals are forced to look
deep within and discover their own needs and value systems,
and this is difficult for many.

We thus find women, out of their own confusion and
insecurity, attacking the lifestyles and values of other women

who have chosen differently. Some feminists seem compelled to criticize the traditional housewife-mother role not only for themselves but for others. We also find traditionalist women raging against the feminist movement. They are threatened and fear the loss of what they interpret as the unique and favored position women in our society hold.

Women opposed to the feminist movement are becoming active in organizing and fighting back. Some feel they are battling for the very foundations upon which their cherished family life is built and they have become vehement. Often they attack with derogatory slurs which are calculated to question the femaleness of the liberationists. A group called the Pussy-cats states that the feminists are not "real women." They go on to say:

> Why, the poor querulous creatures. They're mostly obese and have skin problems. They're afraid they'll never get a man to love them. That's why they have razor blades sticking out of their elbows. And feminists they call them-selves. They should call themselves masculinists. Heaven knows they try to look like men and act like men.[5]

Such colorful rhetoric does nothing except evade the real issues and expose the insecurities and deep antagonisms which have developed as the feminists and traditionalists gird for mighty combat.

Women with traditional values are being challenged by a variety of feminist-inspired sources. In Emily's case, the threat came primarily from her more liberated girl friends while her husband-to-be was clearly in agreement with her values. Husbands, fiancés, and boyfriends, however, are increasingly being influenced by the feminist movement and at times they directly challenge the conventional beliefs of the women they are involved with. The situation which Marleen found herself in shows how some men are beginning to want and demand a more liberated woman for their lifetime mate, resulting in dire consequences for the traditional woman.

Marleen was upset over her younger sister's upcoming marriage—to the point where she was withdrawing from friends and finding it difficult to concentrate on school work. She described herself as typically vivacious and somewhat of a comedienne, in essence a dynamic and outgoing individual. Now she was sullen, morose, and in danger of not graduating from college as scheduled.

"My sister Terrie is getting married in several weeks, and I become more upset as the date draws near. The way I'm carrying on you would think it was *my* marriage. I am caught up in the wedding plans . . . all the commotion and bustle . . . but that should be fun and exciting. It's what I've always wanted for myself. Terrie is having a big church wedding. It's an important tradition in my family."

Marleen stopped and drew back, physically demonstrating her discomfort and fright at being in my office. We chatted for close to fifteen minutes about nothing in particular, playing out the social ritual of first contact, and Marleen gradually relaxed. As the fright disappeared from her eyes, I asked her why the marriage plans for a younger sister might be upsetting.

"Yes, I've thought about that. I never thought my kid sister marrying before me would be traumatic, but that was before John and I started fighting. We've been engaged over a year now, waiting until we both graduated this coming summer. When Terrie showed me her diamond, it seemed O.K. for John and I would be marrying soon thereafter. Now it isn't so certain."

As her eyes moistened, Marleen tried to put up a brave front by laughing and making some inane joke about marriage, but I could tell she was deeply hurt by some problem with John. It was easy to draw her out about the conflict in her love relationship.

"John has become downright nasty. The nearer we get to graduation, the more he criticizes everything about me . . . my hair, the way I dress, my plans, my family, and on and on until I can't stand it. He's obviously avoiding making plans for our wedding. The closer to our planned time, the more threatened he becomes."

"Do you have any idea what he's scared of?"

"We've got a real conflict of values going. I don't know if we can work it out. I want a marriage like Mom and Dad's . . . that way I know I'll be happy. I never intended to work and have a career, and John has been increasingly upset about that.

"It isn't that I want to stay home and be bored. I'm too active for that. There are so many things I'm interested in that I wouldn't have time to be tied down to a career. Art and music are a part of me . . . this is what I've studied in college. And this environmental pollution mess is so serious that I'm on a committee to achieve political action. I want to be active and take my children places . . . teach them about culture and politics and all the things that make life interesting."

As we explored Marleen's many interests in life during the next several interviews, she became more animated and any vestige of moroseness disappeared. Gradually a very outgoing, spirited, artistic young woman emerged from the rather tense, sullen person who originally entered my office. Kid sister's marriage happened and passed, Marleen managing to put on a stiff upper lip and perform as bridesmaid during the ceremony, albeit most anxiously and jealously.

Marleen's serious problem remained—the troublesome relationship with her fiancé. Things seemed to go from bad to worse as she grappled with the basic differences in values which emerged as their marriage date grew nearer. Marleen was not a weak person, and she realized that it was better to work these issues out before marrying.

As I felt Marleen might be in conflict about her basic values, we examined the mores she had been exposed to in her family. It developed that I was very wrong; there was no conflict but rather a young woman who had most thoroughly learned what she wanted out of life.

"Mom and Dad have a wonderful marriage . . . so good I hope to do as well. Dad is successful as a physician and provides well for all of us, Mom never needing to work outside the home and take attention away from her children. She's artistic herself and has an active social life. She's president of her women's auxiliary unit and these activities take all her spare time. This is really the kind of life I want.

"Maybe I've been spoiled, at least that's what John says, but I don't feel that describes it. Certainly I've been well taken care of, the folks paying for all my schooling and anything else I want. But I've never misused this by spending a lot of money . . . only taking what I need to get along. The family has always had long vacations together—skiing, boating and things like this that we can do together."

Marleen continued to paint the picture of a family that enjoyed financial and social success along with a great deal of happiness and rewarding togetherness. She relished her role as the beautiful and talented daughter in this successful family. Life was rewarding and relatively easy (some might say pampered but Marleen did not see it this way) and Marleen had no intention of parting with this pattern which she considered to be her basic right as a female. She wanted to be a dedicated mother and housewife and had no doubts about assuming the responsibility. which this would entail. Her feelings about the feminist movement were direct and the product of her own experience.

"I can't understand this women's liberation business. A couple of my girl friends are motivated in this direction, but I can't see what they have to gain. Why they're even nice girls and very pretty. They wouldn't have any trouble finding a husband. I know there are women who have to work because their husbands aren't successful enough to support the family, but I can't conceive of a woman actually doing this voluntarily. Why women aren't discriminated against at all if they stick to their own business and quit interfering.

"This is what John expects me to do, give up my femininity and compete with men. We've been talking more about this, but things only seem to get worse. The other day he called me lazy and said he had no intention of supporting all my hobbies."

"Do you have any idea, Marleen, why John is pushing so hard for you to have your own career?"

"I think it relates to his family, especially the way his mom is stuck at home. He's much more of a women's libber than I am . . . he keeps reading *Ms* magazine and shows me articles that he thinks are good or could pertain to our marriage. I get sick of hearing about the damn thing. I'm not angry at feminists, I just don't understand them the way John does."

"What about his family? You said his mom has been stuck at home."

"She's a most unhappy woman, and John thinks it's because she never worked or had her own life. I've met her a few times, and I must admit she seems pretty bored. She's bitchy around the house and has a lot of fights with John's dad. John says he never wants me to be trapped by cleaning and children. He doesn't realize I'm a very active woman and would never be bored with life."

I had to agree with Marleen. She was most energetic and enthused about the world around her and she was so attached to the concept of being a wife and mother that it was hard to imagine her feeling trapped at home.

For awhile I wondered if this fighting over whether Marleen should have a career or not was just a side issue, covering up other problems in their relationship. At an opportune time, I queried Marleen about her general relationship with John.

"Everything else goes fine. It's hard to understand how one thing could become such an issue. John and I always had fun together, so much in fact that I was convinced we loved each other. No, we don't fight or disagree about anything else that seems serious. Sex has been great. John is the first one I've slept with, and nothing goes wrong there. We've always been tender and considerate with each other."

Finally I began to realize that John's attraction to women's liberation was real and was causing an irreconcilable split in this relationship. As I went on seeing Marleen, his reasoning emerged more clearly and forcefully. He had become involved with feminism as a cause through his reading and through some friends at school. He was determined that no wife of his would ever be passive and dependent and function as an auxiliary to his success. His insistence that Marleen have a career of her own was an outgrowth of these feelings and was based at least in part on theoretical grounds rather than on understanding Marleen as a person. As I was never to meet John and obtain first-hand information, I can report no detailed understanding of his ideas. These beliefs, however, were in major conflict with those of Marleen and a major confrontation was about to occur.

Precipitating the acute, stormy upheaval was a derogatory comment by John on the life Marleen's mother was leading. A fight ensued and in the aftermath both Marleen and John realized the fundamentally different values they held regarding the role of a woman in our society. No "meeting of the minds" could possibly occur, and a wise mutual decision was made to terminate the relationship. As Marleen said, "Better to break up now than face bitter years of struggle and turmoil over how I am to lead my life. Why John and I would end up hating each other."

Marleen emerged from counseling as a rather healthy young woman with a clear idea of her value structure and the type of life pattern which would fulfill her as a woman. That this was a conventional, traditional style was obvious, and Marleen's task was to now find a mate where close harmony could exist and where she would be free to pursue her ideals of being a socially active wife and mother without the burden of being a "liberated" woman with a career. Marleen and I were mutually confident that this should present her with no great difficulty as long as her goals were kept clearly focused. She had developed the basic inner security and confidence to meet any challenge to her traditional value system.

The traditional woman is vulnerable to the changes occurring in our society. No longer can she count on those close to her supporting her value structure. She is being challenged from many directions. She must use great caution in order to choose a life-mate who will agree with her basic life philosophy and support her ideas through the turbulent years ahead. At times this will mean, as it did with Marleen, that a close relationship will need to be terminated and a new beginning will have to be made.

Chapter 10

There is no group other than slaves that has been singled out for such systematic and total exploitation and suppression as the class of women.   **Barbara Mehrhof and Pamela Kearon**[1]

"Poor Me" Woman

Walking our streets in embittered rage and feeling martyred to the core are the recent casualties of the feminist movement—the "poor me" women. Having accepted literally the radical rhetoric on the slavelike tyranny of females to justify their own internal problems, these women are paralyzed by feelings of oppression, anger, discrimination, helplessness, and self-pity. Spotting the "poor me" woman as she enters the office is a simple task.

The day was springlike and sunny in contrast to Cindy's glum exterior. Hurt and suffering were deeply etched into her facial musculature and one sensed pent-up anger which was about to explode. A sullen recital of her symptoms was the preoccupation of Cindy's first visit.

"These last few months have been terrible . . . I don't see how I can go on. I feel miserable, so terribly miserable. There must be something you can give me to feel better . . . you can't leave me like this."

Cindy's helpless, demanding qualities were showing through, but she continued to explore the details of her discomfort. Tears were beginning to coalesce in the corners of her eyes and soon they would be streaming down her sunken cheeks.

"The world discriminates against me, and I have to pay the price. I hurt all over . . . my body aches with this pressure and I don't even want to get out of bed. I've missed so much work that my sick leave is gone, and the boss said I'll have to take a leave without pay if this continues. But I feel so rotten. What can I do?"

Cindy's tears emphasized the degree of her pain.

"I'm thin enough as it is, and now I've lost another five pounds. It's as though I hurt too much to eat. I sit and stare at the walls and nothing interests me. Life is one big ache."

Cindy had a real need to talk about her anguish, and I was rather quiet during this first hour. She was depressed and feeling sorry for herself. This set the stage for the explosion during the second interview.

"Cindy, last hour you mentioned how the world discriminates against you. Could you tell me more about this?"

For the first time Cindy showed some animation, and she immediately launched into a diatribe against men and society.

"Women are terribly oppressed in our culture. We're treated like slaves and used for our bodies. Men keep all the rewarding work for themselves and force us into a position of servitude. It's been this way for ages and women have to put up with it. Men have all the advantages so why do anything. Life is dismal for a woman with so much inequity going on."

My question had tapped a reservoir of wrath and indignation, and Cindy continued to express her feelings of resentment and futility.

"This really angers me, the way women are abused. There's no use in working, the world is going to crap on me anyway. The more I realize how men structure things in their own interests, the less I try to accomplish. Why strive only to be used by someone else?

"And this sex thing really bugs me . . . the way men want to use a woman. They plaster pictures of our bodies all over the country, using us to sell their junk and make a nice profit. Those billboards on the freeway are so bad I won't drive anymore . . . especially the ones to sell milk with their nude women. What an exploitation of the female.

"Why I'm so upset about this I can't even watch television. All you see is men making a sucker out of us, especially our bodies. Those ads drive me up a wall . . . and they go on and on and on. There's nothing to be done except sit in my room and be miserable.

"I'm sure it's always been this way, but I never noticed it so much until I started my women's consciousness raising group. They opened my eyes to the injustice and discrimination against women. Now I notice it everywhere. There seems to be no escape. The group helped me realize how women are innocent victims in a world controlled by men. I can't stand the sight of men anymore, the way they leer and look you up and down. I don't even want to be where there are men around."

My attempt to help Cindy in group therapy was a disaster. She came to one meeting but could not tolerate a mixed group, the presence of men being too much for her. She clashed immediately with the males, accusing them of mistreating her before they even had a chance to say hello. She rejected the suggestion of some women in the group that maybe she was playing a part in her problems. It was somewhat predictable that I was never to see Cindy again.

In my brief but memorable contact with Cindy, she presented many of the qualities of the "poor me" woman. She was depressed and miserable with little motivation for life. She was finding it increasingly difficult to function and was withdrawing from almost everything around her including work, men, television, movies, and driving. She was filled with self-pity and feelings of helplessness about her condition. Oppression of women was the most dominant theme, and she used it to justify all her internal problems. Anger at men was massive for "using" her, and she played out the martyr role. It was easier for Cindy to find discrimination and injustice in the external world and blame her problems on this than make efforts to improve her situation in life.

Foremost among the traits which characterize the "poor me" woman is the overwhelming feeling of oppression and discrimination which permeates her consciousness. All sense of perspective is lost as she identifies with the most down-trodden and enslaved of human beings. Subjugation is her presumed fate in life, and she finds evidence for this in a ubiquitous fashion. Although characteristically white and middle- or upper-middle class, she compares her position to that of a serf or vassal. In her world view, only women are discriminated against, sex role stereotyping never working to the disadvantage of the male.

While many women are making continual efforts to combat sex discrimination when they encounter it, the "poor me" woman has none of this constructive motivation. Rather, she is found to wallow in feelings of self-pity and misery, collecting each little injustice for her life scrapbook. There is often a manipulative quality to this feeling sorry for oneself—a subtle attempt to coerce others through depression and despondency.

The unique persecution which the "poor me" woman perceives herself as undergoing leads to sweeping generalizations about men and women which have little factual basis. One hears how men are incapable of love or affection, only women having the tender emotions. Men are unwilling or unable to communicate, women alone possessing the qualities for openness in conversation. Large families are conceived in order to satisfy the male ego, the female of the species never being desirous of having several children. And on and on with colorful creations of fantasy which impress one with their originality of thought.

A salient characteristic of the "poor me" woman is the marked degree of her anger. This rage is frequently hidden behind the sullenness and dejection which she presents on first contact. Anger, however, is near the surface (as with Cindy) and is easily tapped by the right type of questioning. This can be therapeutic as the open expression of pent-up anger frequently helps alleviate the more obvious and incapacitating depression.

Anger can be a healthy, motivating emotion which leads toward positive change in one's life, but no such constructive approach is to be found in the "poor me" woman. Her anger is of a different quality, more inhibiting in nature and leading toward a paralysis of functioning. This anger is accumulated and stored, being nursed along with a fervor which makes release and forgetting impossible. It becomes self-defeating in the extreme and turns life into a quagmire from which escape is next to impossible.

Such a wrath permeates to the depths of one's being and becomes a devitalizing burden to carry through life. It is exhausting to be furious all the time, especially when this ire makes it impossible to communicate with the opposite sex in peace. As with Cindy, this bitterness emerges primarily at the male of the species. Men are the oppressors and conceived of as the arch-enemy who enslaves and tyrannizes the helpless female. Men have created a power hierarchy in which they keep all control and advantages, using women only to perform menial tasks and satisfy their sexual needs on demand.

> Life in this society being, at best, an utter bore and no aspect of society being at all relevant to women, there remains to civic-minded, responsible, thrill-seeking females only to overthrow the government, eliminate the money system, institute complete automation and destroy the male sex.[2]

Behind the surface of the "poor me" woman reside major adjustment difficulties. Her serious problems have led to a hostile depression with a significant withdrawal from her environment. As her anger is primarily directed toward men, this creates a real bind in terms of basic need satisfaction. A fundamental conflict has developed in which it is impossible to meet needs for love, sex, intimacy, and family without turning to a homosexual identification, a direction most women cannot take.

The self-imposed alienation of the "poor me" woman, especially from men, leaves her in a difficult position where she will be unable to satisfy any heterosexual desires. Sexual pleasure will have to come from self-stimulation or physical contact with other women. A close, affectionate relationship with a member of the opposite sex is unthinkable when anger reaches such massive proportions. Any urges for a family and children will of necessity have to be supressed when withdrawal from men becomes so complete. The "poor me" woman has indeed cut herself off from satisfying some primary human emotions.

Early developmental history is crucial in understanding the origins of such an onerous dilemma. The young girl has usually been exposed to open hatred of the male in the family setting and has learned her lessons all too well. Specifics will vary from one situation to another but they center around a general milieu of anger, contempt and fear of the male. Men are often absent from such a family either through death or design or else present on only a part-time schedule. If there perchance is a full-time father present, he is commonly weak or ineffectual and likely to be an alcoholic. Mother is free to hold sway and mold her daughters in her own image. Relationships with men have been bitter and frustrating for mother and she openly verbalizes her own dissatisfactions. "Men are mean and cruel and a species to be avoided at all costs" is the direct message. Often the mother's problems with men are matched only by her own hatred of sexuality and she communicates this via diverse mechanisms. Sex is sinful and painful, something which offers nothing to the female, and men are sexual brutes seeking their own pleasure. Thus is the fear and anger at men transmitted from one generation to another.

Such messages are of course not new, and they antedate by eons the arrival of women's liberation. But with the feminist movement, women with this basic hatred and fear of men have a cause to espouse their doctrines. Like a powerful magnet, women's liberation attracts these women and reinforces their feelings of oppression and fear of men. Some, like Cindy, enter women's consciousness raising groups and have their consciousness raised right through the ceiling. They become so sensitive to any discrimination and so angry at any injustice, imagined or real, that they are unable to function.

The "poor me" woman thinks she finds a ready justification for her beliefs in the tenets of women's liberation. She construes these messages to fit her own setting and ignores other ideas of the feminist movement which might slant her in a different direction. The end result is an externalization of problems, a ready excuse to avoid confrontation with herself. Internal developmental difficulties are thus conveniently ignored, but the price paid is an extremely high one in terms of depression, frustration, and a life full of bitterness and unmet needs.

I am not talking about most women who feel a kinship and elemental truth in women's liberation. The great majority of women attracted to the feminist movement experience it as a positive motivating force in their lives. They are able to discriminate between imagined and real injustices and keep things in somewhat of a reasonable perspective. They are not content to wallow in feelings of self-misery, instead actively using the messages of women's liberation to improve their status in life. Their early developmental history does not contain such fear and bitterness toward the male, and they are not consumed with anger at men.

The "poor me" women are not battling down our doors in droves, and they surely must constitute a small minority. What they lack in numbers, however, is made up for in amount of human suffering. Women's liberation is adding to the plight of these most unfortunate women as they have their already overdeveloped feelings of oppression and rage at men intensified to the point where they are unable to meet life in any self-rewarding fashion.

I would like to close this section with a detailed account of one woman's life which will exemplify some of the above points while at the same time revealing how no human being can be neatly encompassed into some preconceived category.

My knowledge of Mabel began over lunch with one of my medical colleagues. We were long-time friends, but seldom conversed about professional topics. Today was different as my friend, who is a family physician, explained some of the details of one of his more perplexing patients. Mabel, who had been in his care for many years, was plagued in recent months by a severe case of hives which covered her face, extremities, and upper trunk. The hives would flare up once or twice a month in a painful, itching manner and were refractory to any type of treatment he instituted.

My colleague was wise in matters pertaining to the psyche, and he suspected that emotional factors were playing a strong role in Mabel's skin disease. He sensed an increasing amount of depression and had recently placed her on antidepressant medication. This brought about little improvement, however, and he was now wondering if I would be interested in seeing Mabel for a trial at psychotherapy.

I was struck by Mabel's appearance during our first meeting. She appeared five to ten years older than her thirty-two years, and her facial expression revealed sadness and disinterest. Her face was marred by swollen, red blotches which she continually picked, and her bodily movements were sluggish and lethargic.

Doleful, meloncholic spirits did indeed reveal themselves as Mabel outlined her problems. Her presentation was more of a lamentation or sorrowful dirge, and she seemed to have a world sorrow or Weltschmerz. She bared that particular type of self-pity and dissatisfaction with the world which was immediately reminiscent of the "poor me" woman.

Some important details of Mabel's life were covered during this initial contact. She was a highly skilled computer programmer and worked full or part time until the past ten months. Marriage had occurred seven years ago and she now had a five-year-old daughter. Open problems with her husband were denied but sexual difficulties were hinted at.

I asked Mabel why she quit her job some months ago, and her feelings about a woman's role were quickly revealed along with her underlying frustration and bitterness.

"Sure the job was good . . . it paid well and I liked the work. But I'm not going to let *myself* be used any more. Those days are over and done with. That course I took in Women's History at the extension school opened my eyes. Women have been ignored for centuries. We do all the work and men get all the glory. Our contribution is ignored; we're seen as inferior beings who can only do men's scud work. A civilization has been built by our sweat and we're not even acknowledged."

"How did the company discriminate against you, Mabel?"

"They treated me pretty decently. I was valuable to them and they knew it. I earned more than a lot of the men, and the bosses were nice to me personally. But that's not the point. They discriminate against women in general; they mirror the attitudes of society. Why there isn't one women executive in the company, and they underpay the secretaries. Why should I let them make money off me? The world is full of injustice to women. You should know that!"

Yes, I did realize that women are often discriminated against, but I couldn't fully comprehend why this meant Mabel had to quit a job she liked and found rewarding.

"Now I'm stranded at home . . . nothing to do except squaw work. Austin does most of the cooking and cleaning . . . he tries to help. But I'm bored. Life's one pile of emptiness. A woman's lot in life isn't a happy one. And then Austin gets upset when I don't want sex."

Since Mabel alluded to sexual difficulties in the marriage on several occasions, I decided it was important to meet her husband.

Austin fit well the role of a successful drug company representative. He was immaculately dressed in the latest fashion, his manner was outgoing and boisterous and he attempted to impress one with overwhelming manhood by a crushing handshake. He was open about his ideas and the relationship with Mabel, and a pattern quickly emerged.

Austin accepted the tenets of women's liberation hook, line, and sinker. He felt women were picked on, exploited, mistreated, and used by chauvinistic males and that years of peonage had left women in a difficult position. He had a well-developed sense of guilt which led to personal acceptance of blame for any discrimination against females. Behind his surface show of strength and masculinity resided a basically insecure male with strong feelings of inadequacy in the sexual area.

Austin was a ready prey for any woman like Mabel who was motivated to exploit his underlying insecurity and guilt. Everytime his wife complained about some supposed inequity, Austin performed cartwheels in an attempt to remedy the situation. He was like a trained circus dog jumping through the hoop.

Mabel spent much of her day complaining about the role of women in our society, and Austin buttressed every injustice she brought up. She had verbalized considerable resentment against the treatment of secretaries by her former firm, often threatening to quit. Austin supported her and the threats became a reality; Mabel terminated her rewarding career. She resented the expectation that a wife perform the house maintenance chores, and Austin assumed the cleaning, cooking, and shopping duties. Mabel grumbled about the mother's role in child care, and Austin hired household help to provide this during the day while he took over in the evenings. He was literally burning the candle at both ends in an attempt to placate his wife and make certain he was not a male chauvinist, and there was no energy, time, or money left for anything else.

Mabel was left with nothing to do but read detective stories, her one love in life. She had maneuvered herself into a boring situation and was left with frustration and bitterness. Some initial attempts were made to establish new meaning, but these efforts were doomed to failure. Volunteer work of any type was quickly rejected as being "too demeaning to women," and an attempt to enter local politics was abandoned because "people won't vote for women anyway." With support from her husband, she began a craft shop at home, but this was also dropped with the reasoning "no one will buy things a women creates so why make things to begin with."

The most serious problem, however, was in the sexual area. Mabel verbalized this well.

"I can't stand sex . . . never have and never will. Men pawing you all over, treating you like some animal. It's degrading . . . disgusting that a woman has to submit to such debasement. It's just one more way men use women."

Sex is where Austin really paid the penalty for being a male. Mabel would put him off night after night, and Austin would try his best to control the sexual urges which his wife referred to as "the beast in him." Finally nature would have her way as Austin's pent up libidinal desire could no longer be contained, and he would demand that Mabel "submit." His hour of aggressiveness was followed by remorse and guilt as Mabel cried and berated the "beast in men." It would be several weeks before the behavior was again repeated.

It was Austin who noticed the pattern with Mabel's hives.

"You know those red splotches Mabel gets, Doctor. I've been realizing that they follow any sexual contact we have. Mabel hates sex so much. Do you think there could be any connection?"

Yes, Austin, there most assuredly was a connection. Mabel's hives were an outward manifestation of her fear and resentment of sexuality, and they followed each "submission" with clockwork regularity. These unsightly blemishes were a most effective punishment for sexual indulgence and both Mabel and Austin suffered.

Mabel externalized her problems. Discrimination against women was a convenient scapegoat and she used it to avoid any "looking in" which may have led to rewarding solutions. Her sexual difficulties had their roots deep in childhood experiences. Father was an alchoholic who drank up whatever meager money he was able to earn. His periodic violent outbursts would at times result in physical abuse of both Mabel and her mother. Mabel's mother was a long-suffering martyr whose main role in the family was to feel sorry for herself and preach on the evils of men. Sex was openly condemned as the "male's pleasure" and denounced at every opportunity. Because of Mabel's reluctance to examine her own personality, I was unable to obtain more than this rudimentary outline of developmental history.

Mabel was of course not the sole cause of current problems in the marital situation. Austin's lack of masculine confidence and ready tendency to feel guilty in his relationships with women served to compound the difficulties. Personalities of wife and husband meshed in a most pathological manner leading to the development of very unrewarding life patterns.

Mabel effectively resisted any suggestion I made that maybe she was contributing to her own problems. She was able to find abundant evidence for mistreatment of women, past and present, to justify her behavior, and Austin would jump in and support this viewpoint. Therapy slowly moved nowhere except that Mabel became less depressed as she ventilated her anger. I confronted Mabel and Austin with this lack of progress, and we discussed alternatives.

Mabel decided she would return to my colleague for medicative treatment as "talking doesn't help, anyway." As usual, Austin readily agreed, and we terminated our contacts.

The sexual problems of Mabel and Austin are typical of those experienced by the "poor me" women and the men they at times attract. A fundamental abhorrence of sexuality is generally present in the "poor me" woman, usually learned directly from the mother. Sex is thought of as pleasurable only for the man, the woman obtaining no sexual joy herself. It is a painful experience inflicted on the suffering female. Sex thus becomes just one more way men use women, further evidence of the way women are mistreated in our society.

The massive anger at males and the disgust with sexuality usually prevent the "poor me" woman from entering into any lasting relationship with a man. Occasionally we find a situation like Mabel's where a marriage has occurred. Men who associate with "poor me" women are generally insecure sexually, lacking adequate masculine identification. They have much guilt surrounding the sexual area and readily believe sex is something men inflict on women. Their sexual guilt makes them a ready prey when "poor me" women accuse them of being beasts because they desire sexual contact. As with Mabel and Austin, rewarding sexual patterns for the "poor me" woman and her consort thus become impossible.

Chapter 11

Since marriage constitutes slavery for women, it is clear that the Women's Movement must concentrate on attacking this institution. Freedom for women cannot be won without the abolition of marriage. Attack on such issues as employment discrimination is superfluous.   **Sheila Cronan**

Some Marital Effects

Many traditional institutions draw fire from the feminist movement, but marriage is often singled out for special castigation. Attacks on marriage come with a machine-gunlike frequency and verbal virulence which are calculated to wither the sworn enemy on contact. Young women are admonished to avoid marriage if they strive toward freedom and independence. Aspiring feminists are exhorted to save their energy for building the movement and not waste themselves on holy matrimony.[1]

Reasons advanced for this frontal assault revolve around a conviction that marriage serves to oppress women. Marriage, so the argument runs, is a social institution designed by men to further their own interests. It is one of the primary devices the male power structure uses to stabilize its dominance and authority. Wives are signed on for life and then exploited while men reap all the advantages. Marriage serves to keep women in an inferior position by consigning to them all the menial drudgery and maintenance tasks.[2]

Furthermore, marriage is a contrivance to meet the sexual needs of men at the expense of women. Marriage is denounced as legalized rape and compared with prostitution. As compulsory sex is given legal sanction, the female is turned into an innocent victim in order to benefit the male. Women are repeatedly forced to have this boring and painful experience while the man satiates himself with libidinal pleasure.

Undoubtedly, this titillating, vitriolic attack represents an extremist position. Many feminists are working toward an improvement in, rather than the destruction of, marriage. Women's liberation is seen as a force which can ameliorate much of the conflict between the sexes. As stereotyped sex roles are abandoned, men and women will be free to relate as individuals without preconceived ideas of masculinity and femininity intervening. Affection and tenderness will develop and prosper in a setting where each of us is encouraged to develop our potential to the fullest.

As we descend from the clouds and enter the mundane world of reality, we observe that marriage continues to endure— thrive and prosper, no; exist, yes. It has not been destroyed nor has it become a modern utopia. What effect is the women's movement actually having on couples as they struggle through life? What are some individual ways in which marriages are reacting to the new messages permeating our culture?

Predictably enough, conflict is intensified in some situations. This is especially likely when a wife "gets the word" and is faced by a rather conventional man at home. The tradition bound husband is confronted by new ideas and increasing demands for change, and if he feels threatened, a struggle of fundamental importance can ensue.

I am reminded of the young couple who recently came to my office, fighting even before they were comfortably seated. Conflict was primarily over permissible role behavior and expectations of each other. The wife was increasingly impressed with feminist ideas concerning desirability of a career for the woman, sharing of maintenance tasks, and more equality in money management and decision making. Her husband, however, was firmly rooted in being "head of the household" and had no intention of assuming a more active role in cleaning, cooking, and shopping. He was menaced at the thought of his wife following a more independent direction in life and felt dejected and humiliated by his wife's demands for more equality.

Fighting and bickering were intense and dramatic as polarization occurred. Each was fighting for issues which they held dear, and their marriage was at stake. The outcome would depend on mutual ability to compromise and understand their spouse's viewpoint as well as on their dedication and affection for each other.

This is a typical situation, a gestalt which is being repeated in numerous households throughout the land. It is not a surprising nor perplexing development but rather one that is easily anticipated in view of the forces sweeping our nation. It has been well publicized and most people are quite cognizant of its occurrence; it needs no further treatment here.

Women's liberation is bringing about change in the traditional marital format as the sexes experiment with newer ways of relating. In an attempt to avoid the dependent all-or-nothing type relationships which can so easily lead to possessiveness and loss of freedom, some women and men are loosening the expectation of strict monogamy. Communal living arrangements are set up in a wide assortment of styles with most, but not all, dedicated to greater equality and sharing between the sexes.

Some couples choose to work within the marital framework and modify its structure to encompass a greater degree of freedom and independence, including a departure from sexual restrictiveness. Ursula and Murray were such a twosome.

Marrage was a constant source of reward and gratification to both Ursula and her husband. As a young woman, many fears of marriage and commitment had plagued her, and it was only after months of doubt that she had been able to say her marriage vows. That was four, almost five, years ago. Now Ursula could look back and better understand what had motivated her reservations.

"I always feared being trapped at home . . . never did want to be a traditional housewife and mother. I was fearful I wouldn't make a good wife. What man would want a woman who didn't stay home and take care of him? But Murray was different . . . he said I could work out any marital pattern I wished, and he would cooperate and help me. Well, I didn't really trust him then, but it has worked out better than I expected.

"Murray and I both have our careers. We share the housework and shopping, and Murray is more than willing to do his share. He thinks my profession makes me a more interesting person, and with both of us working at well-paying jobs, we have all the money we can use for travel or doing exciting things. I think we were both supporters of women's liberation before we even heard the term. I read what some of the feminists are saying about marriage . . . how it enslaves the woman and only makes her life miserable. I guess that's what I feared, but it hasn't worked out that way. Maybe I was lucky in the man I chose."

I suspect that rather than chance or luck being involved, Ursula had made a wise choice based on knowledge of her own needs. There were some early rough spots as they departed from traditional husband-wife role behavior, but these problems had long been overcome. Now they were reaping the benefits.

Ursula was a warm, affectionate woman who seemed to possess an innate capacity to enjoy and partake of life to its fullest. She undoubtedly brought a great deal of enthusiasm and tenderness into her marital relationship. I never had the opportunity to meet her husband and therefore know him only through Ursula's eyes, which were undoubtedly a bit prejudiced on the positive side. She described him as a nonchalant man who sort of floated through life without becoming unduly upset. He was evidently an easy guy to relate to and cooperate with.

Life was working out so well for Ursula that she was now considering bringing forth a new being who would also be able to participate in this great adventure. The problem was a potential conflict between career and child-raising, and this is what brought Ursula in to see me. She was a cautious woman and did not want to have a child if this would conflict with her independence and career.

Freedom within marriage was crucial to Ursula, and she enjoyed talking about this whenever possible. One session she started talking about the unrestraint in her sexual life.

"Murray and I lived together for about seven months before we were married. He wasn't my first lover, but neither of us had a great deal of sexual experience before we met. I laugh as I look back and remember how clumsy and awkward we were . . . sort of like two naive kids. Murray turned me on like no other man had, and I began to realize how exciting sex could be. I learned to feel comfortable with my body, and Murray and I shared sex like we shared everything else. We were possessive of each other physically for a couple years, even though we talked about having other lovers. I think we had to go through a period of building trust—learning that we would never deliberately hurt one another, and that we could always count on each other for support and affection.

"It was about three years before we seriously considered expanding our sexual horizons to include others. I guess this was initially my idea, but Murray seemed to be intrigued. By then, I was seriously involved in women's liberation and this helped me realize how restrictive sex with one man could be. Not that it wasn't fun, but I wanted the freedom to choose my lovers and not feel like I was a piece of property that had been sold to the highest bidder. I don't like the idea of anyone having exclusive rights over me. Some of my feminist friends have structured extramarital relationships into their marriage contracts, and it goes O.K. for them. Well, Murray and I spent a great deal of time talking this through . . . we finally decided our marriage was solid enough so that sexual freedom would present no threat to our relationship."

With that, Ursula glanced at me with an expression that can only be described as full of pride. She was relating a sexual pattern which many describe as difficult to achieve, and she was obviously pleased at how well it was working out for her and Murray.

"It sounds like this has been rewarding for both you and Murray."

"It really has . . . I think it's a tribute to how good our marriage is. We trust each other so much that jealousy doesn't seem to enter the picture, and I feel so free and independent, just like a woman should. I know I can have all the male friends I want, and if I feel close enough to sleep with one, that's O.K. too. I've had about five affairs during this two year period. Some were better than others, but they have all been rewarding. And I don't have to worry about Murray being jealous or upset. He has the same freedom I do, and I know he has occasional affairs. One day Murray came home early from the office and I was screwing with one of my friends. I must say, he handled it well. While Jim and I finished our little get-together, he went in the kitchen and started dinner for the three of us. No jealousy, no complications—just acceptance and trust."

There was little for me to comment on. Ursula was not presenting this as any problem, but rather as a carefully chosen, well thought out pattern which she was proud of. For her it was a sign of liberation and independence, a tribute to the depth of trust and loving which were present in her marriage. Ursula had developed her own way of combining marriage and freedom, and she did indeed appear to be happy with her solution.

Ursula gradually began to realize that having a child would not mean giving up her career. She was quite insistent that Murray share in the child-care tasks, and he was willing and excited about this possibility. Ursula really didn't need any help from me in working this out, but as I said earlier, she was a most cautious woman who wished to talk over her solutions with an outside party. She wanted to make certain she would be able to handle the mother role without feeling too restricted and trapped.

Not all such efforts at openness and lack of possessiveness, especially in the sexual area, turn out in such an idyllic fashion. There is some suggestion that more often than not serious problems for all participants arise. Confusion and jealousy can develop when ideals which sound good on paper are put into actuality. Attempts to adopt what some interpret as the ideals of the feminist movement can lead couples into a morass of confusion and bitterness.

"My wife's lover was over again watching TV, and finally I exploded . . . threw him right out of the house . . . right in front of Ruby. How will I ever be able to live with myself? I had no right to be upset."

In this rather dramatic fashion, Frank announced himself and his problems. He was worried and guilt-ridden because of difficulty in tolerating his wife's paramour lounging around the house. It took several sessions to unravel the background which led up to this situation.

To make a somewhat long subject short, Frank had a strong theoretical commitment to women's liberation. This evolved during the past several years out of his reading, studying, and interest in basic human equality. While such a development is increasingly seen in young men, Frank carried it a step beyond the ordinary.

"Ruby and I worked hard during these four years of marriage trying to set up an ideal situation. We wanted only the best for each other. 'Share all' was our motto—money, housework, friends, sex—everything we could think of."

"I have a real commitment to women's rights, you know . . . not just lip service either but the real thing. Marriage has been a place to test out these ideas . . . put them into action so to speak. I suppose more of the push has come from me than Ruby, but she agrees how important equality is.

"We really had a chance to prove ourselves two years ago when Oscar was born. Before that it was easy . . . now we had to work at it. I'll bet I've put in as many child-care hours as any father has."

Here Frank stopped and beamed at me with the proudest smile I've ever seen, but then his face darkened as he continued.

"I guess a problem did come up. Of course both Ruby and I worked before Oscar was born . . . equality in everything, you know. But Ruby hasn't gone back to work in two years. She always says she will, but it seems like one excuse after another. She can't find a job or it doesn't pay enough or it's too far from home. I want to work only half time and devote more of myself to the home and Oscar, but I have to work forty hours as long as Ruby doesn't earn any money.

"I've been patient though. I figure it's just a matter of time until we can share more equally again. I do talk with Ruby about it several times a week, and she always agrees with me."

This, however, was little more than an interesting, incidental aspect of Frank's life. While being a matter of some concern to him, it was causing no great psychic stress. Frank's main problems were in the sexual area.

One day Frank was talking about his guilt for not being able to tolerate Waldo, his wife's handsome lover.

"I thought I had it figured out . . . share equally with everything . . . no possessiveness, no jealousy, no ownership of another being. Feminists write about how insulting it is for a husband to have exclusive sexual rights over his wife . . . how this humiliates the woman and treats her like a piece of property.

"I know the feminists are right. A woman should be free to have sex with whomever she pleases. In order to work, a marriage can't be restricting . . . but I couldn't handle it. I tried so hard and blew it."

Frank was crushed as he relived these unpleasant memories, but he continued as I asked for details on what had actually happened.

"Ruby never thought we had to have such permissiveness in the sexual area. I guess that was my idea of what a liberated woman would want. She liked all the other sharing, but this one bothered her. I kept trying to convince her though . . . you know I can be rather persistent. [By now I fully realized that Frank could be a downright nag.] Ruby finally said I could have an affair if I wanted to but that she had no need for sex with another man.

"I did have an affair or two, but it was never all that great. I think it must be more important for a woman than a man. I had to try, though . . . it was part of the sharing and not being possessive with each other."

"What started Ruby on an affair, Frank?"

"I guess it was my continual urging. She started to fantasize sex with another man, wondering what it would be like. Ruby never had relations with another guy, and she started getting curious. I don't know . . . you know how it is . . . maybe it was the trouble in our own sexual relationship."

This was a new dimension, and I asked Frank what he meant.

"Well, sex had become a bore. I suppose we fell into a routine. And then Ruby said I didn't excite her very much. She didn't know if any man could . . . always did have trouble reaching a climax. She wanted me to be more aggressive, and I resented that. You know how I feel about sharing and equality. Women should have the same rights as men . . . they need to initiate sex and take a more active part.

"Ruby, she didn't see it that way . . . or at least her feelings didn't. She would agree with me, but it didn't change her behavior. At times she wanted to be thrown on the bed and raped. I think she liked to say no and then be talked into it, but I always respected her right to decline. I refuse to dominate a woman."

It was the next session before we could get back to Ruby and her affair. Frank started right in.

"Well, Ruby met Waldo. What more can I say? I suppose he's a better lover, or at least Ruby says he is. We talk about everything . . . you know how I feel about sharing . . . open communication is essential in a marriage between equals. Right away Ruby told me about Waldo and what they did in bed . . . how she was excited by him in a way she never was with me . . . of course I encouraged her . . . it was the least I could do. But you know something—it bothered me."

Frank was becoming noticeably upset at this point. He was struggling to contain frustration and rage, feelings which he thought a liberated man should not have.

"I kept it all in . . . never once let Ruby know it bothered me . . . that is until I exploded and threw him out of the house. If only Ruby hadn't started inviting him over every evening to eat with us and play cards or watch TV. I couldn't stand seeing him around any more. I went berserk."

Frank's intellectual fascination with the feminist movement had led him into this eccentric, almost ludicrous situation. I began to suspect that his wife was pushing things further and further, hoping to get some sort of assertive action from her dear, all too accommodating husband. Subsequent events were to bear this out.

To Frank's complete astonishment, Ruby was not at all upset about his banishing the hapless Waldo from the scene. When he finally calmed down after several frantic, guilt-ridden weeks, he began to realize that Ruby was actually delighted. She praised him for his behavior, stating that time had wearied her of Waldo, and she made no effort to recontact her exiled lover.

Frank stopped badgering his wife to have extramarital sex relations although he continued in many of his other delightfully wacky ways. He never did understand why things hadn't worked out; he only realized what a confused mess things had become. I tried explaining to Frank that some women don't want this type of sexual freedom, that they enjoy just one man—not all feminists throw monogamy to the winds. He could still be a feminist and believe in equality for women without playing cards with his wife's lover. I was talking to deaf ears— Frank never got the message.

As memories of Waldo faded into the background, Frank's spirits improved. Residual scars, however, were left in his sexual relationship with Ruby. She pressed him even harder to be more aggressive and dominant in their sexual contact, and she urged him to try techniques the romantic Waldo had shown her. Frank responded stubbornly with hurt and incomprehension; he wanted Ruby to be more assertive as this is what the liberated woman should be like. When I last saw Frank, his marriage was strong and constant but sex had degenerated into a quagmire of accusations and dissatisfaction.

The sexual problems experienced by Frank and Ruby are not uncommon in couples structuring a great deal of sexual freedom into their marriages. Jealousy of a mate's lover is a commonplace reaction. Direct comparison between a spouse's and a lover's sexual technique can result in insecurity and loss of sexual confidence. This is what happened with Ruby and Frank, along with the resulting sexual dissatisfaction. Male impotence or premature ejaculation and female inability to reach orgasm are frequent reactions to such conflicts over sexual fidelity.[3]

As marital roles change under the influence of the feminist movement, pressure is brought to bear on wives and husbands. Often the marriage survives but one or both members of the dyad may experience a degree of stress which they are ill-equipped to handle, leading to rather disastrous consequences.

Kate called me earlier in the day, asking to be seen as soon as possible. I had never met her before, but she sounded desperate enough to need an appointment as soon as I could work her into my schedule. Now it was later in the afternoon and she was in my office, agitated and distraught.

"I'm a casualty of women's liberation, Doctor. My husband finally agreed that we could move so I can accept a new teaching job, but I can't handle the responsibility . . . thirty-eight years old and I'm acting like a child."

Kate flung out these words as though they were eating her insides and then she commenced pacing the room. She was visibly disturbed and looked as frightened as she sounded. Her thinking was evidently too confused to permit any elaboration of her opening statements, and she launched into a description of her emotional state.

"Never, never have I felt this way before . . . it's as though someone's controlling my thinking. I can't follow my own ideas . . . they come and go and blur before my eyes. Why, I never thought of suicide before, and now it just pops up when I'm trying to concentrate. I would never kill myself, would I?"

At this point, I really had no idea whether Kate had suicidal potential, but she certainly sounded disturbed enough to consider this a possibility.

"You're staring at me . . . just like people on the street. It's funny. I could hardly find my way to your office and yet the future is so bleak. Why I forgot to water my plants today."

More chaotic, depressed thinking was revealed during the session, and there was no chance to pursue Kate's intriguing opening remarks about women's liberation. Her thought processes were too disintegrated, and there was an immediate need for relief of her symptoms which were becoming incapacitating. I placed her on an appropriate medication and told her to return in a couple days, sooner if needed.

Kate was a much different woman during our next meeting. Although still despressed and agitated, she was thinking in a more integrated, rational manner and reported feeling better. I was now able to investigate the precipitating factors of her near psychotic reaction.

"During our first meeting, Kate, you mentioned how you were a casualty of women's liberation. Could you tell me more about this?"

"It's not really women's lib. I've had these ideas since I was married nineteen years ago. Always blamed Dennis and the marriage restrictions . . . then suddenly things change. I can have what I want and I'm afraid."

"Slow down, Kate, you've got all hour. Why don't you start at the beginning and explain what's happening?"

"I was married young, too young to know what I wanted. I guess you could say I was programmed for marriage. My parents expected it and no alternatives were considered . . . and then two children with all that housework . . . enough to drive you crazy.

"I never gave up my interest in history, though . . . dabbled in it now and then with an occasional night school course. Sure I was angry, damn angry . . . sacrificed my career to make the marriage work. Dennis isn't such a bad guy, but he could never understand why I wanted something outside of the home."

Kate was wound up now and talking fast. She was making sense and needed no prompting to continue. I sat back and let her run with the conversation.

"All along I cursed the marriage for everything that went wrong . . . not really Dennis but the damn institution itself. Sure he was content to have me trapped at home . . . but no different than most men. And then I began to lose interest in sex. All the old excitement seemed to disappear. My life seemed boring and it carried over into the sexual area. And you know something, Doctor? I was angry for being stuck at home. I couldn't respond to Dennis sexually when I felt so cheated.

"Eventually Dennis and I started talking about this. He finally realized how discouraged I was, and then he began to change . . . slowly at first, and I hardly noticed it. He started to encourage my schooling and helped me get out in the evenings. I don't know why, but I think it had something to do with understanding how important it was for me. All the recent publicity about women's rights must have sunk in.

"For years I harped on having more of an independent life . . . a career and my own money to do what I want with. Sure Dennis earns a reasonable living, and he isn't stingy, but I felt like a child being taken care of.

"Finally things began to work out . . . or so I thought. My evening school courses were successful and Dennis started encouraging me to enroll in the full-time teachers' program I was interested in. All was great until a few weeks ago. I found this position teaching high school history, but we would have to move. Dennis didn't want to quit his job . . . he does so well . . . but finally he agreed. Said we could move when I graduate this summer. I could support the family for awhile."

Here Kate became visibly upset; her agitation increased, her face darkened and her voice drifted off. Because of her increasing disturbance, I attempted to give verbal support and reassurance, and the hour ended with Kate in relatively good spirits. The next session was a stormy one. Kate was distraught when she entered the office, and she quickly revealed what was troubling her.

"All week I thought about moving and taking that teaching job. All week . . . I couldn't put it out of my mind . . . it's driving me crazy . . . I can't sleep . . . I can't eat . . . if only something could relax me. My thoughts are playing tricks on me. I'd swear the neighbors are watching . . . they must be laughing at the way I'm going to pieces.

"I want that job so bad, and yet I'm afraid. All my life I've waited and worked for a chance like this . . . now I'm going to blow it. I'm one big failure . . . just a bunch of hot air with no substance. Dennis says we can move so I can take that job, and I can't do it . . . so much responsibility . . . I'd have to support the family, at least for awhile. What if I failed? People would laugh . . . just another female who can't take care of herself."

Kate was in a panic, petrified at the thought of working and assuming financial responsibility for the family. The reality of what she had dreamed of for so many years was too much for her. A reversal of marital duties had sounded good to Kate in the abstract, but the reality of taking on an unaccustomed role by being the bread winner was terrifying. Her husband's increasing acceptance of her ideas removed the grounds for Kate's complaints. The end result was a disturbance of major proportion.

Kate was definitely more upset today. The agitation and confused thinking had returned, and she was finding it impossible to function. I still felt, however, that Kate possessed many underlying strengths and had the potential to solve many of these problems. Events were to prove me wrong, at least for the time being.

During the week, I received a frantic call from Kate's husband. Kate was severely disturbed and was now actively talking about suicide. She was asking to go in the hospital and Dennis felt this would now be necessary. I surmised that there was no practical alternative and arranged to have Kate hospitalized under the care of a colleague who did hospital work.

The only feedback I received on Kate was four or five weeks later when my colleague called to say Kate was quite a bit better and he was discharging her from the hospital. He also mentioned that Kate decided there was no way she could move and take on a career—the responsibility was beyond what she felt capable of assuming.

Kate, in her own words, was a victim of women's liberation. Most certainly this is an oversimplification, but her depressed, near psychotic reaction was clearly related to changing roles within the marriage. Feminist ideology had held out to Kate the promise of escape from problems, but instead brought her misery and suffering.

In a recent issue of the *American Journal of Psychiatry*, psychiatrist Dr. Ruth Moulton discusses emotional difficulties in women precipitated by the "new feminism." One problem she discusses in some depth is the severe panic a long-homebound woman can experience when returning to work outside the home. She labels this syndrome "reentry anxiety," a condition Kate certainly suffered from in the extreme. Describing four major syndromes which are increasing in women because of feminism, Dr. Moulton writes: "There is much evidence that the new freedoms have brought new anxieties."[4]

Chapter 12

I feel we do have a surplus of hostility, of undirected hostility,
because we refuse to take part of the responsiblility for the things
we find ourselves caught in.   **Anais Nin**

Divorce

Women's liberation is commonly seen as the enemy of marriage, the new force which will discourage the young from
marrying and cause the breakup of countless families. This idea
is not surprising in view of the frequent, bitter attacks on
marriage by some feminists and the challenge women's liberation can present to traditional institutions.

Most assuredly, the feminist movement is having an affect on
divorce. This influence, however, is varied and difficult to
measure. More women do appear to be expressing dissatisfaction with their marriages. This theme receives repeated publicity. The number of runaway wives has skyrocketed. We read
that fifteen years ago, husbands ran away from marriages 300
times more frequently than their wives. This ratio has now
changed so that twice as many wives as husbands are fleeing
from their marital homes.[1]

The increasing divorce rate is frequently noted in our public
media with new statistics contantly being quoted. We read:

> Married couples now are divorcing at nearly twice the
> rate of the 1950s. Escalating divorce is prevalent through-
> out Western society. Roughly one in every three American
> marriages now ends in divorce.[2]

Alarmists project these figures into the future, questioning the
very survival of marriage as an institution in our society.

That the divorce rate is increasing can easily be misinterpreted. Many of the statistics come from studies done in California where the divorce rate is high, and they cannot be taken as typical for the rest of the nation. Furthermore, much of the increase is due to the number of people being divorced for the second or third or fourth time.

In actuality, marriage is not dying away at all. The 1970s have ushered in a great wedding boom. Some surveys indicate that marriage may be healthier than ever. "One accurate description of the success of marriage is that 80 percent of all first marriages are permanent."[3]

The actual number of marriages ending in divorce is on the increase, however, even if much of this comes from the "repeaters." While the feminist movement is probably one of the main causes, it is certainly not the only one. Moreover, the thrust of the women's movement does not just bring about the breakup of marriages. In previous sections, we have seen how it is causing an actual restructuring of marriage with a realignment of sexual roles. This often results in the strengthening of a marriage as the relationship attains a more equitable foundation.

The effect of women's liberation on a specific marriage is very much an individual matter, varying from one situation to another. In some marriages, it acts as a powerful force for improving the relationship while in others it can cause a disintegration of the union.

The changing emotional climate surrounding divorce is one of the areas where the feminist movement has had the most impact. Women are receiving new messages. It is alright to be divorced. To terminate a marriage is not a sign of sickness. In fact, it may be an indication of strength. A divorced woman is not a failure. Her ability to lead a constructive and enjoyable life, her attractiveness as a woman, and her sexual desires will not be adversely affected by her new choice. Her worth as a person is not destroyed.[4]

Women are being informed that they do not need a man to complete their identity. They can be complete human beings even though they are not married. Furthermore, women are becoming more independent. They are learning how to do things which have traditionally been reserved for the male. The increasing number of women undertaking auto mechanics, home repair, and hard physical labor are excellent examples of this.

Women are becoming independent financially. More women are working and establishing careers, and their salaries are increasing. The ability of women to support themselves means women no longer have to tolerate an unworkable relationship just to obtain financial protection.

This all adds up to an increasing self-esteem and confidence for the woman who decides to divorce. The feminist movement is definitely making it easier for women to leave marriages they are dissatisfied with.

I am reminded of a recent situation related to me by a colleague. A sixty-three-year-old friend of hers was ending her marriage of almost forty years duration. The love had gone out of her relationship, and she was going to remarry for "romance." As my colleague remarked, this woman would not have dared do this if she had not been a career woman who was independent financially.

There are specific elements in the feminist movement which can precipitate problems in a marriage, eventually leading to divorce. Many of these factors influence one partner to change while their mate undergoes no such transition. Marriages which appear well-founded at first can dissolve as one member becomes more independent and liberated.

Colleen was a full-time housewife for two years, that is until she was forced to find a job because of money problems in her marriage. These first years of marriage had gone well, and Colleen rather enjoyed her role as the somewhat pampered, well-taken care of newlywed. Her husband, Oliver, was a reasonably good provider, and he enjoyed buying things for his new bride. In fact, he relished surprising Colleen with presents so much that he consistently overspent. Credit cards were just too tempting.

When the credit companies closed in, Colleen was angry. She had not been extravagant; her husband had. Now she had to pay the price by finding a job to bail out the family finances.

Now, almost three years later, Colleen was singing a different tune.

"I never planned on having a career. But by the time we

straightened out our finances, I was pleased with my job. I meet such interesting people, and the work is rewarding. And I enjoy the security of earning my own money. I can understand this women's liberation business now. My life is much more fulfilling since I'm not staying at home.

"The problem is Oliver. He's so possessive. He's trying to force me to quit my job, but I won't. Everytime I go out at night with my friends from work, he gets jealous. It's reached the point where he checks up on me. He thinks I'm having an affair.

"And it's getting worse. He expects me to tell him exactly where I'm going to be and what time I'll be home. He treats me like a child. The other night he came into this restaurant to see if I was there and who I was with. It was so embarrassing to be humiliated that way in front of my friends.

"Money is a problem, too. Not in the old way for there is plenty to go around. But Oliver tries to control how I spend my money. When I opened my own checking account, he didn't talk to me for days."

I was to meet Oliver on only one occasion, a joint session I had with him and his wife. Colleen's description of his possessiveness was not exaggerated. The increasing social and economic independence of his wife was threatening the core of his masculinity. He reacted with jealousy and increasing attempts to control her behavior. He refused to return for further sessions even though his marriage was in dire straights.

Things rapidly went from bad to worse. Colleen was not about to give up her new independence, and Oliver was unable to feel more secure and adapt to the change in his wife. Fighting broke out in the sexual area. Whereas sex had previously gone well, it now became a battlefield. Colleen's contact with other men at work was menacing to her insecure husband. The more suspicious he became of her behavior, the more upset Colleen became. Temporary bouts of impotence occurred. Finally, out of anger at her controlling husband, Colleen had a brief affair. The outcome of the marriage was no longer in doubt. It could only end in divorce.

This is a common pattern that has received much publicity. As a result of the feminist movement, women are changing, and they may terminate their marriages as they develop increasing dissatisfaction with their conventional husbands. I am becoming aware, however, that it is often men who are attracted to women's liberation—frequently leaving their wives behind as they aspire toward new equality between the sexes.

When Lyle and Rose married several years ago, probably neither had heard of women's liberation. They were childhood sweethearts and had seldom dated anyone else. Marriage seemed to occur naturally out of this situation, and the early years went well.

After working for two years, Lyle decided to finish his college education. He was becoming more confident and ambitious, and he achieved a great deal of academic success. On campus he was now exposed to the feminist movement, and their messages began to influence his outlook on life. He also noticed women with personalities and value structures considerably different from his wife's, women who were stronger and more motivated toward independence and a career. It was at this point that I first met Lyle.

Lyle was depressed, like so many other people when they first contact me. The fascinating part of depression is the sleuth work which is sometimes necessary to unravel the causes. With Lyle this was not difficult—his depression was clearly related to feelings about his wife and marriage.

"I'm so damn upset about my marriage. Rose and I have known each other close to six years. She's the only woman I've ever been close to, and she's so content. But it's not working . . . the old feelings are gone. I suppose I've changed a lot. That's not fair to Rose, is it?"

What emerged as Lyle continued talking was a growing dissatisfaction with his wife and marriage. These feelings were annoying and troublesome and left him perplexed—he felt no right to be discontented and yet he was. Guilt permeated his being as he was overcome with unacceptable thoughts.

"What leads you to be so down on Rose?"

"I can't stand a housewife, that's all there is to it. Rose is so damn satisfied being at home . . . it drives be buggy. I shouldn't feel this way . . . never used to . . . it's a betrayal of Rose, that's what it is."

Lyle tended to hide from unpleasant thoughts and this led to an initial difficulty in expressing his frustration. It was several meetings before he really opened up.

"Rose is too dependent on me. I suppose this reflects the way she was raised. Her mom is a housewife and that's all Rose wants to be . . . why that's detrimental to human beings. She's been willing to work for a few years until we have children, but there's no interest in a career or achievement . . . she does any sort of secretarial work . . . never aspires to anything higher."

Lyle was wound up now and releasing his pent-up emotion. Many of these thoughts were ones he had never previously dared admit to himself. He now charged full steam ahead.

"Rose really bores me . . . it's hard to say, but it's the truth. All she wants to do is stay home and tend the drapes. It puts so damn much pressure on me. I have to satisfy all her needs . . . she depends on me for everything. It feels so restrictive . . . like Rose wants to possess every inch of me.

"It's the same thing sexually. Rose relies on me to do everything. She just lies there, waiting for me to stimulate her. Sure, she enjoys sex, but all the responsibility is mine. Just once, I would like her to initiate something. It's scary, the way she depends on me.

"This feminist movement has really had its affect. I can't tolerate a superior-inferior relationship any more. And this is just what Rose does. She idolizes me and puts herself in a subordinate position . . . how degrading. Rose is the type of woman who looks out for everyone else's needs, but not her own."

Anger finally began to surface . . . bitterness at being caught in a marriage which was proving to be unrewarding. Before Lyle could act on this frustration and begin setting up a better life for himself, he had to come to terms with his guilt feelings. This took some time as he was committed to Rose and felt personally responsible for any conflict—after all, so he reasoned, the change was in him, not his wife. It was many weeks before divorce could be considered.

Lyle spent these weeks trying hard to make things work. He knew Rose would not change—she was as natural and content in her housewife ways as a tree was in having leaves. He would adjust to the situation and make do as well as possible. The trouble was, the harder he tried the more resentful and frustrated he became.

Lyle reluctantly concluded that divorce was the only practical course. Once this decision was made, the rest fell into place with reasonable ease. As he separated from Rose, new feelings of strength and independence took hold. Guilt diminished and depression lifted as he recognized his own right to have a more equal relationship. Lyle was able to enter his school work with new vigor; he no longer need feel guilty for studying instead of being home entertaining Rose.

In a short time, Lyle was telling me about his new relationship.

"Guess what? I have a new girl friend . . . one of the women I've been working with at school. She's really different from Rose . . . a career is fundamental to her plans . . . such a stimulating person to be with."

Lyle was excited and talking a mile a minute. For some time he had recognized how much he wanted a relationship with an independent woman, and now he had a chance to bring this to fruition. After his initial outburst of enthusiasm, he calmed down somewhat.

"What appeals to me is her strength and assertiveness. She's an active feminist and doesn't cling all over you. Women's liberation certainly helps a woman establish her own identity . . . she doesn't have to depend on a man to feel worthwhile.

"The more I find out about this girl, the more I like her. She insists on making her own decisions and won't let me boss her around like Rose did. I can learn things from her . . . she isn't some rubber-stamp machine that agrees with everything I say. She has real potential to go somewhere in this world.

"You know something funny . . . I think most people would like Rose better. She comes across as sweet, docile and nice . . . doesn't challenge anyone . . . just smiles and looks pleasant. My girl friend appears assertive and capable and never takes a backseat. But other people be damned. I know what I want."

During my final interview with Lyle, he summed up some of his thoughts in a rather clear manner.

"I've been thinking back on my relationship with Rose and what went wrong. It scares the hell out of me to provide all the support for another person. What an impossible situation to be in . . . drains you dry. It's not right for one person to live through someone else. We each need our strength and independence so that we can meet as equals."

Although not true with Lyle and Rose, the sexual area itself is increasingly a cause of divorce. While frequently leading to a more compatible sexual relationship, the messages of women's liberation can stimulate sexual problems which eventually lead to the breakup of a marriage. Women are increasingly expecting full sexual satisfaction within their marital relationships. As their expectations rise, they are less apt to tolerate sexual frustration or even partial satisfaction. They may put pressure on their mates to meet their sexual needs. And if these needs cannot be met in the marital bed, some women will turn elsewhere.

The feminist insistence on independence for women and the abolishment of the double standard can lead to increasing sexual freedom. As women demand that they not be owned as a piece of property, they may feel excessively restrained by the demands of strict sexual monogamy. Sexual experimentation with someone other than one's mate not uncommonly results, and this can lead to eventual divorce.

Bess had never been all that pleased with the way sex went in her marriage. She had slept with two or three men before marriage, and sex seemed exciting enough then. Premarital sex with her husband-to-be was somewhat disappointing by comparison, but Bess had been told there were more important things in marriage. Besides, she rationalized, sex would be sure to improve after she said her marriage vows and settled into a committed relationship.

But sex did not improve for the disappointed Bess. Sex was frequent, but her husband, Titus, ejaculated before Bess could reach orgasm. Furthermore, Titus was little interested in foreplay or the tenderness of love. Following intercourse, he was quick to roll over and sink into the sleep of oblivion. Sex went fine for Titus—except that he repeatedly left his wife frustrated.

As a student on a small college campus, Bess was continually exposed to women's liberation. Whereas in previous generations she would have been apt to put up with a mediocre sex life, this was not the case now. As she read articles by feminists, she was reassured that she had a right to her own sexual satisfaction. It was at this point that Bess consulted me. She was genuinely concerned about a marriage which she felt was basically an excellent relationship, that is except for sex.

"I'm so tired of not getting any sexual pleasure for myself. What a paradox. My marriage is 90 percent good. Titus isn't at all restrictive, and we're so compatible in most areas. But sexually, he seems to think I should function just to meet his needs."

Titus was not about to come in for counseling. After all, there were no problems for him. I encouraged Bess to confront her husband with her dissatisfaction and see if the two of them could work out a sexual pattern which would be more mutually satisfying. Several months later Bess returned.

"It's no use. Titus was threatened when I said we had sexual problems. According to him, his sexual functioning is perfectly normal. When I complained, he said I was getting too demanding. It seems that the more I ask him to pay attention to my sexual needs, the quicker he ejaculates.

"Titus said that my not reaching orgasm is my problem, not his. But I know he's wrong. I never had any trouble with my earlier sex partners.

"This women's studies course I'm taking helps. I'm seeing how men often put women down. That's what Titus does. He wants to put all the blame on me.

"And I'm talking with other girls in the class. Their sexual response doesn't seem any different than mine. A woman needs to be stimulated to climax, it doesn't just happen."

I had to agree with Bess. There was basically nothing wrong with her sexual responsiveness. Her sexual troubles with her husband did not mean she had to doubt her own sexual capacity. It was crucial for Bess to not accept the total blame that her husband was placing on her and end up with many self-doubts. Feminist messages were helpful in this regard.

Sex destroyed Bess's marriage. Sexual troubles are often symptomatic of other problems in a marriage, but they can be the primary problem. This was the case with Bess.

As Bess became strengthened in her feminist ideology, she realized she did not have to tolerate this poor sexual relationship. If Titus would not cooperate, she would have to be independent and manage things on her own. And this is what she did.

Bess decided to seek sexual satisfaction outside the marriage. Finding a partner was relatively easy, and Bess's sexual confidence was confirmed. When she was with an adequate lover, her sexual response was all that she desired. It was shortly thereafter that Bess decided to terminate her marriage. Titus strongly objected, but it was too late. Bess had decided she wanted no part of a man who didn't treat her as a full equal in the sexual relationship.

Increasingly, women will terminate a marriage out of discontent with the institution itself rather than the relationship. This is a direct influence of women's liberation. In these cases, marriage itself is seen as too restricting and demeaning to women. Marital customs are felt to promote inequality, forcing the female into a position of inferiority. Anger at the conventions of marriage can lead a feminist-inspired wife to divorce.

The feminist movement is raising people's goals regarding marriage. Women and men expect to have their needs met in many areas, and they are less inclined to accept a relationship in which this does not occur. This can cause couples to break up a marriage which is only partially rewarding. Equally important, it can also stimulate partners to work for the improvement of their relationship. Marriages which do survive will perhaps be stronger.

Chapter 13

Women's liberation is men's liberation! This is an attitude often overlooked by both the opponents and proponents of the liberation movement.   **Garvin Holman**[1]

Male's Best Friend?

As the clarion notes of the feminist movement are sounded, developed, and recapitulated, the male cannot sit idly by as an uninvolved spectator. He is not a bystander at a drama designed for his amusement, but he is willingly or unwillingly a main participant. The swirl of feminist ideology is encircling the American sire with strident, incessant demands for change. Some men will be engulfed and consumed while others will grow, thrive, and prosper, the outcome depending upon individual circumstances and personalities. Opportunity awaits at the male's threshold, but only those who can open wide the doors and respond positively to the new messages will reap the gains. This section will examine some of the unique ways in which women's liberation can benefit the male of our species.

The effects of the feminist movement on the male has been a most neglected area of inquiry. Publicity, when it does occur, is concentrated more on the negative impacts, the positive implications being largely ignored. This is not surprising in that, at least in its initial stages, the feminist movement has been mainly conceived and promulgated by females for the benefit of females. Few men, except in some unusual circumstances, have been a powerful motivating force behind the movement. The paradox is our realization that men·are potentially as much affected as women.

There has been a gradual awakening within the past several

years as men slowly realize the feminist movement can benefit them. A few books have recently been written by men which deal with the positive effects of women's liberation on males. Two of them, *The Liberated Man* by Warren Farrell[2] and *The Male Machine* by Marc Feigen Fasteau,[3] attack the masculine stereotype and show how it has worked to the disadvantage of men. Both are excellent books, and they are helping to raise the consciousness of men.

Some feminists have long been cognizant that liberation of women can also help lead to the liberation of men. With some degree of regularity, one runs across comments such as the following in the feminist literature.

> I am so sure in my mind that the liberation of women means liberation of men as well. Men have been chained and trapped, too.[4]

In her well-known book, *The Female Eunuch*, Germaine Greer indicates her awareness that the women's movement will necessarily lead to the liberation of men.[5] Feminists have in general been more cognizant of this than males.

Men have been slow to understand the advantages women's liberation might hold for them. Seldom have they formed men's liberation organizations or worked for male consciousness raising. Such groups that have been formed are often a backlash to the feminist movement, being more concerned with protection from loss of power than with pursuing positive implications arising from role change.

On occasion, one reads of a vehement attack claiming that women have most of the advantages in our society and that it is males who need more equality. One of the most significant examples is a book written, interestingly enough, by a woman. In *The Manipulated Man*, Esther Villar develops at length the thesis that women are the oppressors and men their slaves. She sees mothers pitilessly training their male children to perform in stultifying jobs. Girls are conditioned to think men are going to work for them, and even those women who have a career are really not emancipated because they have the option of quitting, an option the man does not have.

Sex is the cornerstone of Ms. Villar's thesis. She writes:

By the age of twelve at the latest, most women have decided to become prostitutes. Or, to put it another way, they have planned a future for themselves which consists of choosing a man and letting him do all the work. In return for his support, they are prepared to let him make use of their vagina at certain given moments.[6]

According to her view, sex is the carrot, the reward women use to control men. The sexual drive in man is so strong that he voluntarily enslaves himself to woman in order to obtain sexual pleasure. Woman denies herself a sexual appetite, but she ruthlessly exploits man's sexual appetite for her own selfish purposes—that is, to be taken care of and have money.

By taking such a far-out position, Ms. Villar falls into the same trap as the radical feminists who claim man is the exploiter and woman the innocent victim. These extreme positions are composed largely of sweeping generalizations which are an oversimplification of a complex reality. They quickly degenerate into a fruitless effort to prove which sex is the most oppressed, obscuring the fact that both women and men are victimized by inequality and rigid role structuring. Dichotomizing the problem into good and evil is usually motivated by anger toward the opposite sex and distracts from the crucial question of exactly what can be done to eliminate inequality in our society.

Equality is a two-sided proposition, a basic truth which many seem to conveniently forget. As women obtain equal rights in areas where they have been discriminated against, men will likewise find previous injustices toward their sex being removed. The equal rights legislation which so many states have recently passed (and the possibility of the Equal Rights Amendment to the United States Constitution being ratified) is an especially powerful double-edged weapon. Already we are witnessing ramifications in widely diverse areas as equality is ordained by law. Men (as well as women of course) are rapidly becoming the beneficiaries as change develops in legal, economic, sexual, professional, and social areas.

Mike's marriage was a shambles. Sexual conflict had been extreme for several years, culminating in his wife having several affairs. Mutual hostility was now rampant and divorce was imminent. No reconciliation was possible.

Several years of sexual problems in the marriage and

discovery of his wife's affairs had shaken Mike's self-esteem. Now, after several months of counseling, Mike was handling the separation well and was looking forward to setting up a new life for himself. He had gained self-confidence and developed a fair understanding of what had gone wrong in the marriage. The big problem now was a divorce settlement and custody of the only child, a nine-year-old boy.

Mike was dedicated to his son. He was a most attentive and caring father and the relationship with his child was an excellent one. Through the years he had provided much of the child care and found this role greatly rewarding. Mike's main reluctance in seeking a divorce earlier in the marriage was his fear of losing this close bond with his son. He felt he could provide a more satisfactory home and be a better parent for the boy than his wife ever could. In his eyes, his wife Susan was more interested in pursuing her career than taking care of their child. She was frequently gone evenings and at times weekends, ostensibly because of the demands her bank job placed on her. Mike now realized that much of the time Susan spent away from home was in the company of her lovers. He considered this to be gross negligence of her responsibilities as a parent.

For years, Mike assumed that the courts would discriminate against him as a male by giving his wife custody of the child just because she was a woman. Several years ago I would have had to tell Mike that he was probably correct and that there would be no use in his pushing the matter in court. Due to the new emphasis on equality, however, I could now give Mike a different message—divorce and child custody courts are attempting to end their age-old discrimination against men and are increasingly awarding child custody to the father when this is in the best interest of the child.

Mike carefully examined these new changes in our society and decided to ask the court for custody of his son. It was many weeks before the matter was resolved and he burst ecstatically into my office.

"I won! I won! The court awarded me sole custody of Jamie. Susan's affairs had become almost public knowledge, and the court was swayed by this. Susan has visitation rights, but that shouldn't cause any trouble. I never thought we could do it. My lawyer said three years ago we wouldn't have had a chance. And guess what? The divorce settlement was great. Because Susan is a working woman and I won child custody, there's no alimony involved. Maybe in a year or two I can cut back on my work like I've always wanted to and spend more time with Jamie. By then I should be able to collect child support from Susan."

Mike is just one example of the many men who are now benefiting from changes in the legal structure of our society brought about by the momentum of women's liberation. Well-publicized in recent years is the more equitable treatment of men in alimony, child-support, and child-custody cases. A *Newsweek* article tells how a judge in Washington, D.C. not only awarded custody of three children to the father but ordered the mother to contribute child support payments of $200 a month. The column goes on to state:

> Awarding custody to fathers is perhaps the most signifi-
> cant new trend in the handling of broken families.
> Although still quite small, the number of children living
> with divorced fathers has burgeoned 50 percent in the last
> two years.[7]

Along the same line, the trend in alimony payments and property division in divorce settlements is flowing into more equitable channels. Another article tells us:

> As feminists began asking for equal opportunity, equal pay
> and equal responsibilities and more and more women
> entered the job market, the courts began taking women at
> their word by passing out 50-50 divorcee settlements.[8]

The women's movement has championed the concept that women should be self-supporting and the legal system is now adopting this principle. The end result is, "courts are getting stingier with alimony awards. More judges are willing to reduce or end them at a former husband's request.[9]

As inequality in our laws based on sex is remedied in some situations, the ending of discrimination against men in other legal areas is a hypothetical promise for the future. Complex conditions can often not be changed by simple removal of an old law or passage of a new one. This is the case in our system of criminal justice enforcement where the male is commonly prosecuted and punished with a zeal which does not apply to women. A psychiatrist from the Albert Einstein College of Medicine states:

> Although women clearly pay a heavy toll because of sexism, men do not get off cheaply either. To become convinced of this one need only note such glaring evidence as the disproportion between prison sentences given to men and women for the same crime, where it is not uncommon for a woman to get a suspended sentence while her male partner goes to the penitentiary.[10]

He then remarks on the much greater probability that a man will be executed under capital punishment than a woman. As equal rights legislation takes root, men can hope to see gradual improvement in a criminal justice system which so blatantly discriminates against them.

In no situation has discrimination against males been more obvious and deadly than in our draft system. Feminists have been quick to realize this and many are outspoken on their right and duty to be drafted on an equal basis with men. In answer to the common question of whether women liberationists wish to be drafted, a feminist publication states:

> If anybody is going to be drafted, yes. Women should be allowed equal access to all the functions of society, including everything from combat duty to decision-making in the Pentagon.[11]

Although temporarily in abeyance, few would doubt that with America's propensity for war the draft will one day again be instituted. The benefits to men of having a coed draft are so important and obvious that no more need be said.

As the women's liberation movement permeates society, economic benefits to women have been real and they are well publicized. Less well known but equally important are the economic benefits to men. The financial advantage that a household obtains when a wife earns equitable pay for her labors in the work force is manifest. Thousands of dollars are lost to a family when a working woman is discriminated against in job placement, advancement, or pay scale. How can a man help but benefit if his spouse is encouraged to enter more highly skilled and responsible positions which provide lucrative remuneration?

The onerous duty of the American male to provide full financial support for the family will be lessened in direct proportion to the number of women entering the work force. As wives increasingly establish their own careers and become successful, men will be able to decrease their hours of toil and sweat. They will have more time to be with their children and an increase in leisure for sports, hobbies, reading, creative efforts, community activity, and crafts. The part-time work week will indeed become a reality for many as wives and husbands share financial responsibility and house maintenance tasks.

Job-splitting by a married couple is already gaining in popularity on college campuses. Colleges are increasingly willing to allow a husband and wife to split an academic position, and their areas of expertise need not be the same. Some predict that this will become a universal trend. A *Wall Street Journal* article, analyzing this development in depth, quotes Felice Schwartz, the president of an organization exploring nontraditional work patterns as stating:

> Our whole society is moving toward part-time work, as women want to work and make a contribution, and men become less concerned with the Protestant ethic of work for work's sake.[12]

The same article goes on to indicate how job-sharing on a part-time basis by husbands and wives is likely to enter the business world and industry due to the push to employ more women.

Young women are coming under increasing pressure to pick up their share of the tab in the dating scene and other heterosexual encounters where the male has traditionally assumed full monetary obligation. Numerous college men with whom I talk are delighted with this development and relate with great relish the joy of dating a liberated woman who pays for her share of the evening. These same women are assuming more freedom in becoming aggressive and asking men for dates, a condition greatly appreciated by men who are tired of taking all the initiative. Shy, inexperienced young men are especially heartened when their coveted ladylove makes the first overtures.

This egalitarian approach to dating allows healthier reasons for choosing a marriage partner. Man-hunting for economic reasons becomes less of a motivating factor. As women become more independent financially, they will have less need to zero in on men as primarily a means of support. Personality and sexual compatibility can assume more importance in choosing a mate.

Other direct economic benefits accruing to the male from the effects of the women's liberation movement are numerous. Each one seems small in itself but they add up to a general trend—the gradual removal of sex bias in employment and related practices. A *Wall Street Journal* article tells how some states are now making unemployment compensation payments to men—and not just women—who quit jobs to follow working spouses who transfer or move to new jobs.[13]

A tax help publication informs single men that they are now allowed to deduct the expenses of dependent care while they work, a deduction which was previously limited to single women.[14]

Attempts are made to remove the sexual discrimination from our social security system. Witnesses at a congressional hearing testify that an aged wife automatically receives benefits when her covered husband retires while a husband who isn't covered is eligible for benefits only if his wife was providing more than half of his support. A suggestion is made that men be allowed the same benefits as women if they are divorced or widowed, and soon thereafter we read:

> The Supreme Court unanimously struck down a section of a federal law that denies widowers with children the same Social Security survivor's benefits as widows.[15]

In May of 1973, the Supreme Court ruled that male dependents of women in the military services are eligible for the same housing and medical benefits as female dependents of male servicemen.[16] Men will now be freer to join and live with their wives who are on active military duty.

The common conception that only females are economically discriminated against is false. As financial injustices based on sex are eliminated, many men as well as women will benefit.

Moving into the sexual arena brings us into contact with one of the more important blessings to men of the women's liberation movement. For years men have complained about the sexual passiveness and disinterest of their mates. Victorian woman has been an anathema with her inhibitions and lack of sexual pleasure and enjoyment. An adventurous, responsive, sexually aggressive woman who is an equal partner in the coupling process is the dream of many a man.

One of the most frequent complaints men make to me concerns the sexual inhibitions of their partners. Prudishness and lack of sexual initiative in woman have been decried and denounced by countless men. "If only my wife liked sex" reverberates from the lips of many a husband, and this lamentation is undoubtedly one of the main factors in the male's fascination with prostitutes.

Eons of sexual myth have proclaimed males as the main possessor of sexual drive. Young boys are taught that it is they who desire sex, not girls, and that they must conquer and subdue the unwilling female. "Men want sex, not women" is a burden that society has placed on the male of our species.

One interesting situation which sheds some humorous light on the sexual attitudes of our society is contained in the following witticism: if a man undresses in front of a woman he is arrested for exhibitionism; if a woman undresses in front of a male, the man is arrested for voyeurism.

Although this is an obvious overstatement of fact, it does contain a pathetic amount of truth. Our society has historically assumed that women are not excited by looking at the nude male body, that men are the main possessors of sexual energy and interest.

Women's liberation is changing all this. As we saw in earlier chapters, women are now receiving different messages concerning their sexuality and responding accordingly. Sex magazines for women, such as *Playgirl*, have become commonplace, and women are realizing they can be excited by nude male centerfolds. No longer is the male thought to be the sole repository of sexual drive. Multitudinous women are now taking a new, more active, participating interest in the sexual act. The female's tremendous capacity and innate interest in sex have been recently brought to the foreground and publicized by the feminist movement. Women are becoming more aggressive in the pursuit of sexual contact. The advantages to the male (and the female) are monumental.

As women pursue sex more actively, the male has an opportunity for increased sexual contact. The cultural tradition of man needing to seduce the reticent female becomes less relevant. As women recognize their own needs and rights for sexual pleasure, sexual contacts can occur on a mutually desired basis. Both men and women can have a more active sexual life, one in which both participants share equally.

The stereotype of the reluctant virgin "saving" herself for marriage is fading into the background. As women become independent financially and more confident of their ability to support themselves, they have less need to barter sex in exchange for the supposed economic security of marriage. They can use their own sexual desires as a guide rather than feeling they must use sex to trap a man into commitment.

Women are becoming more stimulating partners in bed, and their orgastic response is increasing. No longer is the female expected to lie flat on her back and be "used" by the male. This passive approach to intercourse in which the man must take all the responsibility for the sexual responsiveness of both partners is changing.

The feminist movement is publicizing sexual techniques which are more stimulating and rewarding to the female. Men have not always been good lovers; in fact, many have been downright inept. They have not understood the differences in female sexual response and the love act has suffered accordingly. As women assume more responsibility for making their sexual needs and wants known, the enjoyment of sex by both partners will increase.

Futhermore, women are learning how to better stimulate the male sexually. Feminist influenced young women often show a refreshing eagerness to learn about male sexuality and what turns their lovers on. They are less prudish and less inhibited and more willing to consider techniques previously considered to be appropriate primarily for the prostitute. Oral sex, anal sex, and masturbation of the male partner are looked on with a new favorable light.

Under the sway of the feminist movement, the bed can thus

become the scene of greater sexual pleasure for both men and women.

Abundant case histories are available to exemplify the increase in the male's sexual pleasure as women become more liberated and follow the messages of the feminist revolution. Many of these are along the conventional lines of husbands and wives enjoying sex more. Marcus immediately comes to mind, however, as his situation was somewhat different.

An understanding of Marcus is best gained from an entertaining quote from George Bernard Shaw's *Man and Superman* in which Tanner is expostulating on the holy sacrament of marriage.

> Marriage is to me apostasy, profanation of the sanctuary of my soul, violation of my manhood, sale of my birthright, shameful surrender, ignominious capitulation, acceptance of defeat. I shall decay like a thing that has served its purpose and is done with; I shall change from a man with a future to a man with a past; I shall see in the greasy eyes of all the other husbands their relief at the arrival of a new prisoner to share their ignominy. The young men will scorn me as one who has sold out: to the women I, who have always been enigma and a possibility, shall be merely somebody else's property—and damaged goods at that: a secondhand man at best.[17]

Now Marcus never knew Tanner, but his views on marriage were similar. At the ripe old age of twenty-five, he was a confirmed bachelor who was successfully winding up his law degree. Don't get me wrong, Marcus was not down on women: actually he loved them all, too much to give himself to only one.

Marcus's current problem arose out of his incessant sexual energy, a drive which was never but momentarily satisfied. Satiation was an unknown in the life of the youthful, fascinating, debonair Marcus. For several years he had been perplexed on handling his desire for almost nightly sexual contact. His phobic avoidance of spending more than two or three nights with any one woman was due to his fear of even the least suggestion of commitment.

Marcus was not uncaring and unsympathetic to his partners. He had no desire to exploit women and was constantly worried that he was "using" them. He just didn't want any involvement beyond satisfaction of sexual needs. Marcus was under parental pressure to enter his father's law firm and uphold the tradition of worldly success. Freedom from other responsibilities, especially marital or family obligations, was uppermost in his mind.

Marcus was in group and one day was telling us about the recent solution to his sexual problem.

"This women's liberation thing is really great. Imagine, women asking for equality with men . . . why it changes everything. You know how I've been feeling so guilty, always worrying if I am using a woman or taking unfair advantage of her. But if women are independent and don't want involvement either, everything's all right. Some of these young feminists just want a good fuck, and that's all there is to it . . . no hassle, no commitment, no remorse. Why these girls have as much sexual need as I do . . . and to think I always thought only guys were that way.

"I've hit upon this system that really seems to work. I go to the main library in the evening and look for a cute, braless girl . . . if she's wearing a feminist button that's even better. The trick is to find a liberated woman. Well, I approach her and start talking about women's liberation and how great equality between the sexes is . . . how great it is that guys and girls can come together and yet each retain their independence. I feel so strong about this that my enthusiasm must be contagious.

"If the girl seems receptive, I know we can work something out for the evening. It's so easy to be direct and honest and explain exactly where I stand. I tell the girl I'm looking for sexual contact with no commitment and that I admire women who feel the same way. Then I invite her over to my apartment and she usually comes."

Marcus stopped and looked around at the other group members. Finally he continued, "Well, what do some of you think? Am I being unfair to these girls?"

Marcus was looking for validation of his feeling that here was a way to take care of his sexual needs without being a cad in the process. He wanted to make certain that others, especially women in the group, approved of what he was doing. This is exactly the feedback he got. The general consensus was that as long as he was open and honest and stated exactly what he wanted and where he stood, there was no need to feel guilty or worry that he was taking advantage of anyone. One woman remarked on how not all girls interpret women's liberation as meaning this type of sexual freedom, but Marcus was already well aware of this. He just had a knack for finding women who agreed with him.

Women's Liberation had indeed simplified life for Marcus.

Leaving the sexual area and moving on to the professional scene brings to light some recent developments which will serve men in good stead. As equal job opportunities legislation is passed, new fields are opening up to men as well as women. Professions which have been dominated by women, such as nursing, are experiencing a pentration by men. Although still relatively few in number, the number of men entering nursing as a career has moved rather sharply upwards during the last few years. Sex discrimination against males in nursing is slowly disappearing, but problems remain. A male nursing student is quoted as stating, "I'm sick and tired of being called a male nurse. You never hear about female nurses, do you?"[18] Another newspaper article states:

> With the equal employment opportunity ruling, men can now hold the same jobs as women if they are qualified. "From what I've heard it looks like the job opportunities are better for men than women in jobs dealing with interior design."[19]

Home economics is a pursuit where radical change is in progress as more and more males apply. Not only are men entering the field as a career at the college level, but increasing number of high school boys are taking home economics courses.[20]

Other career opportunities which men have traditionally been discouraged from entering, such as secretarial practice, elementary school teaching, and medical technology should become increasingly receptive to males.

Sexuality has been used to discourage men from entering these fields traditionally reserved for women. Men are taught that nursing, interior design, home economics, and similar professions are feminine—that somehow they will be less of a man if they choose one of these careers. Their basic sexuality is questioned, often with homosexual innuendoes. The increasing number of men entering these fields indicates that the scene is changing. Men are now freer to select so-called feminine occupations with less fear of being labeled effeminate, queer, or a sissy.

The move toward allowing men paternity leave on an equal basis with women is occurring. A discrimination complaint on behalf of a New York City teacher was filed with the Federal Equal Employment Opportunity Commission because of the board of education's mothers-only rule on child-care leaves. The case was won on the basis that the mother-only rule "discriminates against male teachers as a class."[21]

Even derogatory job titles for men (and women) are changed by government edict. "Office boys" is changed to "office helpers," "busboys" becomes "waiters' assistants," and "newsboys" reappears as "newspaper carriers and vendors." A government publication states that fifty-two job titles are being revised to eliminate sex-stereotyping. The article goes on to inform us that men will not "apply for job vacancies calling for laundresses, maids, or airline stewardesses."[22]

It is only fair to remark that the bastion of female-only organizations, the League of Women Voters, has been successfully stormed by men. At its national convention, the League voted on May 7, 1974, to amend its bylaws and permit men full voting membership.

Chapter 14

The burdens placed upon men by the myth of masculine superiority far outweigh its advantages. **Eleanor Yachnes**

Male's Best Friend II?

Women's liberation is human liberation. Women's liberation stands for the removal of programmed role behavior which is based solely on one's sex. It is in this context that we can finally understand why males have as much to gain from women's liberation as females. For men have been as restricted and dominated by the concept of "masculinity" as women have been by "femininity."

Gordon and his lifestyle provide evidence of this claim.

In the initial meeting of a new group, the members were introducing themselves, and giving a brief description of their work. When it came to Gordon's turn, he quietly announced that he was a twenty-three year old househusband. His face colored a nice shade of pink as embarrassment took over. A few questions brought out that he had set up housekeeping with his older sister several years ago. While she held a job to provide financial support, Gordon did the cooking, cleaning, shopping, and caring for his sister's two-year-old child.

There was an awkward silence as others in the room looked at Gordon with skeptical, inquisitive glances. They appeared uneasy and somewhat disbelieving in hearing this strongly built young man announce that he was a full time housewife. Sexual stereotypes permeate the culture, and many assume that a youthful, vigorous male would not be primarily interested in house and child care. When they meet a man so inclined, they often make negative value judgments and are uncertain how to respond. Such is the reaction Gordon produced in the group.

Gordon was silent during the next two or three sessions. He had sensed (quite accurately, I may add) that other group members were perplexed by his declaration of occupation and had formed a somewhat doubtful impression of him. Gradually he entered into discussions and revealed more about his interests, hobbies, philosophical outlook, and so on. He became interested in other group members, gave excellent feedback, and in the process became an integral member of the group. Both the women and men began to understand Gordon, and their initial qualms disappeared.

Gordon's interest in women's liberation was slowly revealed. One day he showed up wearing a feminist button and seemed pleased to expound on the ideas and merits symbolized thereon. As the feminists gained momentum and received national attention, Gordon recognized the kinship he felt for the movement. He sympathized with women who were criticized for not fitting in with a "woman's role" in life. After all, had he not been deprecated for his own "unmasculine" behavior?

The women's movement was Gordon's main social and intellectual outlet. Whenever possible, he attended feminist meetings and was present without fail if they brought a prominent speaker to town. He never missed a chance to debate the topic and was always on the pro side. The monthly issue of *Ms.* magazine was read soon after its issue and he followed other feminist publications.

Why this absorbing fascination with women's liberation? Very simply, Gordon quickly sensed that the movement had great relevance to his own life. The promise of an amelioration in forces leading to sexual role structuring held out hope to Gordon—the chance to follow his own interests in homemaking and child care without undue criticism and pressure to follow more "manly" pursuits. He recognized that the women's movement was fighting the conditions which had damaged him during the upbringing process.

Only after Gordon felt accepted and comfortable did a serious discussion of his problems begin. It was well into the second month of meetings before he could reveal the deep humiliations he experienced as a child.

"I always did like to play house . . . can't remember a time when I didn't. Never knew there was anything wrong with it until . . . until . . . do you know what my parents did? They took me to a psychiatrist. I was only nine years old, just a nine-year-old kid and they made me see a shrink. They were worried about my interest in girl-type things, scared I would grow up to be a homosexual."

Gordon was exuding bitterness now, and he became more inflamed as the words streamed out.

"Well, can you imagine what that headshrinker said? Told my parents they shouldn't allow me to play with feminine things. . . actually took my playhouse away . . . my stove, my icebox, my dishes . . . everything I liked went. 'Make him play with boy's toys,' that's what the man said. 'Buy him a baseball bat and glove. Teach him how to act like a real boy. Don't let him grow up to be a sissy. Make him go out and shovel the walk or mow the grass. Toughen him up for sports. See that he plays football with the neighborhood kids.'

"That shrink sure accomplished something . . . played right into my folks' worries and made my life miserable. From then on all I heard was criticism and pressure to do things I hated. 'Don't be so feminine, Gordy. Go out and play soldiers with the boys.' Soon after the visit to the shrink they bought a cowboy gun and holster. They wanted me to go out and play war games . . . pretend I was shooting someone. I had to throw the gun in the river and tell them I lost it."

Gordon had experienced constant, unrelenting pressure to be more "masculine"—that is, live up to the stereotyped image of what a man must be in our culture. His own desires and interests were not only discouraged but openly forbidden. He was made to feel that there was something inherently wrong, something evil or shameful, in his basic nature. His sexual identification was questioned, and homosexual fears were instilled in him at an early age. The end result was a long series of blows to his self-concept, a man with serious damage to his confidence and self-image.

Other members were interested in the homemaking career Gordon set up for himself. During one meeting he explored in more detail the circumstances leading up to his present situation.

"High school graduation left me confused. I didn't know what to do. Everyone discouraged me from babysitting which is what I wanted. My parents and friends laughed when my interest in full-time child care came out. They insisted I work at something 'more becoming to a man.' Well, I tried . . . took this job selling appliances . . . hated every minute of it. It was so boring, so unrewarding. What a waste of life . . . and how I detested leaving home every morning. Never have I felt so trapped.

"Well, Karen, my older sister went and got pregnant . . . bless her soul. She had no intention of marrying the father and was going to give the child up for adoption. We always talked well together, and we finally worked out this system . . . she'd keep the baby and we would rent an apartment. I wanted to stay home and care for the child and she wanted to work. It was an ideal arrangement for both of us.

"It's worked out well, better than anything ever has for me. The boy is almost two years old now, and we get along great. What a joy to raise a baby and help him develop.

"I've had plenty of time for my art. You know how I like to play the viola and paint. I have more time now than ever for these things.

"There is a problem, though. Karen is finally in love and plans on marrying soon. I'm sure they will take the child. I knew this would happen sometime . . . couldn't last forever."

This was a realistic problem Gordon had to face. Someone asked him what his long range plans were, and he began explaining his hopes for the future.

"Someday I want to marry and have my own home and children. I know that this is what I want now that I don't have all those homosexual worries. I never used to feel there was a chance . . . now with this women's lib thing it's different. The difficulty is finding a woman who will work and let me stay home and take care of the kids. It's what I enjoy.

"You know, I've been meeting some interesting women at those feminist gatherings. The girl I'm spending so much time with lately wants a career. In fact she's working now . . . has no intention of staying home. She sees nothing wrong in my being a househusband. Maybe we can work out something together."

Gordon was mildly optimistic for the future. He realized there might be difficulties in setting up such a nontraditional marriage, but he thought a liberated woman would go along with his ideas.

As the months went along, Gordon gradually felt better about himself. The reactions of the men and women in the group were instrumental in this regard. The more they understood Gordon and his ideas, the more they liked him as a person. For one of the few times in his life, he was in a situation where people did not criticize him and try to coerce him into being more "masculine." Gordon sensed this growing acceptance and the sick, oddball self-image he learned as a child began fading into the background.

Coupled with this was a decrease in Gordon's homosexual fears. His parents' worries about his sexuality had taken their toll and left Gordon with serious sexual doubts. This is what caused him to seek therapy. In actuality, Gordon's fundamental sexual drive was toward women. His interest pattern was along so-called "feminine" lines, but this did not mean his sexual preference was for other men. Gordon's task had been to break this connection, and he had now come a long way.

"Women's liberation" was the other factor which helped Gordon accept himself and his nontraditional interests. The movement's emphasis on developing one's own lifestyle irrespective of the role structuring of society provided him with needed reassurance.

Gordon was moderately optimistic about his future, but I would not want to paint too rosy a picture. Serious problems remained. While he liked himself better, it was unlikely he would recover from all the damage his self-image sustained. Furthermore, our society still does not make it easy for men like Gordon who wish to live more of a traditional female life. He will undoubtedly continue to suffer ridicule and scorn because of his chosen ways.

As yet, we have not witnessed a mass movement of males into home and child care on the permanent basis desired by Gordon. His degree of role reversal remains unusual. Envy toward aspects of the female role is growing, however, among some males. Part of this is similar to the "grass is greener on the other side of the fence" phenomenon while a newer element is the male's awareness of how restricting suppression of "feminine" parts of his personality can be.

Women's liberation is turning the spotlight on the limitations and inequities of stereotyped sexual roles for both women and men. A society where both sexes are encouraged to give full expression to their abilities is the goal of many a feminist. One such woman has stated:

> If woman's role has emphasized the reproductive at the expense of other capabilities, so has man's role concentrated on breadwinning, often to the detriment of the quality of his interpersonal relations. Both roles, taken alone, are narrow. Neither, taken alone, is fully human.[1]

As women make vigorous, vocal efforts to heal the split in their own personalities and become whole persons, pressure is exerted on men to examine their own self-definition. A confrontation with the concept of "masculinity" is beginning to occur.

Girls in our society are programmed into a "feminine" role by a variety of family, school, and cultural forces. Boys are likewise channeled into a stereotyped sex role. "Boys over here, girls over there" has ruled the developmental process with a strong hand, limiting the potential of both sexes.

One powerful determinant molding "feminine" and "masculine" behavior is the concept of emotional health versus mental illness. In *Women and Madness,* Phyllis Chesler had done a good job showing how women can be labeled as mentally sick if they do not conform to traditional concepts of female behavior.[2] She has neglected the fact that men are subjected to the same forces. The life of Gordon is a case in point. Boys who develop an interest in "girlish pursuits" are often thought of as emotionally disturbed and the threat of homosexuality is frequently used to discourage any expression of their "feminine" side. Some, like Gordon, are taken to psychiatrists where the concept of sickness may or may not be reinforced, depending upon the orientation of the individual therapist. Men who do not wish to work in the outside world but would rather stay home and clean, cook, and sew are all too easily called abnormal. Homosexual innuendoes are whispered behind their backs. They are often thought of as odd or queer and can be forced into treatment for emotional problems. Undoubtedly some therapists tend to reinforce traditional "masculine" personality traits while others are more sophisticated.

The stereotype of "masculinity" is not an easy one to define, but generally it includes qualities such as aggressiveness, lack of tenderness, hardness, rationality, and a motivation for power and worldly success. Pushed to the extreme, the male image degenerates into the hard-hitting, violent, emotionally cold, superstud portrayed by characters of the James Bond ilk. There is a certain ironic tragedy in men striving to fit this grotesque stereotype of manliness.

Commercial and military sources reinforce and take advantage of this strong, aggressive male image. Merchandise is sold by clever advertisements which claim or suggest their product will help one be more "manly." Everything from deadly rifles to cigarettes, from liquor to overpowered automobiles is peddled in such a fashion. Marine billboards blare out their fatal message—enlist and we will make a man out of you. The implication is clear and subversive—you are not already a man but the shrine of "masculinity" can be attained by becoming tough and aggressive. Militant, belligerent, savage man is encouraged, and war is advanced one step.

A salient component of the "masculine" stereotype is the need to take charge and have control. Dominance over one's surroundings, including women, animals, and even nature itself, is sought after in a most pushful manner. To win, conquer, and subdue is the name of the game. Encounters are structured into won and lost categories, and equality is lost in the process.

An outgrowth of this is the ambition a male is supposed to show in seeking success. Outgoing, achievement oriented qualities will help make one's mark on the world. To enter the arena of economic struggle, compete in an industrious manner, and bring home the spoils of one's victorious enterprises is the goal of "masculine" behavior.

This aggressive, conquering attitude enters the sexual area. A red-blooded American male is expected to have a heightened sexual appetite which leads to the seduction of numerous women. A "love them and leave them" mentality is calculated to achieve manhood. Locker-room talk with its boasting of exaggerated sexual exploits is a natural sequence.

A dominant theme in the male image is the fear of emotional expression. Man is taught to be rational, logical, intelligent. The development of a "cool" attitude in which one is immune to emotional upset is widely emulated. Men are discouraged from showing their feelings, the classic example being the difficulty a man has in crying, either in public or by himself. This tends to inhibit the actual sensing and realization of emotion, positive feelings being missed in the process.

Many positive emotions are thus discouraged by the concept of "masculinity," especially those identified with "femininity." These include tenderness, affection, compassion, consideration, gentleness, cooperation, and sensitivity. The man who adheres closely to the traditional male stereotype thus forfeits a great deal in the process. Intimacy with another human, which is dependent upon the development of such feelings, is complicated and made difficult. Man's fear of the "feminine" in himself restricts his humanness, placing an unnecessary limitation on his potential. He ends up being only a part of what he could be, a definite loser as part of his being is denied expression.

Other problems can develop in an individual inculcated with the traditional male image. One of the common difficulties I see in young men is a loss of self-esteem when they do not fit the concept of "masculinity." Not being aggressive enough, failure to bed enough women, lack of athletic prowess, too much sensitivity, and a thousand other imagined "deficiencies" can leave the young male feeling insecure and inferior. Fears of sexual inadequacy are especially apt to arise in this situation, and development of overt sexual problems such as impotence and premature ejaculation can occur. In an article entitled *Sexual Difficulties Due to Stereotyped Role Playing*, Dr. Morton Kurland has examined how belief in the super-masculine man can lead to sexual difficulties for the male.[3] Reassurance and a discussion of the "masculine" stereotype with all its component myths can be helpful in counteracting these problems. The attention women's liberation is directing to the disadvantages of programmed sexual roles is making the deconditioning process simpler and easier to understand.

The role of "masculinity" is certainly not all negative. There are advantages in aggressiveness, rationality, and attaining positions of control and authority, especially in those whose personalities are inclined in these directions. These benefits are, however, often overbalanced by the pressures placed on men in the drive toward achievement and superiority. In an excellent article, psychiatrist Eleanor Yachnes discusses the various myths which she feels make up the "masculine" role. She states:

> It is almost impossible for men even to approach the task of living up to the godlike demands they and society in general, have placed upon them.[4]

Dr. Yachnes goes on to comment on the masculine myth which calls on the male to suppress his tender emotions. She feels this leads men to develop strain, psychosomatic illness, and sexual and work difficulties. This is a concept well recognized in psychiatry. Emotions which are contained and not given expression are one of the primary causes of psychological problems.

Another psychiatrist, Dr. Jerome Kummer from the University of California, addresses himself to this same question. He states:

> Our society, with substantial subcultural differences, imposes restraints on men for both giving and receiving affection. If my thesis is correct, then difficulties should be expected to arise intra-physically in our males because of deprivation both in regard to output and input of affection.[5]

He further speculates that the shorter life span for the male may be due to this very suppression of emotion.

Still another psychiatrist, Dr. Norman Zinberg from the Harvard Medical School, sheds further light on this topic. He appears to be well aware that the women's movement has been instrumental in our recent questioning of the traditional "masculine" role. He states:

> The advantages of this [masculine] role, while obvious on the surface, are debatable when seen in the context of our society, and recently they have been questioned sharply by a number of writers, chiefly women. Our clinical work contributes evidence of its cost to the man.[6]

If feminists and psychiatrists are at last beginning to recognize the inherent disadvantages of the "masculine" role, is the man in the street doing likewise? This is a difficult question, but there is evidence that more men are sensing how limited and trapped they are by the role society has assigned them as a male. This may account for the hostility with which they greet women's liberation. They realize women are being freed and developing new options while they sense no corresponding hope for themselves. It may be tremendously more difficult for the male to shed the negative aspects of "masculinity" than it is for the female to do likewise with her "femininity."

In the article previously referred to, Dr. Zinberg examines this issue. He feels women are having an easier time changing their traditional role because historically they have had many functions other than that of wife-mother-housekeeper. The male, however, has little or no historical precedent for anything other than the success oriented-husband-breadwinner-warrior role.[7]

We are living in an era when it is more acceptable and feasible for a woman to shed the wife-mother role and establish a successful career than it is for a man to abandon the breadwinner role and turn to full-time child and home care. Women have an increasing number of options to choose from—they can decide to marry or stay single, have children or not, stay home and be a full-time housewife, or enter the labor market and work towards a career. Seldom does the male in our culture have such a wide range of options. He is still expected to be the primary breadwinner which influences other choices.

As women's liberation pursues the disadvantages of programmed sexual roles, attention is focused on the "masculine" and "feminine" traits within all of us. The road leading to an integration of these elements can indeed be stormy for some individuals as the following history illustrates.

Joe's attempts to relate romantically to a woman consistently ended in disaster. His more superficial contacts and friendships went fine, but as soon as closeness, trust, and intimacy were called for, he ran as if pursued by the devil.

By many outward signs, Joe appeared to be leading a successful and rewarding life. He was a dignified, calm, considerate young man, who, at the age of twenty-four, had accomplished far more than most. As a technical writer, his abilities were outstanding and he had already received several honors for his lucid and imaginative professional texts. He received excellent financial remuneration and saved more than half his salary. Inwardly, however, he was a maze of conflict and was torn by tension and a fear of inadequacy.

It was during the first meeting or two that Joe launched into his attitudes toward women.

"You bet I'm having trouble with girls. When I begin to know one well, I get disgusted and break things off. I can't believe all women are as bad as the ones I meet."

"You seem to be rather down on women, Joe."

"I suppose I am pretty angry. But they're so darn superficial and inane . . . can't even carry on an intelligent conversation. They don't think . . . just let their feelings hang out all over the place and act hysterical. And the way they play games with a guy . . . never say anything direct and honest . . . always beating around the bush and acting innocent and naive. Why the hell can't they just say what's on their mind?

"The way they play up to a man . . . pretending to be inferior with all their obsequious mannerisms. They hang all over you like an appendage . . . let you win to flatter your ego."

Joe finally glanced at me and laughed.

"You might say I get carried away when I talk about women."

I had to agree with Joe. The subject certainly aroused his hostility. He held a most unflattering view of women which probably had little to do with the reality of the ones he met. He thought of all women as an extreme of the feminine stereotype and forced them, at least in his own mind, into this image.

Although not discernible for some time, it became apparent that Joe's attitudes toward women reflected his early experiences in the parental family. In this situation, he learned stereotyped sexual role behavior. Joe's mother was many of the things he disliked in women. She was dependent, inclined toward the hysterical, unable to think for herself, and servant-like in her relationship with Joe's father. He saw his mother as being a bottomless pit who made insatiable demands on her husband. To think that all women were like this aroused the fear in Joe.

For some time, Joe was in a group therapy situation. Here he met women who differed substantially from his preconceived, negative view. He was confronted with intelligent, independent women who were anything but superficial and inane, women who would in no way act inferior and play up to his male ego. For the first time he heard the messages of women's liberation and began to understand the damage that programmed sexual roles can produce. Before his own eyes, he witnessed women struggling with their own concept of "femininity," trying hard to find room for strength and appropriate aggression within their own personalities. These women would certainly not make the inordinate demands on a man which Joe so greatly feared.

Sexuality had been a common topic in group. Joe's sexual life had been moderately active, and he had no particular trouble functioning. But sex had not been great, mostly due to Joe's feeling that his partners remained passive and expected him to do all the "work." Undoubtedly, Joe was at least in part responsible for this sexual pattern as it fit his preconceived notion of how men and women were different sexually. Now Joe had a chance to hear independent women discuss their sexual lives, and he attained new insight. He was reassured that some women would take equal responsibility for the sexual act and that the entire responsibility would not be his.

A dramatic confrontation occurred, a confrontation between Joe's stereotyped image of females and the reality of the women in the group. Joe did not back down or run, and the end result was a gradual realization that many women did not fit his demeaning view. For the first time, he began to see women as real people and not as a stereotype of "femininity." He gave women a chance, and his liking for them grew substantially.

A confrontation of another kind occurred in group, one that was more painful for Joe. During one of the meetings, a young woman named Becky turned to him and asked, "Joe, I've been wondering why you are so obsessed with proving your masculinity. Are you feeling inadequate or something?"

Joe turned purple on the spot but could not avoid the situation as all eyes riveted on him. He sputtered and fumed and finally muttered a few words about how ridiculous a question that was. He could go no further at this time.

The next session was started by Joe.

"I've been thinking about that question from last week. Maybe there is more to it than I thought at first. Dad is such a cold, calm, rational person . . . just takes over and handles everything. He's really got an iron grip on his emotions. His whole life is his business . . . no time for anything else. I suppose that's what I've thought a male should be—aggressive, have a successful career, and run the show."

Here Joe stopped and glanced slowly around the room. He was visibly upset and showing more emotion than ever before in group. Slowly he regained his composure and continued.

"Do you know something crazy? I don't think that's really me, and that's what I've tried to be all these years. What a tragic fate . . . to try and be something you aren't. I'm not like Dad at all. I've got all this emotion stirring around inside and I try to deny it. When I feel tender or affectionate I get scared and run away. How strange . . . how strange.

"It must be something like you women have been talking about. Now I understand why women's liberation is so important to you. You've been taught to be something you aren't . . . to suppress your independence and aggression and act 'feminine.' But the same thing has happened to me. I was conditioned to be 'masculine' . . . to deny my feelings and act hard and cold like Dad."

Joe was finally putting some pieces together. He had learned sexual role behavior from his parents. Men were unemotional, ambitious, and above all rational. He paid a heavy price, not only in being unable to set up a rewarding relationship with a woman but by having part of his own personality split off and buried. One day Joe started talking about his new feelings toward women.

"I sure am beginning to like intelligent women. It seems the more successful and capable a woman is, the more I'm attracted to her. It's great to realize women aren't all a bunch of clinging vines . . . that they really can be stimulating and exciting to be with. And you, Becky, you make me angry. Here you are, one of the most brilliant persons I've ever met and you say you're afraid of becoming too successful . . . that a man won't like you then. That's bullshit. The more accomplished you are, the more fun you are to be with. I'm tired of women pretending to be inadequate and not living up to their potential."

Becky is the young woman you met in Chapter 4, and she

heard every word Joe said. It would turn out that this was instrumental in helping her overcome her fears of being too "masculine" just as her words helped Joe overcome his dread of being "feminine" for having a sensitive, emotional personality.

Joe could now begin the process of combining the "masculine" and "feminine" parts of his personality. This would not be easy, but at least he had new direction and knew where many of the problems were. No longer would he feel inadequate or less of a man because of his sensitive, compassionate nature. He could stop depositing all these emotions on women and begin giving them credit for being intelligent and rational.

As Joe stopped fighting the tender emotions stirring within him, tension and frustration subsided. Trust and intimacy became less frightening and he ceased running from close, romantic relationships. In short, Joe became more of a complete human being who no longer needed to deny an elemental part of his personality.

Chapter 15

Sexual equality should properly mean sexual fulfillment, the woman realizing her masculinity through man, and the man realizing his femininity through woman.   **Alan Watts**

Spirituality

As women's liberation forces an examination of the male stereotype, more subtle manifestations come to mind. The concept of "masculinity" includes elements such as progress, achievement, working for the future, molding the world into something different. There is an emphasis on outgoing aggressiveness with the goal of change in mind—putting our stamp on the world if you may. An assumption is made that things should be different or better, a belief which leads to a manipulative, exploitative approach toward life.

This aggressive, growth oriented, improvement minded philosophical outlook has tended to dominate the earth, at least the Western world and increasingly of late the Eastern world. It is an outgrowth of Western philosophy in which scientific materialism rules. Goethe's Faustian ideals of ever upward and onward striving toward the ultimate prevail. We have the rule of Nietzsche's "superman" and the worship of an increasing gross national product.

There is another way of conceptualizing and meeting life, a manner of feeling and thinking which is more in tune with "feminine" and spiritual qualities. It is a direct outgrowth of Eastern religious philosophy, and as such is difficult for those raised in the Western tradition to understand and appreciate.

Instead of an emphasis on conquering and subduing life, there is an inclination toward joining and becoming part of the whole. One adapts to nature and flows with it instead of fighting and struggling toward some elusive state of progress. The individual becomes one with creation through a process of co-mingling with the surroundings. There is passive belonging and a deep feeling of acceptance of all that is.

The concept of progress is recognized as an elusive figment of the imagination. There is eternal change, a continual ebb and flow with no forward movement. Life is a circle which cannot be squared and those who try obtain nothing but frustration. We have entered the universe of Lao-tse and the Chinese Tao, the world view of Hermann Hesse and his Siddhartha, the *Magic Mountain* of Thomas Mann—in short, the world of the Buddha himself.

Have we strayed afar from women's liberation? No, not really, for the world of the Buddha is dependent on qualities which have traditionally been described as "feminine." The aggressive approach of "masculine" pursuit and domination is antithetical to this Eastern value of serene acceptance and belonging. Man cannot enter the world of the Buddha until he accepts the "feminine" side of his makeup.

Spiritual qualities have long been identified with the eternal "feminine." Love, tenderness, meekness, service, and acceptance do not mesh with a strong "masculine" stereotype. A more inner-directed, contemplative, ethereal approach to life is an outgrowth of what we traditionally label "feminine." Men who are intent on remaining "masculine" are forever separated from their spiritual nature, at least in an Eastern philosophical sense. This is perhaps not true in Christianity with its historical roots of bloodshed, active martyrdom, the slaughter of the Crusades, the Spanish Inquisition, and Calvinism with its emphasis on worldly deeds and accomplishments.

There is little question in my mind that more males are recognizing and accepting their spiritual or "feminine" qualities. Women's liberation has been a potent force in this direction. As women dramatically encourage and develop their so-called "masculine" characteristics of aggression, pursuit, and outgoing activity, men are examining and confronting the "feminine" aspects of their personalities. Those who listen and like what they find are sensing freedom to develop their spiritual, contemplative nature. The actual number of males moving in this direction, while on the upswing, still appears to be relatively small. They tend to be concentrated on college campuses or other environments where there is an emphasis on the examination of underlying values by which one lives. This affirmation of spiritual "feminine" values by men is manifested in a variety of ways. One of the more abundant and obvious is the movement toward religious expression through meditation. By its very nature, meditation is contemplative and accepting—it is inner directed in the extreme. Meditation is not something that can be successfully pursued through a conquering, aggressive attitude. It is part and parcel of the movement toward Eastern religious concepts which has become so predominant of late.

Young men with whom I have contact are increasingly turning away from the competitive, "masculine," rat-race type life which society has structured for them. They are repelled by the surrounding acquisitive minded culture and attempt to establish a more peaceful way of life. Of prime importance is sufficient leisure time to develop one's inner nature, and work for work's sake is frowned upon.

These young men are motivated to earn only enough money to support a basic, simple life. Many wish to enter service oriented fields which traditionally give little financial remuneration and place no emphasis on advancement or worldly success. Although difficult, some choose to leave our accomplishment stressing culture and opt for the backwoods. Others distance themselves psychologically, living a life of calculated isolation from the hectic bustle surrounding them.

Rejection of the "masculine" achievement minded philosophy leads to a new interest in child care and household tasks. It is not surprising to read that, in some surveys, more men than women favor swapping traditional male and female roles.[1]

For some men, maximizing their potential may mean staying home, meditating, and developing inner spiritual qualities. This is a lifestyle which has been actively discouraged in the male. Now women's liberation is demonstrating to perceptive males that options outside of traditional "masculine" role behavior can offer great rewards.

For many years, Pierre was known to all as the successful, hard-working dentist. He had striven hard to attain this image, and maintaining it took most of his waking hours. As a thirty-seven-year-old family man, he was respected for his professional competence and his efforts at community service. Now his life had reached a crucial phase of self-evaluation.

Pierre's efforts to achieve success had occupied him so completely that there had never been time for an evaluation of his goals—that is until he developed hypertension about a year ago. Medication was necessary to reduce the blood pressure to acceptable levels and tranquilizers were needed to control his tension. Pierre's physician laid it on the line—his ambitious drive for achievement and compulsive dedication to work would likely shorten his life span.

Pierre was finally forced to think about the life purposes he had been raised to accept. When I first saw him he was confused, angry, and blaming many of the difficulties on his wife.

"Sure I'm tense . . . have been for some time but never stopped to think about it. But who wouldn't be? All this pressure to be a success. 'Get ahead! Get ahead in this world!' That's what everyone screams at you. So I work . . . work hard all my life and look what I've got . . . high blood pressure and an excellent chance for an early death.

"I feel like there's a noose around my neck . . . that I'm trapped with no way to get out. My wife spends more and more money, the kids get more and more expensive, and I have to earn the damn stuff. Meg just takes it all for granted . . . she wants to live like royalty.

"What's all this success talk anyway? Some life it leads to. The more I think about it, the angrier I get. Everyone looks up to me, everyone respects me. I'm the man people admire. But what good is that? I don't even have time to spend with my children. There's no time left to live!"

By now, Pierre was livid with rage. He was sweating profusely, his face had turned beet red, and he looked as though he were about to pop a blood vessel. He was taking a hard, long look at his life and felt cheated, as if he had been played for a fool. There was a dawning recognition of what he had missed in life and his whole being was reacting. The fury continued.

"Here I have three kids, three beautiful children, and I don't even know them. The eldest is already fifteen . . . before I know it, he'll be gone from home. I do so little with the kids . . . never had a chance to take care of them . . . spent all my hours supporting the family. We're like strangers to each other. I don't know the kids and they don't know me.

"The worst part, the most pathetic part, is that it's gone forever. No way can I go back and capture what I've missed. Life will be over soon, and I've been left out of the most important part."

In the depth of his pathos, Pierre was probably exaggerating the plight of his life, but I could well understand his feelings. There was dire truth in what he was upset about. Pierre was one more player in the human tragedy of programmed role behavior.

Pierre worked overtime being a full-scale success symbol. He did this for years without ever questioning the ultimate rewards. Now, as he began realizing the terrible price paid, there was bitterness and a deep sense of loss. Pierre's wife, Meg, was blamed for trapping him into this fruitless struggle for achievement. What Pierre didn't realize was that his own motivations, not Meg's, were largely responsible for setting up this unrewarding lifestyle.

Pierre was trapped by forces over which he had little control, of that there was no doubt. They were the forces, however, of an early family upbringing and of a society which inculcated the "masculine" role.

Pierre was raised to be a "real man" with all the implied false glory. This became clear as he talked about his family background.

"Dad's a physician, completely dedicated to his work. I grew up in awe of him. We never were very close. I guess our relationship is what you would describe as formal. We all looked up to Dad as the head of the family. He was clearly the boss. And he was so successful in his work. We admired him for that.

"Mom, she was the weak, sick one. As long as I can remember, she's had emotional problems . . . depression Dad calls it. We humored her and dismissed what she said as complaining. Dad treats her like another patient. He keeps her on drugs for her depression.

"I always liked my mom better . . . she's kind and

considerate. We've stayed pretty close through the years. I like being around her. But you know, she hopes for the same sort of things from me that Dad does.

"The men in our family are expected to achieve and be successful. I have to work as hard as Dad, even if it means killing myself in the process. I was never allowed to relax as a kid. My parents always wanted me to be on the go . . . competing in sports, pursuing this or that project, studying for good grades. I liked to walk in the woods . . . look at birds . . . fish . . . just sit under a tree and do nothing. But I was never allowed to do these quiet things . . . that was being shiftless and unproductive. I can remember Dad saying that if I was lazy I would end up being a failure as a man."

Pierre was thus programmed to work hard, take little or no time to enjoy the simple things in life, and above all become successful. This, he was told, is what makes a real man. Pierre lived out this prescribed pattern. When he married, I suspect that he, rather than his wife, was the primary motivator behind the long hours of work, absence from the home and children, and emphasis on material prosperity.

Pierre's wife eventually pointed the way out of this "success" trap which was killing her husband. She was close to him and sensed his deep frustration. Her interest in women's liberation led her to have more realization of what was going on, and for some time she had been interested in reestablishing her own career. Meg was a registered nurse and had worked for several years before her marriage to Pierre. His conventional attitudes toward the division of labor between husband and wife led to her forced retirement before the advent of their vows. Pierre was to be the sole breadwinner—to accept financial help from his wife would be damaging to his concept of what a man should be. After all, was not this the male's primary function?

Meg had not been unhappy at home. The children came, and she settled into a mother's role which proved to be rewarding. She enjoyed the material things which her successful husband provided, and she appreciated the community prestige in which the family was held. But Pierre was dead wrong—Meg was not dependent on these comforts and signs of worldly attainment. She had accepted them mostly because he was so insistent on providing them.

Now the children were older, and Meg was not needed as much at home. She had wanted to return to nursing for the past two or three years, but the proud, achievement directed Pierre could not allow this. The feminist movement was giving Meg strength and she was about to challenge her husband and insist on her right to more independence. She sensed, however, that Pierre was now questioning his own life values and that she could help both herself and him at the same time.

Husband and wife started talking. Pierre's initial anger toward Meg cooled as he began recognizing how his ambitious drive toward success had trapped him. Long discussions on stereotyped role behavior followed, and women's liberation frequently entered the picture. Pierre was desperate about his life and willing to listen to anything. The rage at his unrewarding life served as a motivating force to explore new behavior.

Amazing things happened. Pierre began to understand how Meg really wanted her own career, and he saw the advantages in sharing the financial support of the family with his wife. The vision of a new future arose where he would be more than a success symbol. If women could abandon the traditional concept of "femininity," could he not leave behind the concept of "masculinity" which had served him so disastrously?

Meg returned to her nursing and Pierre began to relax. He was gradually able to take more time off from work by cutting back on his dental practice. The discussions had been good for Pierre, and he did not feel his manhood threatened as leisure developed. He could now explore all of the early interests which had been forbidden by his parents.

First came Pierre's three children. Time to be with them was precious, and he used it to the fullest. Strangeness disappeared as close bonds were established. Pierre enjoyed being home and sharing in household tasks and family gatherings, elemental parts of life from which he had long been excluded. He developed his dormant cooking talents and learned to sew and knit, and to repair his own automobiles.

Participation in the outdoors took root as Pierre went fishing, hiking, and camping with his children. Deeper feelings of communion with nature developed as he was at last able to "just sit under a tree and do nothing." His suppressed wish for solitude, peacefulness, and contemplation came to the fore.

Pierre became interested in Transcendental Meditation. An inner calm supplanted his previous tension, and daily meditation sessions became a regular part of his life. Tranquilizers were dispensed with. Pierre came into contact with his inner spiritual essence, and a full sense of meaning pervaded his life.

Gradual changes began to occur in Pierre's sexual life. Sex for Pierre had always been competitive with a certain driving, aggressive quality. This is not surprising in view of his need to prove he was a man. As Pierre abandoned the "masculine" stereotype, sex was calmer and more enjoyable. To his surprise, he discovered increasing sexual energy. Furthermore, he had more time to devote to sex.

Pierre summed things up in these words.

"The real breakthrough point was when I realized how my parents taught me a man must act in certain ways. It was ruining my life, actually killing me. Why I'm more of a complete man now than I ever was when success dominated my existence. Sure I'm lucky to have Meg for a wife. Without her willingness to share the financial burden things would have been more difficult to change, but I think it could have been done anyway. I was trapping myself . . . no one else was.

"But one thing we never talked about . . . probably the most important of all. I love my children and don't want them growing up with all the paralyzing stereotypes I had. When I recognized what was happening to my children, how I was teaching them what Dad taught me, then I knew things had to change. This is as true for my girl as it is for the boys. By teaching them that men have to be hard working, competitive, success hungry creatures and women are to be housewives, I was destroying their lives."

Several types of meditation have recently gained acceptance in our culture, Transcendental Meditation as practiced by Pierre being only one form. Zen Buddhist "sitting" or zazen and some types of yoga are other common modes. Although different, these methods of meditation all emphasize an awareness of breathing and a turning of our attention inwards. Through regular practice, contact is established with all the facets of our personality, including elements long suppressed. A feeling of inner completeness and unity is developed.

Sexual stereotypes have interfered with this inner unification and sense of wholeness. Alan Watts has conceptualized this as follows:

> So far from being a form of strength, the masculine rigidity and toughness which we affect is nothing more than an emotional paralysis. It is assumed not because we are in control of our feelings but because we fear them, along with everything in our nature that is symbolically feminine and yielding. But a man who is emotionally paralyzed cannot be male, that is, he cannot be male in relation to female, for if he is to relate himself to a woman there must be something of the woman in his nature.[2]

A corresponding analysis could be developed for women as they have been taught to reject the "masculine" part of their nature.

Meditation searches for a quiet, serene acceptance of all the diversity within us. This cannot be forced or actively controlled. In fact, the harder we strive to attain this lucid calm, the more impossible it becomes. To the beginner or one trained in the aggressive, "masculine" pursuit of goals, this can seem frustrating and paradoxical. If a desired objective cannot be energetically worked toward, how can it be attained? It is at this point that the more "feminine" qualities of passive waiting and acceptance of all-that-is must take over. If part of our personality (which is so often the forbidden "feminine" or "masculine" side) is unacceptable, there is no way to be at peace with the totality of our nature.

Ancient Eastern religions have long recognized that everything is composed of male and female elements. No attempt is made to dichotomize the "feminine" and "masculine" into irreconcilable opposites. No premium is placed on the separation of these qualities. In fact, just the opposite holds sway. The spiritual essence of many Eastern religions is the successful combination of the male and female parts which reside within all of us. The ultimate destiny of the soul is thought to be the achievement of completion through the union of polar opposites within our body. Another way of saying this is that when human beings can accept all the parts of themselves, they can be more deeply in touch with humanity.

Pierre experienced a new sense of relaxation and a decrease in tension as he became involved in daily meditation. This is a common result, one that is not mysterious or difficult to understand. Tension is the hallmark of conflict, of opposing forces struggling within us. If a man tries to suppress his female side or a woman attempts to suppress her male side, anxiety develops and much unnecessary energy is expended. When the female and male within us are recognized, combined, and harmonized, we come to experience a calmness as tension melts away. Our total being can be strengthened as we feel a sense of fullness and harmony.

This calmness is not soporific. It is full of vitality and charged with energy. This comes about in part because our psychic energy is no longer wasted in an unnecessary struggle to repress an elemental part of our being. It also comes about because we use less energy in pursuing futile drives. There is less concern with striving for domination, possession, or control.

As the mind is freed from tensions, the body can undergo beneficial transformations. This is crucial in much of psychosomatic medicine where there is a direct connection between psychic conflicts and physical illness. The improvement in Pierre's hypertension is one example of this. As he became more relaxed, his blood pressure decreased, and he had less need for medication.

Meditation and the amalgamation of our male and female parts into a unitary whole can have a direct effect on sexuality. We no longer have to fight sexual traits which were previously felt to be appropriate only to the opposite sex. When we accept the "feminine" and "masculine" within us, there is no longer a need to prove we can live up to some sexual stereotype. The competitive element is taken out of sex.

Pierre's sex life had a driving, proving quality to it until he was able to accept the "feminine" side of his personality. As the battle to suppress part of his sexual nature ceased, sex became more spontaneous and enjoyable. The essence of good sex is a receptivity to all our inner feelings and sensory responses. When there is a male-female conflict within us, this becomes impossible.

In sex, we must give up control in order to attain full enjoyment. By its very nature, the orgasm is beyond our control. Sexual ecstasy for both sexes involves self-surrender. It has a wild, unrestrained quality as our ego boundaries are loosened.

For those raised in an environment where "masculine" control is emphasized, this is difficult. Eastern religions such as Zen Buddhism are dependent on "feminine" traits where the drive for ascendancy and domination is relaxed. Successful meditation involves an abandoning of the need to control everything within and around us. The effect on sexual enjoyment is often noticeable and salutary.

A common fallacy is that sexual equality will adversely affect sexual pleasure. Many people assume that an abandonment of traditional "feminine" and "masculine" behavior indicates a lessening of sexual desire. As the sexes become more similar, it is feared sexual relationships will suffer.

In actuality, the reverse seems to happen. This is historically demonstrated by those Eastern religions where sex is treated as an art and a sacrament. Tantra yoga is an excellent example of this. By emphasizing the joining of the "feminine" and "masculine" in each of us, the unity of female and male in sexual intercourse takes on a more natural dimension. No longer does our partner seem strange or forbidding. The combining of diverse elements which was begun within us becomes complete through the sexual act. Sexual ecstasy is heightened.

The contemplative, inactive sex of Tantra yoga is in contrast to the hurried, forced intercourse which occurs when female and male are dichotomized into irreconcilable opposites who meet only in the sexual embrace. In Tantra yoga, nothing is done to actively excite sexual energy; instead it is simply allowed to develop its own momentum. This makes it possible to greatly prolong sexual intercourse, a primary goal of Tantra yoga and other Eastern religions which elevate sex to a position of spirituality.

This prolongation of the sexual act can lead to the acme of sexual pleasure. The timing of sexual response becomes less important. The slow, relaxed pace allows for an in-depth exploration of foreplay. Anxiety as to whether orgasm will occur is relieved, and sexual energy flows spontaneously.

Chapter 16

A woman cannot demand potency in a man—she has to elicit it. And since a really gratifying sexual experience for a woman depends on male potency, any attempts to grab at sex cannot be completely successful.   **Natalie Shainess, M.D.**

Some Problems Caused for Men

Not all men respond enthusiastically to women's liberation. This is an understatement of the obvious, a matter readily discernible to all who listen for the male cries of outrage and suspicion. Some men are fearful and alarmed without knowing why. Others feel that the feminist movement is a force to be guarded against and actively battled as it leads to tumultuous problems in their lives. What are some of these difficulties which women's liberation is bringing about for men?

"My wife insisted on getting a job . . . now all we do is fight."

Alexander announced his beastly plight in irate tones. His five years of marriage had gone smoothly—that is until his wife upset the balance with her momentous decision. Alexander was enraged that a wife of his would dare undermine his head-of-the-household authority. He took good care of Irene and felt that he satisfied her needs. Frustration and indignation welled within him when Irene deliberately left the security of the home he had so diligently furnished.

Why would a man become so incensed at his wife obtaining outside employment? After all, this common occurrence is greeted by many husbands with relief and gratitude. It was in response to this very question that the riled up Alexander began his diatribe.

"She insisted on working. I told her over and over that it

wasn't necessary . . . that I would work longer hours if she wanted more money. But all she talked about was women's liberation and wanting her independence.

"Those women's libbers stirred up Irene. She was content at home until those frustrated old maids got her in their clutches . . . then she started bellyaching. I can't see what she has to bitch about. She had it damn easy at home . . . no kids to take care of . . . all she had to do was clean the house and fix my meals.

"And you ask why I'm upset just because Irene wanted a job. You're a man . . . you should know. Don't you provide for your wife? Why, I had to make my own lunch the other day . . . that's what it's come to . . . five years of marriage and suddenly I have to make my own lunch.

"Well, I'll tell you this . . . I won't allow it. No wife of mine has to work. I'm more capable than that."

Alexander was raised to be "masculine," a condition which manifested itself in some curious, at times almost humorous, ways. During high school, he showed an initial interest in photography but soon switched to football because he thought it was more appropriate to his maleness. The fact that he didn't like football was a minor consideration quickly brushed aside. In a calculated effort to obtain power and authority, Alexander ran for class office and was elected. He was carefully building his "masculine" image.

Next came weight lifting and body building with dietary control and weekly measurement of such important things as chest circumference, waist size, and muscle girth. An impressive, manly physique was deemed essential.

This magnificent body could only do things appropriate to strength and endurance. Karate lessons were suitable, but dancing and ping pong were naturally frowned upon. At one point Alexander froze both ears. Even in the dark of severe winter, ear flaps could not be used as others might think he was a softy. Being uncomfortable and freezing were sure signs of male hardiness.

Alexander early realized that a true bona fide man served his share of time in the military. Dreams of heroic glory were his companions as he enlisted in the U.S. Navy. He was upset at being discharged a month early from the armed forces, being fearful people would think he had not done his duty.

Now it was time to obtain a wife. After all, isn't a real man supposed to marry and support a woman? Alexander went about the process much as he did buying a variety of soup from the supermarket. Not any woman would do. She had to possess remarkable beauty and social poise, attributes which would certainly impress others with his desirability as a male. One of Alexander's main pleasures was to buy his woman fancy clothes and parade her up and down the street for all to see.

Sexual attitudes often reveal important dimensions of a person's personality. Alexander was suspicious of sensuous pleasure, fearing that this would distract him from more important life tasks. Before marriage, Alexander complained that women were not satisfied with a kiss—they wanted more. Intercourse with his wife was regular and efficient, his body functioning like a well-oiled machine with worn grooves. Irene never climaxed, but then that was her problem, not his.

More of Alexander's underlying feeling toward women was bared as he reacted to the Equal Rights Amendment placard on my office door.

"I've been noticing that sticker on your door. I can't understand why a woman would want such a thing. They have so much to lose. The law carefully guarantees them all this protection, and now they want to throw it away. It's like Irene . . . she isn't able to think logically, and I have to help make her decisions. She complains that I'm too domineering, that I try to mold her to my ideas. But a man doesn't have any other choice . . . there are things a woman can't do for herself."

Alexander's whole definition of himself as a person was tied in with his masculine image—including taking care of and supporting a wife. When Irene heeded the messages of women's liberation, she destroyed the fragile underpinnings of his confidence. Irene's renouncement of the protective nest which Alexander worked so hard to provide was, in his view, a direct slap at his ability and success as a man.

Such a direct challenge to Alexander's adequacy could not go by without producing major conflict and hostility. Horrendous arguments continued to dominate the relationship. Alexander felt he was fighting for his integrity as a man. He was too insecure to change the ideas with which he was raised, and Irene was not about to give up her right to a career. Survival of the marriage was seriously in doubt.

To the man steeped in the tradition of dominance, authority, and power, women's liberation appears as a distinct threat. As women become independent and achieve positions of greater control, these men sense mastery slipping from their grasp. They view this as an uncalled for usurpation of power, power which belongs naturally to the male by dint of birthright.

In his book, *Sexual Suicide*, George Gilder views this realignment of male-female influence and supremacy with dismay and fear for the future of society. He sees the male ego as extremely fragile and ready to collapse if traditional supports are challenged by the feminist movement. As the male is forever doomed to play an inferior role in the family, he can validate his manhood only in action and achievement of economic success. The female loves her male for his strength and protectiveness, for his ability to protect and support her.[1]

While Mr. Gilder's general picture of the world is open to serious question, some men are indeed as insecure and precarious as he paints them to be. They view the strong, independent woman as a distinct threat to their personal adequacy. These are the men who are finding their lives severely complicated by the women's movement, Alexander being one example. They lack the inner resources to make the necessary change in their lives in a constructive manner.

The male accustomed to unquestioning flattery and adulation experiences shock as he meets women's liberation. Reliance on the girl friend or wife to deprecate her own abilities and build the male image of her loved one has been in vogue in our culture. "Always let the man win" and "make certain you don't act more intelligent than *him*" have been concepts permeating male-female relationships. Now this is changing, or at least changing for those women influenced by the feminist movement. Unqualified support will no longer be available to their men, and those males needing it are in for rough times ahead.

The employment and economic situation for the sexes is changing. No longer can men count on built-in advantages over women in obtaining a job or receiving higher pay. As the movement toward greater equality in employment practices moves ahead, real or implied threat is perceived by many a man. There are powerful forces in our society, notably the labor unions, which persist in viewing this trend with fear and trembling. They foresee a situation where multitudes of needy men are forced into unemployment because women are making off with their jobs.

There is no question that men are under vigorous economic competition from women. No longer is it unusual for a male to work under a woman boss or for a husband to earn less than his wife. Rivalry with women for career advancement and higher salaries is occurring at most levels. To the secure male, this presents no more threat than the normal competition with other men which has always occurred. The man who is worried about his masculine adequacy, however, often interprets this as a special menace and may react with hostile retaliation. Always the advocate of masculine vulnerability, George Gilder has expressed this as follows:

> A man who does not make as much money as the significant women in his life—his girl friend, wife, and closest coworkers—will often abandon his job and will pursue women in the plundering masculine spirit that the women's movement so woefully condemns.[2]

The push to hire and advance more women, often under pressure from the federal government, is causing some realistic problems for men. Increasingly, white males are feeling discriminated against, and their complaints are becoming more vehement.

Affirmative action programs in universities and large industries are frequently leaving aspiring men gasping behind as women with similar or inferior qualifications are promoted ahead. A *Wall Street Journal* article headlines "White Males Complain They Are Now Victims of Job Discrimination."[3] Discrimination charges against a state university are filed by Caucasian males who allege that they are the victims of employment prejudice.[4] And a group of university scholars organizes and protests to the U.S. Office of Civil Rights that male professors are being discriminated against. A well-known political scientist states, "Large numbers of highly qualified scholars will pay with their careers simply because they are male and white."[5]

We have reached the point where the tables have turned in the admission policy of many professional schools. A woman director of career counseling at a private college speaks of her personal experience in helping students gain admission to graduate programs.

> In many cases it is an advantage to be a woman seeking admission to medical or graduate school because they're trying to build up their female enrollment.[6]

Reverse discrimination is used in an attempt to rectify past inequities against women, leaving some individual males paying a high price indeed.

To some men, the male of the species has always been oppressed and dominated by the controlling female. These men react to the recent demands of women's liberation with over-whelming rage. The feminist movement is a living justification of all their fears, a validation of how castrating woman will continually extend her already substantial power over the hapless male. Raised in a family of rigid maternal control and growing up in a school system where women are masters, they find evidence of female tyranny in every nook and cranny. These men are analagous to the "poor me" women who feel like slaves living in a world of perpetual servitude. Their extreme feelings are usually accounted for by early experiences which were anything but ideal, such individuals being damaged in their ability to lead a full life.

Paul was never particularly fond of females, irrespective of race, color, creed or age, but at least he was able to be friendly with them on a superficial level—that is until women's libera-tion came so forcefully onto the scene. The more the women's movement gained hold, advanced, and obtained publicity, the more he became critical and angry at women. Each new TV program, magazine article, or newspaper clipping on women's liberation sent Paul into a corner sputtering and fuming. To Paul, women's liberation was a nauseating spectacle. "Women have always had the best deal in life and now they're trying to increase their advantages" was his viewpoint.

Paul was now having trouble functioning at work or in any mixed social gathering—he was too bitter at any women who might be present. He withdrew from social situations which included women but could not eliminate contact with females on the job. His relationships neared the breaking point as some of the women at work began talking feminist ideology. He was about to terminate his otherwise rewarding employment.

What had happened to produce a man with such sensitivity and anger toward females and the feminist movement? Although never fully understood, clues were provided as Paul ventilated his feelings. He was blunt, and, once started, turning him off was difficult.

"You asked if I were married. What a stupid question. I would *never* marry. A wife does nothing but bitch. That's what Mom does . . . she screams and yells at Dad all the time and other women are a lot worse than Mom. I can't see getting permanently involved with a girl . . . you get a maid who screams and cuts you down. Mom runs around the house complaining she's just a maid.

"My parents get along only because Dad gives in. Dad is the epitome of a nice guy, but he's weak and passive . . . sits around watching TV all the time. Mom controls everything . . . always cutting Dad down.

"It isn't only Mom. Her whole family is just a bunch of bitchy women . . . her mother and her sisters are the same. Grandfather is a great person, but Grandma bitches at him. Most women are dominant. My landlady is that way . . . trying to boss me around and tell me what to do. But I fight her . . . damned if I'll do what she wants."

"How do you get along with women your own age, Paul?"

"It's the same story. They're just as bad. I'm always afraid when I meet a new girl . . . afraid she will criticize me or ridicule me. You have to justify yourself to a woman. That's the way Mom acts . . . criticized every thing I ever did. She took whatever money I earned and bought my clothes. She ridiculed whatever I bought."

Paul always came back to his mother. He felt constantly

criticized and humiliated in this relationship, and it left him with an indelible stamp for the future.

At one point, Paul left the topic of his mother long enough to reveal his attitudes toward sex. As you might expect, they were hostile, full of fear, and at times somewhat contradictory.

"Sure, I've had intercourse with girls, but they're just out to screw a guy. They don't really care . . . only want their itches scratched. Women don't want to give a man any satisfaction. They use sex to manipulate you and get economic security. Then they castrate you. Women aren't sexual beings. They don't reciprocate and enjoy sex. They only use it to perpetuate the species.

"Sex makes you more vulnerable to a woman . . . then she really has you in her clutches. I've been hurt every time. Girls are critical enough sexually . . . and now this women's lib thing . . . telling women to be more active and expect greater sexual pleasure. Now they demand a great performance from a guy.

"Women's lib is just females trying to extend their power and bleed more from a man. They're like spiders . . . take what you have to offer and then dispense with you. A lot of the fellows feel this way.

"It was bad enough with women being masters in the family but now they want to rule men at work. The bitches weren't satisfied having most of the power . . . they insist on having it all. With this women's lib thing, the next thing you know I'll be working for some dame. They even want women governing the country. Wouldn't that be a sorry state of affairs for men . . . women domination of the family, women domination of our schools, women domination at work, and even female domination of the government."

Paul's overwhelmingly negative view of women was full of generalizations, misconceptions, and futility. Women's liberation exacerbated his already substantial fears of female domination and pushed him to the precipice of bitterness. He tenaciously held onto attitudes learned in his family and could not give women a chance. The advent of women's liberation increased his distance and loneliness, and the expectations for his future were not encouraging.

Women's liberation is having a pronounced effect on the

sexual lives of men. In previous sections we have seen the salutary rewards for the male, but it is not all this one-sided. In the past several years, there appears to be a definite increase in the number of young men complaining of impotence, a phenomenon directly related to the spread of the feminist movement. This is confirmed in my own practice and in the journals where other psychiatrists are reporting similar trends.

One psychiatrist has succinctly summarized this course of events:

> It is in the recently increasing complaints of impotence and premature ejaculation that we see evidence of the deep shifts that are occurring with women's quest for equality.[7]

Women's liberation places increased pressure on the male to perform sexually and be a good lover. The feminist message that women have an inherent right to sexual satisfaction means that the male can no longer be concerned only with his own pleasure. He must now make efforts to please his partner. Young men often interpret this as meaning it is their obligation to make the woman respond, and if she doesn't climax once, twice, or numerous times, there is something fundamentally wrong with them as lovers.

Most men greet women's increasing sexual interest with loud applause and cheers, but the insecure or inexperienced male is apt to feel threatened by such expectations and become impotent. Usually this is of brief duration and clears up spontaneously as the man relaxes and gains confidence. A continuing menacing situation, however, can prolong the impotence indefinitely.

Some men are more threatened by theoretical, abstract notions on the sexual capabilities of women than by the reality of the woman lying by their side. They read feminist accounts of how females are sexually insatiable and capable of one orgasm after another. These men fear that women will demand the right to repeated orgasms with one partner after another, leaving husband, home, children, and country in the process. Again, the empirical evidence of the woman they are in bed with is conveniently ignored.

The feminist position that the female has a right to sexual pleasure can cause problems for the male in another way. In previous generations, men who were impotent could largely ignore their problem and remain relatively anxiety free—now this is no longer as easy. A woman interested in her own sexual enjoyment will not passively accept a nonfunctioning lover as bygone generations of women have. She pressures him to seek some type of help if he is consistently unable to perform. Thus the women's movement is forcing the impotent male to recognize his problem. This leads to considerable anxiety and may account for at least part of the recent upsurge in impotent men consulting therapists.

Likewise, in the not so distant past, the young man who did not desire immediate sexual coupling could appeal to conventional morality. Before the advent of women's liberation, most women would accept this with relief and understanding. The passing of each year, however, makes this increasingly difficult. We have reached a point where, if a man does not attempt sexual contact by the third or fourth date, he is suspect of being homosexual.

Contrary to popular opinion, there are still numerous young men who wish to know a woman in depth before engaging in intimate relations. They have a need to build a solid relationship which contains security and comfort before experiencing close physical contact. When such a man is pressured by a liberated partner or his own psychological expectations into premature attempts at physical pleasure, sexual problems such as impotence can result.

Males have been conditioned through the ages to expect a passive, recipient sexual partner. Women's liberation is telling women to be more active, to initiate sexual contact, and to be aggressive once in bed. To some men, this is threatening as they feel their dominant sexual role being challenged. Their concept of being an adequate man is associated with the need to be the sexually aggressive partner. Inability to perform sexually can develop in this situation.

Impotence can also represent an attempt to control women. The male who needs to dominate is easily threatened by an active feminist in his bed. When he cannot control his partner by being the aggressive one sexually, he may resort to withholding sexual pleasure from his partner.[8]

While similar in many respects to impotence, premature ejaculation adds an interesting new dimension. In the Kinsey era, man was viewed as a superior, efficiently functioning sexual machine if he was able to obtain erection, move on to insertion, and reach an ejaculatory climax regardless of the time involved. Intercourse of sufficient duration to satisfy the female was of secondary importance.[9]

Masters and Johnson have redefined the situation so that the normal male is expected to maintain intercourse for a sufficient length of time to satisfy the woman 50 percent of the time.[10] These changing expectations on the male's ability to withhold ejaculation have been included in feminist ideology and are well publicized.

In an article entitled "Effects on Men of Increased Sexual Freedom for Women," psychiatrist George Ginsberg analyzes this development in depth. He feels that premature ejaculation has been redefined so as to become a male problem in situations which were formerly attributed to female unresponsiveness.[11] Thus, while previously considered normal, the male who, for example, ejaculates after two to three minutes of intercourse and leaves his partner unsatisfied would now be considered a premature ejaculator.

Problems in Hector's sexual life can illustrate some of these factors. Hector's sexual difficulties became painfully manifest about six months back at an out-of-state business convention. A married female colleague invited herself to his room for a drink and after an hour or so told Hector she would like to have sex with him. This direct approach by a young, pretty, liberated woman took him by complete surprise, and, before he had time to recover from his confusion, he found himself nude in bed with his horny business associate.

As Hector subsequently related the story, she lost no time in getting down to the business at hand. Her aggressive techniques stimulated the dumbfounded hero, but his erection failed at the crucial moment. The frustrated young woman swiftly left the room, hurling insinuations about Hector's masculinity behind her.

Hector was humiliated. His most prized possession had gone to sleep at an embarrassing time and left him with perplexing doubts about his virility.

I asked Hector if this was his first experience with potency problems.

"I've only had intercourse with one woman and that ended a

year or so ago. Sex went well enough, but it took months before we made it to bed. We were both so young, just out of high school, and she was a virgin. Neither of us wanted to go all the way until we knew each other well."

Hector's first and only sex partner made no demands on him. She had been a passive lover who accepted whatever Hector had to offer. It was a nonpressure situation, and he functioned reasonably well. His personality, however, could not adequately cope with an active, experienced, sexually aggressive woman.

Hector was a self-conscious, shy individual and had been for as long as he could remember. One of his earliest memories was the fear he experienced on starting first grade. The presence of so many children overwhelmed him, and he withdrew from his peers. Throughout these school years, he felt inferior to his classmates and tended to be a loner.

Hector talked briefly about his family upbringing.

"My parents have their problems getting along. Mom is nice, but she has trouble with Dad. When I was in high school they separated for a few months, but then they were back together, fighting as usual. That's when I remember Dad accusing Mom of having affairs. Mom did have men stay overnight when they were living apart . . . I've always felt shame about that . . . never could talk to anyone about it.

"I remember Dad shouting that women couldn't be trusted. I've never forgotten that. It sticks in my mind. Maybe that's why I can't feel confident with women. I worry that they will leave me . . . sooner or later a woman would tire of me. I never have been able to compete for a woman . . . afraid that I'll lose out in the end I guess."

Hector was a socially inhibited, insecure young man who worried about his abilities to establish a long-lasting marriage. He functioned reasonably well until running head-on into a sexually aggressive woman. Now he was anxious, depressed, and acutely worried about his potency.

Since the breakup with his first and only girl friend about a year ago, Hector had not dated. Now he began looking for another girl with whom he could be comfortable and eventually relate to sexually. Several months later he discussed his experiences.

"Well, it's happened twice more . . . two additional failures to notch on my belt. You said if I relaxed and quit worrying so much about my potency it would return. You were dead wrong . . . it hasn't."

Hector felt devastated and took his anger out on me. His natural inclination was to withdraw, but I was encouraging him to seek social outlets, especially with women.

"What actually happened with these women, Hector?"

"It was the same thing in both cases. You told me to be patient and wait . . . to not push anything sexually until I felt confident and ready. Some advice! There's no slowing things down with these liberated girls. You date them once or twice and they want in your pants.

"What's a guy supposed to do? If a girl wants sex and you turn her down, you feel like a fool. All I did was kiss this one girl and she was all over me. If a girl would just take it easy until I'm ready, sex would be good . . . like it was with my first girl friend.

"The more pressure there is, the worse it gets. When these girls made advances, I wasn't even able to get an erection, let alone maintain it. What the hell do these women expect . . . instant gratification or something?"

Hector's underlying insecurity and lack of sexual confidence came to the fore as demands were placed on him. His fear of not being able to please a woman and hold her in a long-term relationship was learned from family experiences. This fear necessitated his having a secure, trusting relationship before he could function sexually.

I was inclined to agree with Hector, that he would again become potent in the right situation. His personality problems, while real, were not all that severe, and he had a past history of adequate sexual performance. The problem was in finding a woman who was herself sexually reticent and passive so that she could wait for the insecure Hector to feel confident. This, as Hector was discovering, was not an easy task in this era of increased sexual freedom for women.

Chapter 17

Didst thou forget that man prefers peace, and even death, to
freedom of choice . . . .   **Dostoyevsky**

The Freedom
of Androgyny

Our culture has been saturated with a "girls over here, boys
over there" philosophy since time immemorial. In the process,
sexual role stereotypes have become so ingrained and pervasive
that we have taken them for granted. Basic human nature has
been split into "masculine" and "feminine" principles, each to
rule its own domain. Inequality for all is the natural sequel.

For too long have we been trapped by traditional sex roles.
Individuals have been discouraged from developing character
traits reserved for the opposite sex. Both women and men are
thus cut off from an intergral part of themselves.

All of us are handicapped when taught to suppress one part of
our being. Not only are limitations put on our human potential,
but our nature is divided into opposing factions. Conflict within
the individual self ensues as large amounts of energy are used in
subduing the feared inner traits. Neurotic anxiety is frequently
experienced and full sexual expression cannot be realized.

Women's liberation is setting in motion forces to counteract
this conditioning process. Women are being encouraged to
develop their so-called "masculine" qualities and men are gradually being given a chance to realize their "feminine" aspects.
Feminist Betty Friedan has expressed this as follows:

> It [feminism] isn't sex-warfare, woman against man, but it
> is woman breaking away from that obsolete role—the

feminine mystique—the other half of which is that man must break away from his obsolete role—the masculine mystique.[1]

The male and female principles have not only been divided but have often been set against each other. With a strong impetus from the women's movement, we are embarking on a great experiment to determine the extent to which these factors can be harmonized. The new messages tell us that the "feminine" and "masculine" are not mutually contradictory but can be combined into a congenial whole. The end result is a more complete, liberated human being of either sex.

Androgyny is the term used to describe this mixing of female and male elements. There is a simplistic beauty in this expression which combines such supposedly diverse traits in a matter-of-fact manner. The word itself derives from the ancient Greek and symbolizes a combination of male and female into one unified whole. *Androgyny* is thus neither a recent word nor a new concept. In a fascinating book, *Toward a Recognition of Androgyny,* Carolyn Heilbrun explores in depth the historical antecedents of androgyny and concludes that it has long represented an unfulfilled wish of the human species.[2]

Androgyny is a large, magnificent concept with sufficient latitude to include the supposedly irreconcilable—the male in every woman and the female in every man. By encouraging individuals to express their inherent nature, regardless of whether the specific qualities are labeled "feminine" or "masculine," the development of more complete human beings is encouraged. Individual freedom is given an important forward thrust as women and men obtain new options to manifest their innate human characteristics. This is the real meaning of human liberation—to recognize and seek these long suppressed parts of our basic nature.

As an outgrowth of this emphasis on developing human potential, women have a wider range of lifestyles to choose from. While these options have always been available, society has made many of them difficult. Now a new freedom prevails, allowing a woman to marry or remain single, conceive children or remain childless, be a traditional housewife or have a career, or terminate an unrewarding marriage. Previously forbidden combinations, such as having children and remaining unmarried, are gaining acceptance.

While men have not as yet been allowed the same wide range of lifestyle choices, this is beginning to change. Society will not for long allow women such flexibility and latitude while locking males into a limiting, stultifying sexual role. The momentum and direction of change are apparent—as a result of the women's movement, men will gain the freedom to pursue other than traditional male lifestyles.

The pursuit of androgyny has been occurring for some time in subculture variants. Most notable among these is the commune movement. Communes do not follow any set pattern, as they are established along a wide variety of lines. Many, however, have made deliberate, systematic attempts to abolish traditional roles for their female and male members. The sharing of maintenance tasks, child care, and economic production is frequently worked toward as an ideal of human development. The premium placed on sharing leads to a decreased emphasis on traditional "feminine" or "masculine" behavior. Members are encouraged to develop their full range of human qualities as old stereotypes are left behind.

It is difficult to evaluate the success or failure of these androgynous efforts in the communal system. Some individuals adapt while others cannot make the necessary change. Unfortunately, communes are often unsuccessful and short-lived, the majority lasting less than one year. It may be that the difficulty of changing traditional sexual roles accounts for the collapse of many communes.

Movements to cast off sexual roles are transpiring in some other cultures. China is a vociferous example. Admirers of Maoist China state that they have virtually eliminated sex roles, especially since the great Cultural Revolution of 1966. Equality of Chinese women and men is proclaimed.[3]

On careful analysis, however, it becomes clear that by elimination of sexual roles, they mean the almost compulsory obligation of women to enter the economic work force. Women are viewed as crucial in the means of production, and any hindrance to their becoming full producing economic machines is dutifully removed. Equality of pay and employment opportunity is undoubtedly practiced, but this is a far cry from the promotion of androgyny.

At its most grandiose, the women's movement is attempting to heal the split between women and men and also between the "masculine" and "feminine" principles. There are those who foresee utopian social results. The great problems of society are to melt away as the female traits of affection, caring, and tenderness temper the mighty steel of the male's aggression.

The feminists who have such upward-looking visions follow a certain type of reasoning. The world has become a dangerous place to live in as "masculine" dominance, pursuit, and exploitation have gained ascendency and ruled. Patriarchal society is unsafe for humanity. As women gain positions of power and political control, we will enter a new era of peace and gentleness. Violence will be eradicated from our globe and the lamb shall forever sleep beside the lion.

The examples of Golda Meir and Indira Ghandi are pushed into the background as irrelevant to the feminist millennium. After all, they are but products of male dominated cultures and as such have not yet learned to control their aggressiveness. As influential women permeate society, females will have an abundance of other women as role models and then things will begin to change.

There is abundant theoretical justification for this feminist position. Competitiveness, violence, and aggression have long ruled our world. Androgynous humans, be they female or male, could soften these influences and introduce more traditional "feminine" qualities into the power hierarchy.

Beneficial social change is not, however, built on wishful dreams. The heterogeneity of individual responses to women's liberation indicates that the movement will not solve broad social problems. Also the weight of reality and the complexity of world problems argue against the arrival of heaven on earth. Much as I would hope otherwise, I cannot envision the feminist movement stopping war, eliminating hunger and poverty, eradicating inequality among nations, and curbing the rape of our environment.

On the other hand, I can in no way share the fears of those who predict nothing but ultimate disaster from the messages of women's liberation. Alarmists abound. On the one hand the prominent psychoanalyst Dr. Ralph Greenson has voiced his startled concern over the blurring of role gender which he observes going on around him.[4] In the other corner, Midge Decter, the protectress of traditional woman, writes about women's liberation:

> We shall all of us, men, women, and babes in arms, live to reap the whirlwind.[5]

Women's liberation ultimately affects the man and woman in the street rather than social institutions. Throughout this book, we have concentrated on individuals and their reactions, witnessing a seemingly incoherent maze of responses to the feminist movement. One observation grew and slowly took form until it cried for expression—women's liberation means different things to different people. For some it is a friend to be welcomed with open arms while to others it has the trappings of an enemy charging out of the rising sun.

Certain individuals do indeed sense a new freedom and equality as the messages of women's liberation permeate their existence—their lives are enriched and there is an increased capacity to develop their human potential. Others are not so fortunate as the feminist movement brings confusion and serious problems their way.

This wide diversity of reaction leads to a safe conclusion: women's liberation will neither lead us into paradise nor propel us all headlong into a chaotic abyss.

The elimination of traditional sex roles and the quest for androgyny cannot just be accomplished by proclamation. A shift of such magnitude occurs only with difficulty. In attempting to bring about this change, an empirical experiment is in the making, one where results are largely unknown. To envision nothing but gain from these efforts would be naive in the extreme.

Biology is probably a more influential factor in this difficulty of role change than many of us would like to recognize. Its function in role formation remains largely an unknown, and we can only speculate on the limitations it imposes. At this point, separating learned behavior from what is ordained by nature is all but impossible.

This does not mean we should ignore the anatomical and physiological as we examine similarities and differences between the sexes. The influence of these factors is too crucial to be denied. The biological is forever present, forming the background on which psychological and social factors operate. Sexual identity is dependent upon genetic factors, hormones, family influences, and cultural expectations.

In the past, there has been a strong tendency to overrate the innate, biological differences between the sexes. Nature has been used too extensively as the primary explanation for male and female sexual role behavior. Indeed, biology has at times been used as a justification for unequal treatment of the sexes.

Now, through the influence of women's liberation, we are aggressively moving in the other direction. We are experimenting to determine the extent to which sexual role formation is learned behavior which can be changed at will. There is danger we will push this to an unreasonable extreme, causing hardship for countless women and men by encouraging them to develop personality traits which defy their basic biological substrata. Both nature and learned behavior are important in personality development, and we ignore either at our own risk.

Recent medical literature contains examples of authors addressing this issue. In an article entitled "Innate Masculine-Feminine Differences," psychiatrist W. J. Gadpaille explores those characteristics of "masculine" and "feminine" behavior which may have a biological base. He concludes "that there are indeed innate biological distinctions between males and females which affect their emotional, mental, and behavioral characteristics and contribute to predictable expressions of masculinity and femininity."[6]

This is a controversial viewpoint but one which needs to be aired. Anatomy need not be destiny nor mean inequality, but it certainly does affect us.

In writing on Freud, Margaret Mead states that "the path he outlined . . . still suggests that the rhythms of human development, patterned during a million years, are ignored at our peril, and understood give us wisdom."[7]

In the final analysis, women's liberation is probably an elitist phenomenon. It is similar to Dostoyevsky's Grand Inquisitor argument that the ability of humans to handle freedom is limited. Women's liberation brings to each of us the potential for more freedom—to abandon limiting, restricting sexual roles and live to the fullest what is deepest within us. It gives us each a chance to be ourselves and not be governed by what we are expected to be. The basic issue is nothing less than the freedom to choose one's own lifestyle and not be molded by stereotypes.

Women's liberation is elitist because many cannot handle this liberty. Those who can tend to be the elite of the human species. It is the most intelligent, the adaptable, the gifted, the visionary, and the creative who will benefit from women's liberation. The feminist movement is a true friend to those who can manage freedom and the increased responsibility which it entails. Change is a blessing only to those able to handle it—we have seen this repeatedly throughout these pages.

The very freedom which comes as a godsend to some causes serious problems for others. This is an unmistakable fact of life which we often conveniently try to ignore. The ability to look within, choose wisely, and decide one's own direction is, unfortunately, not exactly universal in the human species. Many will stumble as they are given an increasing number of alternatives to choose from.

The difficulties that accompany a greater range of choice are vividly manifested in choosing a mate. As never before, it is now crucial to examine not only our own value structure but that of our potential life companion. No longer can one count on traditional sex roles to point the direction the relationship will take. It is necessary to work out ahead of time such important questions as children, career, degree of sexual permissiveness, performance of household tasks, and economic support of the family. Couples increasingly have the freedom to establish any type of relationship they desire. This is not an easy freedom but one that calls for self-knowledge and open, honest communication.

For a man to marry a career woman and then expect a traditional housewife is an invitation to disaster. Likewise, it is folly when a woman motivated to raise children and be a full-time housewife chooses a liberated man who expects equal sharing of economic support. The possibility of such mismating is enhanced by the new role freedom wrought by the women's movement.[8]

Furthermore, there is now an increasing likelihood of basic change occurring in one or both partners after a relationship is established. This can tax the most dedicated of couples and at times cause unresolvable difficulties. At present, society has inadequate mechanisms for dealing with the complications of such growth or change.

Tradition serves a useful and necessary function to many—it provides direction, gives answers, and establishes meaning for those unable to discern their own. To abandon the age-old traditions of sexual roles and substitute nothing in their place except freedom of choice is to shake the very foundations upon which many depend. We have met a fair number of such men and women in these pages. They deserve an understanding and respect which are often denied them by those who stand to benefit from the feminist movement. Women's liberation cannot expect a warm reception from those finding their lives confused, complicated, or deprived of traditional meaning.

With tradition being abandoned, we have more people going in different directions than ever before. No longer are there ready made answers as to what a woman is or what a man is. Each individual must decide for himself or herself.

This responsibility calls for a degree of wisdom, self-knowledge, and courage which many do not possess. An enormous amount of sexual role confusion can result, especially in youth who do not have a fixed sexual identity and no guiding star to steer by.

Because women's liberation is an elitist movement does not diminish its significance or assign it a pejorative label. The greater economic and employment equality which is permeating all levels of society is a solid attainment which is benefiting most people. And the swing away from sexual role stereotypes creates a potential for human liberation which many cherish and look forward to. The difficulty of human freedom only means we must be aware of its negative impact and alleviate resultant problems whenever possible. It does not negate its importance.

Chapter Notes

2 - What Is Woman's Liberation?

1. Cellestine Ware, *Woman Power* (New York: Tower Publications, 1970), p. 107.
2. Emma Willard, Task Force on Education, *Sexism in Education*, 3rd ed. (Minneapolis: 1972), p. 10.
3. Two periodicals with articles on this theme are: *Ain't I a Woman*, Box 1169, Iowa City, Iowa 52240, and *Lavender Woman*, Box 60206, Chicago, Ill. 60660.
4. Helen Victry, "The Male Power Hierarchy," *A Feminist Journal* 1, No. 3 (September 1970): 2.
5. Ware, *Woman Power*, p. 60.
6. *A Journal of Female Liberation*, Issue 5 (July 1971): 91.

3 - Conflict and Confusion

1. Valleda, *Gold Flower, A Twin Cities Newspaper for Women* 1, No. 9 (November 1972).
2. Ibid.
3. Virginia Abernethy, "Cultural Perspectives on the Impact of Women's Changing Roles on Psychiarty," *American Journal of Psychiarty* 133, No. 6 (June 1976): 660.

4 - Intellectual or Career Success

1. Group for the Advancement of Psychiatry Committee on the College Student, *The Educated Woman: Prospects and Problems, Report 92* (New York: GAP, 1975).
2. Emma Willard, Task Force on Education, *Sexism in Education*, 3rd ed. (Minneapolis: 1972), p. 6.
3. M.S. Horner, "Woman's Will to Fail," *Psychology Today* 3, No. 6 (November 1969): 36.

4. Philip Goldberg, "Are Women Prejudiced Against Women?" *Transaction*, April 1969.
5. Constantina Safilios-Rothschild, Commentary on "The Difficulties of Being Wife, Mistress, and Mother," by John J. Schwab, M.D., *Medical Aspects of Human Sexuality*, May 1974, p. 159.
6. Virginia Abernethy, "Dominance and Sexual Behavior: A Hypothesis," *American Journal of Psychiatry* 131, No. 7 (July 1974): 813.
7. Safilios-Rothschild, Commentary, p. 159.
8. *Minnesota Daily*, February 17, 1976, p. 3.
9. *Wall Street Journal*, January 9, 1973, p. 1.
10. Ibid.
11. *Newsweek*, April 21, 1975, p. 82.
12. *Minneapolis Tribune*, November 10, 1974, p. 130.
13. Janet Silliman, *Hamline University Bulletin*, September 1972, pp. 7–8.
14. Maxwell Alvord, *Minnesota Daily*, January 16, 1973.
15. *AAUP Bulletin*, August 1975, pp. 118–122.
16. *Minneapolis Tribune*, November 10, 1974, p. 13c.
17. *Minnesota Daily*, January 19, 1976, p. 4.
18. *Minnesota Daily*, November 13, 1974, p. 5.
19. *Wall Street Journal*, October 15, 1974, p. 1.

5 - Sexual Stereotypes in Literature and Language

1. Fyodor Dostoyevsky, *The Adolescent*, translated by Andrew R. MacAndrew (New York: Doubleday, 1971; Anchor Books Edition, 1972), p. 29.
2. George Bernard Shaw, *Man and Superman* (New York: Bantam Books, 1959 edition), p. 61.
3. Kate Millett, *Sexual Politics* (New York: Doubleday, 1970).
4. Melvin Anchell, *Sex and Sanity* (New York: Macmillan, 1971), p. 204.
5. Hannah Stone and Abraham Stone, *A Marriage Manual* (New York: Simon and Schuster, 1968), p. 199.
6. Anchell, *Sex and Sanity*, p. 121.
7. Betty Friedan, *The Feminine Mystique* (New York: Dell, 1963).
8. Caroline Bird, *Born Female: The High Cost of Keeping Women Down* (New York: McKay, 1968).
9. Millett, *Sexual Politics*.
10. Germaine Greer, *The Female Eunuch* (New York: McGraw-Hill, 1971).
11. Boston Women's Health Course Collective, *Our Bodies, Our Selves, A Course By and For Women* (Boston: New England Free Press, 1971).
12. Phyllis Chesler, *Women and Madness* (New York: Doubleday, 1972).

6 - Sexual Messages

1. Robin Morgan, *Sisterhood Is Powerful* (New York: Vintage Books, 1970), p. 164.
2. David P. McWhirter, *Medical Aspects of Human Sexuality* 7, No. 2 (February 1973).
3. Boston Women's Health Course Collective, *Our Bodies Our Selves, A Course By and For Women* (Boston: New England Free Press, 1971), p. 12.
4. J., *The Sensuous Woman* (New York: Dell, 1971).
5. Morgan, *Sisterhood Is Powerful*, p. 163.

7 - The Pursuit of Sexual Happiness

1. Saul Rosenthal, Commentary on "Effects on Men of Increased Sexual Freedom for Women," by George L. Ginsberg, *Medical Aspects of Human Sexuality*, February 1973, p. 80.
2. Natalie Shainess, "A Psychiatrist's View: Images of Woman—Past and Present, Overt and Obscured," *American Journal of Psychotherapy*, January 1969, pp. 77–97.
3. Germaine Greer, *The Female Eunuch* (New York: Bantam Books, 1972), p. 338.
4. One recent book illustrative of this type is: Ingrid Bengis, *Combat in the Erogenous Zone* (New York: Knopf, 1972).
5. Mary Jane Sherfey, "The Evolution and Nature of Female Sexuality in Relation to Psychoanalytic Theory," *Journal of the American Psychoanalytical Association* 14, No. 1 (January 1966): 124.
6. Julia Cotter, Claudia Leight, Colleen Livingston, Sharon Mulgrew, Karen Shitman, "Feminists in Heterosexual Relationships," *Women, A Journal of Liberation* 3, No. 1 (1972): 30.
7. Mary Jane Sherfey, *The Nature and Evolution of Female Sexuality* (New York: Random House, 1972).
8. Shainess, "A Psychiatrist's View," pp. 77–97.
9. Elizabeth Stanley, "Can Women Enjoy Sex Without Orgasm?" *Medical Aspects of Human Sexuality*, January 1973, p. 106.
10. Dana Densmore, "Independence from the Sexual Revolution," *Notes from the Third Year: Women's Liberation, 1971*, p. 59.
11. Cotter et al., "Feminists in Heterosexual Relationships," p. 32.
12. Boston Women's Health Course Collective, *Our Bodies, Our Selves, A Course By and For Women* (Boston: New England Free Press, 1971), p. 22.
13. Claudia Dreifus, "The Selling of a Feminist," *Notes from the Third Year: Women's Liberation, 1971*, p. 101.
14. Linda Phelps, "Female Sexual Alienation," *Women, A Journal of Liberation* 3, No. 1: 12.
15. Ibid., p. 15.

8 - Homosexuality

1. *A Letter From Mary* (Boston: New England Free Press, 1970).
2. Emma Willard, Task Force on Education, "The Lesbian: A Survey," *Sexism in Education*, September 1972, p. 17.
3. Radicalesbians, *Woman Identified Woman* (Boston: New England Free Press, 1970).
4. Emma Willard, Task Force on Education, p. 17.
5. Marion Furst, "Dear Andy," *Women, A Journal of Liberation* 3, No. 1 (1972): 45.
6. Zira Defries, "Pseudohomosexuality in Feminist Students," *American Journal of Psychiatry* 133, No. 4 (April 1976): 401.

9 - Traditional Woman

1. *Minnesota Daily*, January 16, 1973.
2. Ms. Day Creamer, *Minneapolis Tribune*, February 14, 1973, p. 5.

3. Norman E. Zinberg, "Changing Stereotyped Sex Roles: Some Problems for Women and Men," *Psychiatric Opinion* 10, No. 2 (April 1973): 28.
4. Midge Dector, *The New Chastity and Other Arguments Against Women's Liberation* (New York: Coward, McCann and Geoghegan, 1972).
5. *Daily News,* January 29, 1970. Quoted in Cellestine Ware, *Woman Power* (New York: Tower Publications, 1970), p. 134.

10 - "Poor Me" Woman

1. Barbara Mehrhof and Pamela Kearon, "Rape: An Act of Terror," *Notes From the Third Year: Women's Liberation, 1971,* p. 79.
2. Valarie Solanas, "SCUM Manifesto," 1967–1968. Quoted in Robin Morgan, *Sisterhood Is Powerful* (New York: Vintage Books, 1970), p. 514.

11 - Some Marital Effects

1. Sheila Cronan, "Marriage," *Notes From the Third Year: Women's Liberation, 1971,* pp. 62–65.
2. Helen Victry, "The Male Power Hierarchy," *A Feminist Journal* 1, No. 3 (September 1970).
3. Mary Howell, "The Sexual Revolution and the Feminist Movement," *Medical Aspects of Human Sexuality,* February 1975, pp. 175–176.
4. Ruth Moulton, "Some Effects of the New Feminism," *The American Journal of Psychiatry* 134, No. 1 (January 1977): 1.

12 - Divorce

1. *Wall Street Journal,* October 1, 1975, p. 1.
2. *Wall Street Journal,* March 18, 1976, p. 1.
3. *Minnesota Daily,* March 30, 1976, p. 5.
4. Constantina Safilios-Rothschild, Commentary on "The Difficulties of Being Wife, Mistress, and Mother," by John J. Schwab, *Medical Aspects of Human Sexuality,* May 1974, p. 159.

13 - Male's Best Friend?

1. Garvin L. Holman, *Hamline University Bulletin,* September 1972, p. 18.
2. Warren Farrell, *The Liberated Man* (New York: Random House, 1974).
3. Marc Feigen Fasteau, *The Male Machine* (New York: McGraw-Hill, 1974).
4. Edith Mucke, *Minnesota Daily,* November 30, 1972.
5. Germaine Greer, *The Female Eunuch* (New York: Bantam Books, 1972), p. 9.
6. Esther Villar, *The Manipulated Man* (New York: Farrar, Straus, and Giroux, 1973), p. 14.
7. *Newsweek,* March 12, 1973, p. 48.
8. *St. Paul Dispatch,* January 4, 1974, p. 13c.
9. *Wall Street Journal,* May 29, 1974, p. 1.
10. Bennett Rosner, "Commentary," *Medical Aspects of Human Sexuality,* September 1973, p. 216.
11. Emma Willard, Task Force on Education, *Sexism in Education,* 3rd ed. (Minneapolis: 1972), p. 8.
12. *Wall Street Journal,* April 19, 1974, p. 24.

13. *Wall Street Journal*, April 16, 1974, p. 1.
14. *Physician's Financial Letter*, March 12, 1973.
15. *Wall Street Journal*, March 20, 1975, p. 6.
16. *Wall Street Journal*, May 15, 1973.
17. George Bernard Shaw, *Man and Superman* (New York: Bantam Books, 1959), p. 171.
18. *Minnesota Daily*, January 15, 1973.
19. *Minnesota Daily*, March 20, 1973.
20. Don Brignolo, *St. Paul Dispatch*, May 4, 1974.
21. *Time*, January 22, 1973, p. 43.
22. U.S. Department of Labor, *News*, November 9, 1973.

14 - Male's Best Friend II?

1. Sue From, "An Untitled Essay," Emma Willard, Task Force on Education, *Sexism in Education*, September 1972, p. 16.
2. Phyllis Chesler, *Women and Madness* (New York: Doubleday, 1972).
3. Morton L. Kurland, "Sexual Difficulties Due to Stereotyped Role Playing," *Medical Aspects of Human Sexuality*, June 1975, pp. 8–22.
4. Eleanor Yachnes, "Some Mythical Aspects of Masculinity," *Medical Aspects of Human Sexuality*, September 1973, p. 200.
5. Jerome M. Kummer, "Male Needs for Affection," *Medical Aspects of Human Sexuality*, April 1974, p. 119.
6. Norman E. Zinberg, "Changing Stereotyped Sex Roles: Some Problems for Women and Men," *Psychiatric Opinion* 10, No. 2 (April 1973): 28.
7. Ibid., pp. 25–30.

15 - Spirituality

1. *Minneapolis Star*, May 1, 1973, p. 1b.
2. Alan W. Watts, *Nature, Man and Woman* (New York: Pantheon, 1958), p. 100.

16 - Some Problems Caused for Men

1. George Gilder, *Sexual Suicide* (New York: Quadrangle/The New York Times Book Co., 1973).
2. George Gilder, "The Suicide of the Sexes," *Harper's Magazine*, July 1973, p. 44.
3. *Wall Street Journal*, February 28, 1974, p. 1.
4. *Minnesota Daily*, January 30, 1974.
5. Paul Seabury, *Newsweek*, December 4, 1972, p. 127.
6. Janet Silliman, *Hamline University Bulletin*, September 1972, p. 8.
7. Alan G. Miller, "Commentary," *Medical Aspects of Human Sexuality*, February 1973, p. 78.
8. Arnold L. Gilberg, "Impotence as a Response to Feminism," *Medical Aspects of Human Sexuality*, February 1976, p. 112.
9. A.C. Kinsey, W.B. Pomeroy, and C.E. Martin, *Sexual Behavior in the Human Male* (Philadelphia: Saunders, 1948).
10. William H. Masters and Virginia E. Johnson, *Human Sexual Inadequacy* (Boston: Little, Brown, 1970).

11. George L. Ginsberg, "Effects on Men of Increased Sexual Freedom for Women," *Medical Aspects of Human Sexuality*, February 1973, pp. 69–72.

17 - The Freedom of Androgyny

1. Betty Friedan, "Humanism and Feminism: New Directions," *The Humanist*, May/June 1974, p. 11.
2. Carolyn Heilbrun, *Toward a Recognition of Androgyny* (New York: Knopf, 1973).
3. *Minnesota Daily*, April 22, 1974.
4. Ralph Greenson, *Newsweek*, June 10, 1974, p. 79.
5. Midge Decter, *The New Chastity and Other Arguments Against Women's Liberation* (New York: Coward, McCann and Geoghegan, 1972), quoted in Adrienne Rich, "The Anti-Feminist Woman," *New York Review of Books* 19, No. 9 (November 30, 1972): 34.
6. W. J. Gadpaille, "Innate Masculine-Feminine Differences," *Medical Aspects of Human Sexuality*, February 1973, p. 155.
7. Margaret Mead, *Newsweek*, June 10, 1974, p. 80.
8. Letha Scanzoni and John Scanzoni, "Mismating," *Medical Aspects of Human Sexuality*, April 1974, pp. 9–26.

Index

301.412
B247s

106634

DATE DUE			
MAR 2 '80	FEB 18 '80		
MAR 18 '80	MAR 19 '80		
APR 8 '80	APR 9 '80		
DEC 05 '80	NOV 21 '80		
OC 17 '83	OCT 18 '83		
OC 17 '84	OCT 10 '84		
NO 28 '84	NOV 12 '84		
MR 04 '85	FEB 20 '85		

DEMCO 38-297